Theokritos Kouremenos
Plato's forms, mathematics and astronomy

Trends in Classics –
Supplementary Volumes

Edited by
Franco Montanari and Antonios Rengakos

Associate Editors
Evangelos Karakasis · Fausto Montana · Lara Pagani
Serena Perrone · Evina Sistakou · Christos Tsagalis

Scientific Committee
Alberto Bernabé · Margarethe Billerbeck
Claude Calame · Jonas Grethlein · Philip R. Hardie
Stephen J. Harrison · Richard Hunter · Christina Kraus
Giuseppe Mastromarco · Gregory Nagy
Theodore D. Papanghelis · Giusto Picone
Tim Whitmarsh · Bernhard Zimmermann

Volume 67

Theokritos Kouremenos

Plato's forms, mathematics and astronomy

—

DE GRUYTER

ISBN 978-3-11-068529-9
e-ISBN (PDF) 978-3-11-060186-2
e-ISBN (EPUB) 978-3-11-060148-0
ISSN 1868-4785

Library of Congress Control Number: 20189402984

Bibliographic information published by the Deutsche Nationalbibliothek
The Deutsche Nationalbibliothek lists this publication in the Deutsche Nationalbibliografie;
detailed bibliographic data are available on the Internet at
http://dnb.dnb.de.

© 2019 Walter de Gruyter Inc., Boston/Berlin
This volume is text- and page-identical with the hardback published in 2018.
Printing and binding: CPI books GmbH, Leck

www.degruyter.com

Contents

Introduction —— 1

1		Platonic Forms as Forms only of Mathematical Objects —— 8
1.1		The identification of forms with forms of mathematical objects in the cave simile —— 8
1.1.1		The cave simile —— 8
1.1.2		The forms —— 8
1.1.3		The forms of mathematical objects —— 16
1.1.4		Forms and forms of mathematical objects in the cave simile —— 20
1.2		The problem of the range of forms —— 21
1.2.1		The evidence —— 21
1.2.2		The forms of negations, of similarity and dissimilarity and of opposites —— 22
1.2.3		The forms of artifacts —— 24
1.2.4		The form of number —— 25
1.2.4.1		The Good —— 25
1.2.4.2		The Good-like form of number —— 26
1.2.4.3		The 'generation' of numbers in the *Parmenides* —— 27
1.2.4.4		Aristotle's testimony in *EE* A 8, 1218a15–28 —— 30
1.2.4.5		Aristotle's testimony in *EN* A 4, 1096a10–18 —— 32
1.2.4.6		Aristotle and Plato's conception of the forms of mathematical objects —— 33
1.2.4.7		The philosophical arithmetic of the *Philebus* —— 36
1.2.4.8		Numbers in *Republic 7* —— 37
1.2.4.9		Plato and Aristotle on mathematics —— 41
1.2.4.10		Forms galore —— 47
1.3		Are all forms only forms of mathematical objects? —— 50
1.3.1		The forms of oneness and multitude(s) —— 50
1.3.2		The forms of half and double, third and triple etc., small and large —— 51
1.3.3		The forms of equality and inequality —— 53
1.3.4		The forms of the elements: fire, air, water, and earth —— 53
1.3.5		The forms of compound material substances —— 57
1.3.6		The forms of properties of matter —— 59
1.3.7		The forms of living things —— 60
1.3.8		The Good and the forms of virtues —— 63
1.3.9		The form of beauty —— 67

1.4	The equation of forms with form-numbers, and their principles —— 68
1.4.1	The equation of forms with form-numbers —— 68
1.4.2	The principles of form-numbers —— 70

2	**Plato on Astronomy and Philosophy —— 77**
2.1	Astronomy in the cave —— 77
2.2	Astronomy in Socrates' intellectual autobiography in the *Phaedo* —— 85
2.3	Astronomy in the myth of the *Phaedo* —— 86
2.4	Astronomy and beauty in *Republic 7* —— 89
2.5	Astronomy in the *Timaeus* —— 91
2.6	Astronomy in the *Epinomis* —— 97
2.7	Astronomy in the *Laws* —— 100
2.8	Astronomy and the Good —— 105
2.9	Astronomy and observation —— 108
2.10	Planetary retrograde motion and Plato —— 119
2.11	Planetary retrograde motion and forms —— 132
2.12	Conclusion —— 135

Bibliography —— 139

Index of passages —— 145

Introduction

When Godfrey Hardy told his ill friend Srinivasa Ramanujan that he rode to the hospital in a taxi with a dull number, 1729, Ramanujan protested "No, it is a very interesting number, it is the smallest number expressible as a sum of two cubes in two different ways" (Hardy [1921] lvii-lviii). 5040 is another very interesting number. It is a highly composite number, an integer that has more divisors than any smaller integer has. It was Ramanujan himself who defined the highly composite numbers and also coined their name (Ramanujan [1915]). 5040, moreover, appears intriguingly in a statement that is equivalent to the Riemann hypothesis (Borwein et al. [2008] 47–48), one of the most important, if not the most important, unsolved problem in mathematics (for an eminently readable account of the Riemann hypothesis, the struggle to prove it and its importance intended for non-experts see du Sautoy [2004]). It is also the number of plots into which it is proposed in Plato's *Laws* that the land of Magnesia, the colony to be founded in Crete whose constitution is planned in this dialogue, should be divided: it will be the number of economic units in the state and of the households into which its population will be organized as nuclei of its higher social structure. Plato has the Athenian stranger, the main codiscussant, justify his choice of 5040 on account of the fact that this number not only has more divisors than any smaller number, 59 (if we exclude 5040 as trivial divisor), it also has an abundance of successive divisors because it can be divided by all numbers from 1 to 10 (*Lg.* 5, 737e1–738b1); returning to this interesting number later on, the stranger adds that it is divisible by all numbers from 1 to 12 with the exception of 11, which divides, though, 5038 (*Lg.* 6, 771a5–c7). Various divisions of the population will be needed in the life of the state for administrative, military, tax-related and religious purposes, so it is best to have a number of nuclear units into which the population is organized that will admit of as many divisions as possible. 5040 is given as an example of a number of this sort (*Lg.* 5, 737c1–e3), which hints at the notion of numbers that have more divisors than any smaller number has, Ramanujan's highly composite numbers, a fact that has not gone unnoticed by mathematicians (Kahane [2015] 136).

Plato's mention of the number 5040 in this context illustrates nicely his attraction to pure mathematics, a term that can be traced to his *Philebus* (55c4–57e5 and 61d10–62d3), and the inextricable link between the abstract and the concrete, the theoretical and the practical, in his thought. The Athenian stranger says that lawmakers must know at least that much about numbers: what number and of what kind, one that we call highly composite today, is the most useful for all cities (*Lg.* 5, 737e7–738a2). Their knowledge of mathematics, however, is assumed to go much further than that. For, as the stranger observes elsewhere, lawmaking is patterned on the 'music' in the intimate links relating the branches of mathematics to one another that emerges from hard work in mathematics much more advanced than what all citizens must learn at school (*Lg.* 7, 817e5–818a3, and 12, 967d4–968a4). It also requires the ability to give an account, as guarding the laws also does (*Lg.* 12, 967d4–968a4). Giving an account means looking up from the many and dissimilar, e.g. beautiful and good things, to one unifying form: an expert craftsman and guardian must not only be able to look at the disparate many but also know a unity over them, one form that explains how each of them is like the others, so that, having grasped the form, he will be able to arrange or ordain each of them in relation to it and view them as a system thanks to it (*Lg.* 12, 965b7–c8). This ability marks the lawmaker and guardian of the laws in the *Laws*, who is a mathematician, as philosopher too, a descendant of the more famous philosopher-kings of Plato's earlier *Republic*, since it and the objects in terms of which it is defined, the forms, define the philosopher in Plato's view (there is no reason to think that this definition is not operative in the *Laws*; that it is presupposed is suggested by *Lg.* 12, 965c9–967d3, esp. 967c5–d3, where the term *philosopher* occurs).

In the *Laws* there is no characterization of forms. It can be safely assumed that they are conceived as in the *Timaeus*, another late work (pace Owen [1965]), where, though, forms are characterized as in the *Republic* and other dialogues grouped chronologically with it. The forms, objects of true knowledge after the love of which the philosopher is named, are objectively existing entities accessible not to our senses but only to our intellect, for they are neither bodies nor anything existing in space, though in an inexplicable manner they are related to bodies, which deficiently 'copy' them and which are themselves form-'copies' in the 'malleable' space (the concept of space is introduced in the *Timaeus*, where Plato gives an account of physical bodies not hinted at in earlier dialogues but consistent with them); they are clearly 'copied' in non-bodily things too such as laws and customs since rational human souls also 'copy' them as also do their other products such as proofs, theories and whole branches of knowledge (*Smp.* 209e5–211b5). Unlike physical objects, their properties and all human cultural products, therefore, forms are not subject to change, as befits their epistemological role as objects of stable knowledge that must have unchanging objects if it exists: beings, things serving as referents of the answers to the question "what is…?", e.g. the beauty or the goodness itself, not the beauty or the goodness in any of the many disparate beautiful or good things around us that are objects only of changeable opinion, though they can be brought within the compass of knowledge if related to forms. Forms are not only the objects philosophy strives to know by Plato's lights: they are also the objects really studied in mathematics (on Aristotle's reports that Plato posited the so-called intermediates as special objects of mathematics see Kouremenos [2015] 1.1). This is not stated in the *Laws* (where the relation between philosophy and forms too is barely hinted at), but it is one of the central themes in *Republic* 6–7 (again there is no reason to think that Plato somehow changed his mind about the nature of the objects studied in mathematics after the *Republic*; the opposite is suggested by the *Timaeus*).

Arithmetic does not study 'bodily', hence tangible or visible, numbers, groups of physical objects, but intelligible beings, form-numbers (*R.* 7, 521d4–526c6); similarly, in geometry one really aims at understanding unchanging beings, forms, not at knowing their 'copies', the geometrical objects that can be constructed and variously manipulated in geometrical reasoning either physically, as diagrams, or mentally (*R.* 7, 527a1–b11). Plato, as far as we know, was the first to put forth the familiar view that "mathematics, and not only its basic concepts, exists independently of us. This is a notion that is hard to credit, but hard for a professional mathematician to do without" (Langlands [2010] 6; Plato himself expresses a similar sentiment about professional mathematicians in *R.* 7, 527a1–b1). Mathematics is contrasted with philosophy in that it relies heavily on form-'copies', while its problematic definitions of its objects, which are in sore need of accounts, manage to lay only a tenuous hold on the relevant forms, which are seen as if in a dream, and function only as the starting points of proofs, chains of consistent steps that lead to conclusions about the objects they define, without illuminating the nature of the definienda; philosophy hopes to provide full accounts of forms only through forms (*R.* 6, 509d6–511e5, and 7, 533a10–c6). Insofar as it aims to do this, it will be to mathematics as a cornice is to the building it crowns, an integral part of an edifice which is higher than all other parts and in which all of them will find their completion (*R.* 7, 534e2–535a1).

In *Republic* 6–7 Plato makes relatively modest claims. He does not think that his philosophy of forms is really more privileged than contemporary mathematics as far as direct access to forms is concerned (Fine [1999] 235–242), which must be why he has his mouthpiece Socrates demur from explaining its methods (*R.* 7, 532d7–533c6). Contemporary mathematics is also immature by Plato's lights, but he is confident that it too will grow in the future even if it continues to be studied in the non-philosophically ruled states existing in his time (*R.* 7, 528a6–c7, 530b6–c4, 531b2–c5); the fundamental autonomy of mathematics is not threatened by his wish to bring the discipline under the auspices of an 'ideal', philosophically ruled state, which would grant institutional support to its study, thereby helping focus the collective attention of mathematicians to important open problems, and would counter the slight of uselessness habitually hurled against it by relating it to governance and societal welfare through philosophy. It is not contemporary but future mathematics that he thinks will be useful for an heir of his philosophy of forms as its propedeutic, a mathematics his contemporary mathematicians would definitely marvel at (R. 7, 530c3–4, 531c5), and he insists that, in order to be useful for philosophy, mathematics must simply advance; as for its empirical fields, astronomy and harmonics, he does not wish them to be cut off from the sensible world and focus on forms but to become more or fully mathematical and reveal new mathematical objects by trying to understand it, thereby pushing further the boundaries of the realm of known forms, the true objects of mathematics (Kouremenos [2015] ch. 1).

Apart from the nature of the objects mathematics studies, forms, it is mainly through its unity that mathematics will be useful for philosophy as its propedeutic, through the unifying connections among its distinct branches (R. 7, 531c9–d5 and 537b7–c8) or their 'music', as it is called metaphorically in the *Laws*, which in the mathematics of Plato's day could barely be heard (Kouremenos [2015] ch. 2): it is very unlikely that he envisaged that this unity would lead to disunity, to philosophy as a foreign importation into mathematics, an unpleasant discordant note spoiling its 'music'. Philosophy will be to mathematics as a cornice to the building it crowns, a part of a unified whole. Plato seems to consider number the most basic mathematical concept (R. 7, 522c1–e4), but in the *Timaeus* he locates its origins, and thus the origins of mathematics, where he locates the origins of philosophy too (47a1–b2): since he says that the study of future advanced mathematics will pave the way to future advanced philosophy of forms by bringing out the 'kinship' of all branches of mathematics to one another, it will introduce the philosophy of forms as its 'relation', not as an overbearing outsider.

The best evidence for this comes from the passage in *Republic* 7 where philosophy is likened to law and mathematics to the law's preamble (531d6–7). The metaphor follows the requirement that the 'kinship' of the diverse fields of mathematics stand out in order for the study of mathematics to aid philosophy propedeutically and the acknowledgment of the difficulty of this task. Likening philosophy to law is to be expected since the philosopher is an expert lawmaker who, feeling compelled to mold human affairs to the rational order of the unchanging forms he studies, is interested not in the welfare of one class of citizens but of the whole community and tries to bring all citizens into harmony with one another so that they share the benefits each can offer to the community (R. 6, 500b8–d10, and 7, 519e1–520a5). The preamble to a law is an important concept in Plato's legal thought introduced in the *Laws*, a complement to the prescriptive necessity of the law proper; it is addressed to those who are expected to obey the law and aims to make them understand it too (4, 718b5–723d4). These introductions to the laws are "a sort of stirrings" and "skilled approaches to what will be brought to completion" by the laws (4, 722d4–6). Although their difference from the laws is emphasized, they fall within the remit of the same expertise (4, 723a4–b8), clearly in that they serve the same goal in distinctly different ways, the law by force and its preamble by gentle persuasion and understanding which, as the accompanying persuasion shows, is not the full understanding of the lawmaker. Force and persuasion are the two ways by which the law is said in *Republic* 7 to attempt to bring the citizens into harmony with one another, which is the ultimate goal of law and lawmaking in the later *Laws* too (1, 628a4–b5): thus, when in the same book mathematics is likened to a law's preamble and philosophy to the law after the demand that mathematics pave the way to philosophy through the 'kinship' of its fields, the metaphor suggests that philosophy is envisaged to join in the harmony of all mathematics as distinct part of a single intellectual endeavor, a single edifice.

Although philosophy studies forms, abstract entities not existing in space and time, in the sense that all truths about them do not refer to time, though temporally they are eternal, it has a prominent practical dimension. This is clear from the fact that it comprises lawmaking, from the demand in the cave simile at the beginning of *Republic* 7 that the philosophers return to the cave from which they have fled to help its benighted inhabitants, and from the detail in the education of the philosopher-kings in the same book that their ten-year-long study of all advanced mathematics and their subsequent, five-year long, study of philosophy must be followed by a fifteen-year long service in various administrative roles as prerequisite for their ascent to the peak of philosophy. There can thus be no doubt that Plato does not envisage the wholesale absorption of philosophy into mathematics or vice versa, the aid mathematics can offer to lawmaking and governance notwithstanding. But it is plausible to assume that he envisages the absorption into mathematics at least of the philosophical investigation of its foundations as he conceives them, definitions of forms which need to be given complete accounts. Although he notes that mathematicians are indifferent to giving full accounts of the objects they define and only deduce busily theorems about these objects (*R*. 6, 510c2–d3), he admits that a few, apparently philosophically-minded, mathematicians are actually capable of providing accounts (*R*. 7, 531d6–e5): it thus stands to reason that the philosophers who will start elucidating the real nature of the objects mathematics is really about after their prolonged study of advanced mathematics itself will do so not only as philosophers but also as expert mathematicians interested in foundational issues. In the *Timaeus* Plato might envisage the eventual absorption of fundamental physics, if not of all physics, into mathematics as another field of applied mathematics next to astronomy and harmonics. However, for philosophy and mathematics to be viewed as a single edifice, like the expertise within whose remit fall the laws and their preambles with which philosophy and mathematics are compared, full absorption of one into the other is not needed. The ultimate goal of the prolonged preparatory study of advanced mathematics by the future philosopher-rulers is said to be the comprehension of the 'kinship' not only of the diverse fields of mathematics but also of "the nature of being" (*R.* 7, 537b7–c8). "Being" here can only refer to forms, the forms of those objects that are studied in mathematics, indirectly and as if in a dream, but the way these forms are referred to in Greek by a singular used collectively for plural suggests that they exhaust the entire range of forms: mathematics does not see through a haze a part of the abstract realm which philosophy will see in full clarity and in its entirety but lays out its entire topography, catalogues and describes its denizens to the extent it has explored it up to a certain time for philosophy to further study it. Mathematics and philosophy share the same goal, as is the case with a law and its preamble, obtaining knowledge, and this shared goal is directed at the same range of objects. The preamble to a law does not touch upon the true nature of what it attempts to make broadly understood, for it is addressed to the average citizen, and also skips all details about how the general understanding it tries to offer will be turned into a specific statute. Likewise, mathematics does not inquire into the true nature of the objects, the forms, it studies in its characteristic manner, nor can it be interested in how these objects exfoliate everywhere into the multifaceted sensible world: fleshing out fully the bare bones of forms is the job of philosophy, which in this respect is comparable to the specific law and, together with mathematics, will form a single intellectual enterprise insofar as they study exactly the same objects and will attempt to reveal jointly their real nature as the cornice crowning the rest of the single edifice they together will constitute.

This amounts to two theses: according to Plato, it is philosophy that came up with the concept of beings, which he calls forms, and highlighted their importance, first to natural philosophy (viz. the pioneering investigation of Parmenides and the different takes on his beings, all corporealist, by Empedocles, Anaxagoras and the atomists) and then, widening the scope, to ethics (viz. Socrates' search for definitions of the virtues), but the things that do qualify as beings are inchoately revealed by mathematics as raw materials that must be further processed by philosophy (mathematicians, according to *Euthd.* 290b7–c6, do not invent the theorems they prove but discover beings and, like hunters who must hand over what they catch to chefs if it is going to turn into something useful, they must hand over their discoveries to philosophers); hence, even those forms that do not bear names of mathematical objects, such as the well-known forms of beauty and goodness mentioned above, are forms of mathematical objects. The first chapter of this study is an attempt to defend this thesis. The second argues that for Plato philosophy's crucial task of investigating the exfoliation of the forms into the sensible world is already foreshadowed in one of its branches, astronomy.

1 Platonic Forms as Forms only of Mathematical Objects

1.1 The identification of forms with forms of mathematical objects in the cave simile

1.1.1 The cave simile

At the climax of Plato's cave simile in *Republic* 7 a former prisoner who has been forced to exit his subterranean prison and ascend to the surface can see directly first the night sky, the moon and its other luminaries and finally the sun itself as it is, which hitherto he could see only indirectly, e.g. reflected in the surface of water. He now sees that the sun causes the seasons and the year, governs everything in the visible realm and is even responsible in some way for everything he used to see as prisoner in the cave. As is clear from the end of the previous book, the sun is a metaphor for the Good, the good itself or the form of the good, the highest object studied in philosophy. Metaphors for the other forms, the rest of the objects of the enquiry crowned by the Good, are the people, animals and all artifacts existing outside the cave: shadows cast on the cave's wall facing the prisoners by simulacra of such things as they are being carried by prison employees above a low wall, behind the prisoners and in front of a light source, are the only things the prisoners in the cave can see, constrained as they are to look only forward. The shadows and reflections of real people etc. outside the cave, the only things the former prisoner, blinded by the bright daylight, can bear looking at right after his exit from the cave, stand for forms studied indirectly, as in mathematics, the propedeutics to philosophy according to *Republic* 7. The things seen directly by the former prisoner when his eyes get used to daylight, first the things immediately around him, then the night sky with its luminaries and finally the sun, stand for forms studied directly in philosophy.

1.1.2 The forms

The forms have been introduced in *Republic* 5 as the objects philosophical knowledge is about after the famous claim that, unless philosophers rule or rulers philosophize, there will be no end to humankind's troubles (473c11–e4). The first forms mentioned in this context is the form of beauty, the beautiful *itself*, and implicitly of ugliness since Plato has Socrates refer next to the forms of justice and injustice, of the good and the bad and to an indefinitely large multitude of other forms (475b4–476d6). Forms are not subject to sensory knowledge but can be apprehended only by the intellect. Each form is unique but is somehow related to many sensible things and appears multiply in many places (the form of beauty e.g. appears in all beautiful things; cf. *Phlb.* 15a1–b8): as is explained in the *Phaedo* (100c10–e3), the form causes their having a character named after it (e.g. their being beautiful).[1] Forms lack all sensible features and are immaterial, which is why they are not themselves sensible and can be apprehended only by the intellect (see *Phdr.* 247c3–d1 and *Sph.* 246a7–c3; their lack of sensible properties is also implicit in *R.* 5, 476b4–7). They seem to be timeless and to exist outside space (see *Ti.* 37d1–38b5 and 51e6–52b5), though from our temporal perspective they are eternal (everlasting).[2] In terms of the traditional ontological categories, they can be thought to be universals non-definable in observational terms.[3] Forms, as is shown by the elaborate discussion of the form of beauty in the *Symposium* (209e5–211b5), are related not only to sensible objects but also to human souls and actions, to the products of human social life, e.g. laws and institutions, and to the contents and products of human intellect, to any knowledge it might have, whose real objects are forms, to any proof or theory it might construct or understand and to branches of knowledge.

The relation of something to a form is called participation in, or partaking of, the form: it results in this thing's mysteriously 'resembling' the form according to which it is described—mysteriously, for a form is completely unlike anything participating in it, as is emphasized in the description of the form of beauty in the *Symposium*.[4] As is suggested by the definition of justice in *Republic* 4 (443b9–

---

1 Plato is imprecise in *Phd.* 100c10–e3 on the nature of the relation between forms and sensibles: a form might be present in sensibles or associated with them in whatever manner it might be associated with them; cf. *Phlb.* 15a1–b8, *Prm.* 130e5–133a10 and Arist. *Metaph.* A 6, 987b13–14.
2 On whether forms are timeless or everlasting see Sorabji (1983) 108–112. That they exist in space, thus in time too, being immanent in sensibles, has also been proposed; see Harte (2008) 206–208. I assume that timelessness is existence outside time, on which see Lowe (2002) 370–372.
3 See e.g. Fine (1995) 20–25 and (1999) 215 n. 1. As Harte (2008) 208–214 argues, however, important as the distinction between universals and particulars may be to Aristotle and us, it does not seem to be essential to Plato's metaphysics; cf. Vlastos (1965) 252–253. For forms as particulars see Owen (1957), Allen (1965), Geach (1965) and Mohr (1985) 43–52. Cf. next. n.
4 Talk of participation in forms seems to imply their instantiation and thus that forms are to be understood as universals, whereas talk of resembling forms as paradigms or models seems to imply that they are to be understood as particulars of a privileged sort; Cleary (2013b) 417–421 argues that paradigmatic forms can be viewed as classes (cf. below n. 9). That forms are paradigms is not in itself incompatible with their being universals; see Fine (1995) 61–64. Aristotle

444a9), some participants in forms partake of the relevant forms indirectly, insofar as they depend on what participates directly in these forms: actions are just insofar as they are performed by persons whose souls, the primary participants in the form of justice, are just, and similarly laws, state institutions and states are defined as just in their dependence on the souls of the citizens. Participants in forms cannot be objects of knowledge in themselves but only of changeable opinion.[5] The objects of knowledge must be stable and unchanging but everything participating in a form is subject to change. Non-philosophers, however, think that such things are the only existents, and confuse them and their properties, changeable too, with beings, the stable entities referred to in the answers to such questions as "what is justice?" or "what is beauty?", whose subjects cannot but be the names of unchanging existents, the forms (see *Phd.* 78d1–79a11 and *R.* 5, 478e7–480a13).[6]

Plato thinks of them not as independent but as tightly interrelated. The crucial topic of the interrelationships of forms takes center stage in dialogues generally assumed to have been written after the so-called middle dialogues such as the *Republic*, but it is already present in the earlier phase of Plato's thought. He has Socrates imply at the end of *Republic* 6 (511b2–c2) that forms cohere both with one another and with the principle of their universe, which seems to be the Good: a philosopher, having gotten hold of this principle, can pass from it to the forms cohering with it, from them on to other forms with which they cohere in turn, and so on down the whole structure; the philosopher is assumed to have ascended to the principle of the realm of forms from "true hypotheses", accounts which can be understood as ideally (cf. n. 22) full explanatory definitions of forms in terms of their relationships to other forms they directly cohere with, springboards whence one can ascend to higher and higher reaches of the structured realm of

---

considers Plato's forms to be both universals and particulars (*Metaph.* M 9, 1086a31–34), but this need not imply that forms are particulars; see Fine (1995) 61 and cf. previous n.

5 They can be objects of knowledge, however, if referred to forms; see below.

6 Change has been understood as compresence of opposites (the fact that property x is F in one context and non-F in another at the same time t, which means that x cannot be the F itself, the form that explains why something is F and is thus unchanging in that it cannot be non-F) rather than succession of opposites (whereby thing x is F at time t_1 and non-F at time t_2) and coming into/going out of existence; see Fine (1995) 54–57 (cf. 167 n. 26 on *Phd.* 74a9–c3). This seems to be so in the *R.* 5 passage, but not in the *Phd.* passage. All of these kinds of change are clearly ruled out for the form of beauty in *Smp.* 209e5–211b5 (cf. *Ti.* 51e6–52b5 and Fine [1995] 57 n. 58). Any perceptible number n is said in *R.* 7, 524d8–525a9, to also be in(de)finitely many other perceptible numbers, obviously at the same time, in implicit contrast to the intelligible form-number n, which cannot also be non-n.

forms, whose principle is said to be "unhypothetical" probably in the sense that it does not lead to anything higher. In the seventh book of the *Republic* Plato has Socrates define the philosopher as a synoptic viewer (537c6–7), one who takes a comprehensive view of a whole, presupposing that, ideally, a philosopher studies forms not in isolation but in the full richness of their mutual interrelationships and ultimately as a single coherent system into which they are unified by these connections: the context of this definition leaves no doubt that the synoptic view, though it is directed at a multitude, does not consider each of its diverse objects in isolation, or all of them as an amorphous heap, but brings them together into a whole as its parts, whose relations are described by a term (οἰκειότης) evoking the familiarity of kinship, friendship and marital intimacy (537b7–c3). Each part of the whole can be known not in isolation but only as part of the whole, in its relations to all other parts, a coherentist or holistic view of philosophical knowledge presupposing a symmetrically coherentist conception of the objects philosophical knowledge is actually about.[7]

In the *Philebus* Plato illustrates the foundation of philosophical knowledge using that of grammatical knowledge as parallel (16c5–17b10 and 18a7–c6).[8] This consists in understanding that the seemingly indefinitely large vocal multiplicity of speech boils down not only to a number of elemental sounds produced by the human vocal apparatus but also, and much more importantly, to a number of their classes, the largest of which divide into sub-classes and so on until the elemental sounds are reached: similarly, the foundation of philosophical knowledge consists in realizing that a form, which is a unity, although it seems to be extensionally conceived since the full set of e.g. the consonants stands for it, 'divides' into, and 'contains', a number of other extensional forms, all of them unities for which stand the broadest classes of consonants, and so on with each one of them down to the 'atomic' forms answering to elemental sounds. In view of this parallel between the elemental sounds and their classes, on the one hand, and forms, on the other, Platonic forms seem to be not only 'atomic' entities of some kind but also various collections or sets into which such related entities are arranged, sets of these sets and so on (the term *set* is not used in any technical sense here and below will be used as a synonym of *class* et sim.).[9] Good candidates for forms

---

[7] On Plato as a holist about knowledge, see Fine (1999); cf., though, Silverman (2002) 207–217.
[8] On this parallel, and on the following one with musical knowledge, see Harte (2002) 199–208.
[9] Kahn (2013) 172–173 thinks that Plato uses terms for forms intensionally, for the stable objects of cognition, as well as extensionally, but only for the classes of transient participants in forms. Cleary (2013b) 417–421 argues that the description of forms as self-predicative paradigms suggests their extensional conception as classes, presumably of each form and its participants; see, though, Fine (1995) 52–54 on the self-predication of forms.

conceived as sets are the forms of evenness and oddness or even and odd number(s), which play a prominent role in the last argument for the immortality of the soul in the *Phaedo*.

There is no reason to deny that here "three and five and each number in half of all numbers" (ἡ τριὰς καὶ ἡ πεμπὰς καὶ ὁ ἥμισυς τοῦ ἀριθμοῦ ἅπας), every one of which is always odd, though it is not what the odd is, are primarily form-numbers which earlier in the dialogue are described as beings, by participating in which things are three, five or as many as they are (101b9–c9; cf. 104d1–8). The same can thus be plausibly assumed to be the case with "two and four and each number in the other row of numbers" (τὰ δύο καὶ [τὰ] τέτταρα καὶ ἅπας ὁ ἕτερος αὖ στίχος τοῦ ἀριθμοῦ), every one of which is even, though it is not what the even is: the two forms of even and odd number(s), "what the even is" and "what the odd is", can be naturally identified with "half of all numbers" and "the other row of number" respectively, the sets of even and odd numbers as is suggested by the image of the row (103e2–104b5; on the form of number, which 'divides' into them, see 1.2.4).[10]

Grammar as metaphor for philosophy and the elemental sounds and their various classes as metaphors for forms appear also in the *Sophist*. Just as a grammarian knows not only which class of elemental sounds goes through all the rest as a bond, in that its members must be present to combine into syllables the elemental sounds in other sets, but also which classes of elemental sounds can have their members joined to produce syllables, a philosopher knows both which forms combine by means of which and which forms do not (252e9–253d4). Cast in extensional language, the explication of the analogy that follows next (253d5–e7) can be plausibly illustrated by extensional forms such as those of evenness and oddness as understood above: the philosopher can 'see' one form extending throughout a multitude of non-overlapping forms (either the 'atomic' form-numbers in the forms of even and odd number(s) or disjoint, i.e. mutually exclusive, and exhaustive sets of even or odd form-numbers, e.g. the prime form-numbers and the composites, viewed as forms in themselves); many different forms being

---

10 ἀλλ' ὅμως οὕτως πέφυκε καὶ ἡ τριὰς καὶ ἡ πεμπτὰς καὶ ὁ ἥμισυς τοῦ ἀριθμοῦ ἅπας, ὥστε οὐκ ὢν ὅπερ τὸ περιττὸν ἀεὶ ἕκαστος αὐτῶν ἐστι περιττός· καὶ αὖ τὰ δύο καὶ [τὰ] τέτταρα καὶ ἅπας ὁ ἕτερος αὖ στίχος τοῦ ἀριθμοῦ οὐκ ὢν ὅπερ τὸ ἄρτιον ὅμως ἕκαστος αὐτῶν ἄρτιός ἐστιν ἀεί (*Phd.* 104a7–b4). The translation of ὁ ἥμισυς τοῦ ἀριθμοῦ ἅπας as "each number in half of all numbers" and ἅπας ὁ ἕτερος αὖ στίχος τοῦ ἀριθμοῦ as "each number in the other row of numbers" construes ἕκαστος as appositive to each ἀριθμός such as ἡ τριὰς καὶ ἡ πεμπτὰς and τὰ δύο καὶ [τὰ] τέτταρα (ἕκαστος cannot be plausibly construed with ὁ ἥμισυς τοῦ ἀριθμοῦ ἅπας and ἅπας ὁ ἕτερος αὖ στίχος τοῦ ἀριθμοῦ as well, as if these phrases referred to an odd and even number respectively, unless each phrase is understood as totum pro parte).

contained in one form (again the prime form-numbers and the composites, as forms in themselves, are contained in the superordinate form of oddness); one form not only extending throughout many other forms but also being joined together with another form (if two forms, of F and G, are "joined together" in the sense that the predicates F and G are extensionally identical but intensionally distinct, an arithmetical example would be the sets of even-times odd numbers and odd-times even numbers conceived as forms); finally, a number of forms being wholly separated from one another (e.g. the sets of even and odd form-numbers conceived as two forms). The upshot is that forms are studied not in isolation from one another but as communing (κοινωνεῖν) with one another and as not communing, i.e. as separated.

According to the *Philebus*, each elemental sound, and thus each form, cannot be grasped in itself, independently of all the rest and the classes into which they are grouped together and separated: all these make up a system, a single bond of its parts which somehow turns them into a coherent unity, allowing all of its components to be treated in a single discipline, grammar or philosophy (18c7–d2).[11] To illustrate this point, Plato uses in the same context as metaphors for forms the musical notes, pitched sounds which are the elements of musical scales, and the intervals, the relations between pitches that are expressed as ratios of whole numbers and actually build up the scales;[12] metaphor for philosophical knowledge is now knowledge of music (*Phlb.* 17b11–e6). To know music one must have learned not only that high- and low-pitched sound is not indefinitely variable but also the numbers expressing each sound as pitched in relation to others and all the different ways in which these intervals unite into wholes, scales structured by ratios of numbers and called here "systems" and "harmonies". The basic structural units of these harmonious patterns are the intervals defined by the highest and lowest of four successive notes, a "tetrachord": they have to each other the ratio 4:3, the "fourth", and the four notes in a tetrachord form each with its immediate lower successor intervals expressed in ratios which, multiplied together, give the fourth. The musical scales, Plato's harmonies, are continuous sequences of tetrachords divided into incomposite intervals in various ways, some tetrachords being linked together so that the highest note of the lower tetrachord

---

[11] As is clear from the above, it is assumed here that Plato understands the entire structural arrangement of all forms, i.e. what in the case of forms answers to the "single bond" of the elemental sounds in the *Philebus*, as the principle of the realm of forms mentioned briefly at the end of *Republic* 6 and thus as the Good, a form unto itself that communes with all other subordinate forms and ultimately allows them to commune with one another; for further discussion of the Good see 1.2.4.1 and 1.3.8–9. On structure in Plato see Harte (2002).

[12] On the difference of Greek from modern scales see Barker (2007) 8.

is also the lowest note of the tetrachord above, whereas between other tetrachords there is an incomposite interval, always the same (a "tone", i.e. 9:8).[13] Leaving aside the divisions of the tetrachords and the range spanned by their continuous arrangement, what matters in connection with forms is that notes build intervals, which build larger intervals until the basic structural units of the fourths are reached (or, if there is a tone between two tetrachords, of a fourth and a "fifth", 3:2 = 4:3 × 9:8), all of which cohere into an overarching structure, just as the groups of the elements of speech do: each note and interval is defined by its place in the substructures of this structure and ultimately by its place in this entire structure itself, by the relations in which it stands to all other notes and intervals in the system.

As in the case of the elements of speech, this system holds its parts together and turns their multitude into a unity, thereby allowing all its components to be the subject matter of a single discipline, harmonics: whether Plato presupposes as fundamental structural units of this system only two tetrachords joined by a tone and spanning an octave (2:1) or its elaborate extension to the span of two octaves (4:1), the purpose of this system "was to make it possible to locate all acceptable melodic patterns and structures and to identify the relations between

---

13 Two tetrachords joined by a tone and spanning an octave (2:1 = 4:3 × 9:8 × 4:3). On the left column are shown the names of the Greek notes, from lower (bottom) to higher (top).

νήτη	τετράχορδον τὸ διὰ τεσσάρων (4:3)	
παρανήτη		
τρίτη		
παραμέση		
	τόνος (9:8)	τὸ διὰ πασῶν (2:1)
μέση	τετράχορδον τὸ διὰ τεσσάρων (4:3)	
λιχανός		
παρυπάτη		
ὑπάτη		

them within a single, integrated scheme".¹⁴ Plato envisages forms as arranged into a similar integrated scheme that gives philosophy its unity as a discipline.

Insofar as it is synoptic, philosophical knowledge is not only of forms but also of their participants which turn into objects of knowledge if referred to the relevant forms, although in themselves they cannot be objects of knowledge but only of changeable opinion.¹⁵ Full knowledge, according to Socrates in the *Philebus*, is not only of justice itself and every other being, e.g. the divine sphere itself and the divine circle itself, but of the human spheres and circles too used in arts such as building, which are clearly sensible participants in the forms of the sphere and the circle, and thus by implication of justice in human affairs, both private and public: although knowledge of forms, which are not subject to coming into being and passing away and are always unchangeable, is different and truer than knowledge of what comes to be and passes away, i.e. of the various participants in forms, a difference reflected in the description of the former as pure and the latter as impure, nevertheless both kinds of knowledge are necessary for full knowledge, with precedence given understandably to the pure knowledge of forms (61d10–62d3).

As a synoptic view, true philosophical knowledge is, therefore, wider and requires substantially more than mere knowledge of forms, though it is because of them that everything else which falls within its remit does so: to repeat the examples Plato gives in the *Philebus*, in order to know the human spheres and circles used in building etc. one needs to know much more than the divine sphere and circle, whether we approach them indirectly in mathematics or directly in philosophy, as the intelligible exemplars in which sensible artifacts we use in various areas of life participate. Full knowledge of music requires not only the pure knowledge of harmonics with its synoptic integration of all scales into a single arithmetical and proportion-theoretic framework, thanks to which the infinitely

---

14 Barker (2007) 16, referring to the so-called Greater Perfect System whose core are the two tetrachords in n. 13 which are linked by a tone thus spanning an octave: extending the core by the addition of two extra tetrachords, one above the upper and one below the lower, so that the highest note of the lower tetrachord is the lowest note of the tetrachord above, and by the addition of a tone to the tetrachord at the bottom, we obtain the Greater Perfect System, which spans two octaves. If we take only the lower tetrachord of the core and, having adjoined a tetrachord to its bottom and the tone to the new bottom, we continue by adjoining a further tetrachord to its top, we obtain the so-called Lesser Perfect System spanning an octave and a fourth. The two systems are clearly the two branches of a single Perfect System; see Barker (2007) 16. Its core seems to have been extended in late 4th cent. BC; see Barker (2007) 12–13, according to whom only the central octave is presupposed in Plato's dialogues.
15 See Fine (1999) 215–225. Conversely, forms can be objects of opinion too.

various heard melodies constitute music. It also requires its impure counterpart (cf. *Phlb.* 62c1–2), the knowledge of music based not on reason and exact mathematics but rather on the senses, experience, practice and approximation: this is the knowledge of how to produce harmony not by relating one pitch to another in a ratio but by a set of practical rules for the successful construction e.g. of a wind-instrument with such an arrangement of finger-holes that it produce pitches in a certain pattern, whose intervals will be, however, only approximately those determined by pure, or theoretical, harmonics for this pattern (see *Phlb.* 55d1–56a8 and cf. *Ti.* 68e1–69a5).

That philosophical knowledge is synoptic because it not only aims at viewing forms in their mutual interdependence as parts of a coherent whole but also brings sensibles under its survey is already suggested by the demand in the seventh book of the *Republic* that the freed prisoners from the cave, metaphor for the philosophers who have escaped the prison of the sensible world and accessed the forms, return to the cave, and not bask blissfully in the intelligible light of the Good aboveground: they should not despise the only things one can see in the cave, shadows cast by mere simulacra of the things themselves which they have been privileged to see directly outside the cave, but get used to seeing and learning these things and not shy away from the pain involved, for the willing returnees will see all images and simulacra in the cave far better than their unlucky fellows since they will have viewed the originals outside the prison (519c8–520d5).

1.1.3 The forms of mathematical objects

The forms named after the objects studied in mathematics, geometry and arithmetic, are introduced at the end of *Republic* 6 in the simile of the divided line as the objects mathematical theorems are really about (509d6–511e5): a theorem about e.g. the square concerns not any sensible square such as the one that might be drawn by a mathematician or a student in carrying out the theorem's proof but the square itself, the form of the square.[16] This type of realism according to which

---

[16] Plato does not argue for this claim. His only argument for the existence of forms of mathematical objects occurs in *R.* 7, 521d4–525c7, esp. 524d8–525a9, where the intelligible nature of numbers is shown by a reference to the argument in *R.* 5, 478e7–480a13, which suggests that these numbers are beings, form-numbers (cf. above n. 6); cf. Cleary (2013b) 417. As for the objects of geometry, in the subsequent discussion of geometry it is simply assumed as self-evident that geometry aims at knowing not what comes into existence and goes out of it but instead beings, i.e. forms, which can only be those of the various objects studied in geometry (*R.* 7, 527a1–b11).

mathematical objects exist objectively, independently of our thought and neither in space nor in time, is perhaps what is best known as Platonism.[17] It does not go out of fashion and we can plausibly guess that "it will persist through generations yet unborn. It is an instructive response to the very experience of many mathematicians".[18] As the objects mathematics is really about, forms are best viewed not as universals but as abstract particulars.[19] Geometry does not study a single square: it assumes an indefinitely or infinitely large number of copies of each of its objects such as the square. In view of the imagery of the cave simile, these are in each case multiple 'shadows' cast by a unique form, which is approached by the mathematicians only via the study of its 'shadows'.[20] In the simile of the divided line Plato has Socrates locate the difference between mathematics and philosophy in the way each studies forms. Mathematics studies forms indirectly in that it relies (a) on their sensible 'images', the 'shadows' forms cast on the sensible world and which in this context are the figures usually accompanying Greek mathematical proofs but can also very well be their visualizable counterparts in a mathematician's active mind; (b) on problematic definitions of forms, non-true "hypotheses".[21] Ideally, philosophy has no need for crutches and approaches the

---

Ep. 7, 343a5–b3 shows that the argument like that in *R.* 7, 521d4–525c7, could have been used to establish the existence of forms of geometrical objects. Forms answering to geometrical concepts, of the equal and the commensurable, are shown to exist in the third argument from the sciences and the arguments from relatives for the existence of forms, which Aristotle had discussed and criticized in his treatise *On forms* (Alex. Aphr. *In metaph.* 79.11–15 and 83.6–16 Hayduck). The other two arguments from the sciences (*In metaph.* 79.5–11 Hayduck) can also establish the existence of forms of mathematical objects. The relationship of all three arguments from the sciences to *R.* 5, 478e7–480a13, is fully discussed in Fine (1995) 91–97 (cf. her treatment in ch. 10 of the argument from relatives); see also Cleary (2013a). That geometry studies objects which do not behave like sensible objects seems to have been first pointed out by Protagoras (Arist. *Metaph.* B 2, 997b35–998a4 = Protag. DK 80 B 7); see Pritchard (1995) 140–143.

17 Cf. e.g. Annas (1976) 3–4, Panza & Sereni (2013) 1–26, Hacking (2014) 191–222.
18 Hacking (2014) 206; cf. *R.* 7, 527a1–b1.
19 Abstract is used in the sense 'existing outside space and time'. On what is studied in mathematics as abstract particulars see Lowe (2002) 375–376; cf. Panza & Sereni (2013) 1–6. In mathematics, what does not look at all like a thing, e.g. a function, is often treated as such; cf. Gowers (2008) 10.
20 On the so-called intermediates, see below 1.2.3.
21 Pritchard (1995) 94–95 connects hypotheses with forms but does not call them definitions of forms; for hypotheses in the divided-line simile as definitions see Bostock (2009) 13. The use of mental visualization in geometry is not mentioned by Plato but it is very unlikely that he does not tacitly presuppose it alongside the use of visible diagrams. In *R.* 7, 527a1–b11, Socrates says that the habitual talk of performing on 'geometrical' objects such operations as squaring, adding and applying areas presupposes that these objects do come to be and pass away, although in

forms in themselves to give satisfactory accounts of them; as said in *Republic* 7, mathematics sees beings not in the state of wakefulness, as philosophy does, but as if in a dream (533a10–c6).[22]

The unsatisfactory definitions of forms in mathematics are the definitions of objects, e.g. of the square, studied in mathematics. They are the foundations of mathematics, as Plato conceives them.[23] Compared to the definitions of forms philosophy aims to give, full explanatory accounts of forms in the light of their interrelationships with one another (see 1.1.2), the foundations of mathematics are deficient probably because they are incomplete: they are not "true" hypotheses, springboards from which one can reach other regions in the structured domain of forms, but mere beginnings of proofs, chains of consistent steps leading to certain conclusions about the definienda without illuminating their true nature (cf. *R.* 7, 533a10–c6). The objects they define, moreover, are mental idealizations of

---

fact they are beings, forms, which implies that it cannot be they themselves that are treated by the geometers as if they were coming to be and passing away but some other things similar to, and partaking of, them. The fact that contemporary geometry can study forms only by means of their participants necessitates its prominently operational and constructive character. Nothing suggests that for Plato the concrete objects on which geometrical operations can be performed are only sensibles, not their mentally formed 'images' as well.

22 As Fine (1999) 235–242 notes, this description of philosophy does not apply to Plato's own philosophy in the *Republic*, for it is like mathematics insofar as it too necessarily relies on images and non-true hypotheses. Indeed, Plato believes that contemporary philosophy is undeveloped since in his view mathematics must pave the way for true philosophy but contemporary mathematics has not sufficiently progressed to do so; see below 1.2.4.9.

23 He seems to imply that the foundations of mathematics are unsatisfactory not only from a philosophical but also from a mathematical point of view. Aristotle reports that Plato rejected points, the first kind of object to be defined in Euclid's *Elements* (1 Def. 1), as fictions of the geometers (*Metaph.* A 9, 992a19–24), but the context leaves unclear whether Plato found the concept of point in itself objectionable, and if so why, or simply the assumption that points are principles of lines (see also next n.). Judging from the Euclidean definitions of other basic geometrical objects and number (*El.* 1 Def. 2–7 and 7 Def. 1–2), Plato would have certainly had good reasons to find them problematic; see the remarks in Mueller (2006) 39–40 and 58–59 on the principles of *El.* 1 and the Euclidean definitions of unit and number respectively (the latter are subjected by Plato to dialectical scrutiny in *R.* 7, 525c8–526b3; see 1.2.4.8). Aristotle mentions an apparently pre-Euclidean definition of the line as what is produced by the motion of a point and of the plane as what is produced by the motion of a line (*de An.* A 4, 409a3–5); in Euclid's *El.* 11 the sphere, the cone and the cylinder are defined kinematically (Def. 14, 18 and 21) but, since Plato thinks that the objects mathematics really studies are forms, he would have denied that kinematic definitions of geometrical objects illuminate the forms of these objects, though he would have certainly considered the reliance on intuitive assumptions about motion in geometry to be equally indispensible to contemporary geometry with performing operations such as squaring (cf. above n. 21).

sensible participants in forms of mathematical objects, rarefied 'shadows' of forms in the souls of mathematicians or in the product of our intellectual and social activity called mathematics, which transcends any individual intelligent soul, though it cannot exist apart from souls. However, the forms of mathematical objects such as the square, the geometrical objects themselves, are not themselves geometrical. As stated in the *Phaedrus*, forms lack shape (247c6–8); indeed, there is no reason to assume that the form of any geometrical object should not be as fundamentally different from its 'images' as famously is the form of beauty according to the *Symposium*.[24] That these forms were defined in contemporary mathematics geometrically, i.e. as idealized material objects, and form-numbers similarly as groups of at best ideal units indistinguishable in all these groups (see 1.2.4.6), also explains in part the unsatisfactoriness of their mathematical definitions.

---

24 Aristotle's testimony that Plato rejected points as fictions of the geometers and considered not points but indivisible lines to be principles of lines (see previous n.) perhaps suggests that the lines themselves, the forms of lines which are the true principles of the 'shadowy' lines geometry is proximately concerned with, are non-extended, hence indivisible and not really lines, unlike the things depending on them and studied in geometry; for forms of geometrical objects as indivisible entities see *LI* 1, 968a9–14, where, though, it is not specified whether these forms are themselves geometrical objects or are merely called so misleadingly after the objects that resemble them in the physical world and in mathematics, for lack of better terminology. If Plato did speak of the forms of lines as indivisible lines, the plural perhaps reflected the fact that in Greek geometry a line determines an infinite class of rational lines commensurable with it both in length and in square, opposed to which is an infinite class of irrational lines commensurable with a member of the rational class neither in length nor in square (Euc. *El.* 10, Def. 3). What might possibly be the aspect of non-geometrical forms which is manifested in their material and mental 'shadows' as the phenomena of commensurability and incommensurability and how it is so manifested were in all probability questions Plato did not try to answer. That the forms of geometrical objects are not themselves geometrical is clearly suggested by the author of *Ep.* 7, 342a7–d3. As Proclus will point out much later (*in Euc.* 54.1–8 Friedlein), in the realm of the immaterial causes extended things exist without extension, divided things without division, magnitudes without magnitude and figures without shape. It is implausible that Plato regarded the forms of geometrical objects as paradigmatic cases of the objects that were defined in the hypotheses of contemporary geometry: e.g. as a square and a circle that not only lack the slightest deviations from true straightness and circularity but are also not subject to any kind of change whatsoever, unlike all their sensible and mental 'shadows' resembling them, as a single square and a single circle that are different from, but as perfect as, countless mathematical circles and lines over which they each preside.

1.1.4 Forms and forms of mathematical objects in the cave simile

Mathematics seems to differ from philosophy also in that it is concerned with a limited range of forms, those of mathematical objects, not all of them, unlike philosophy, though this is not noted. However, the cave simile seems to hint that all forms are of mathematical objects. The shadows and reflections of people, animals, artifacts etc. outside the cave stand for forms as are studied in mathematics, i.e. indirectly. These forms can only be the forms of mathematical objects. But since the people, the animals, the artifacts etc. themselves outside the cave, the things that cast the shadows and are reflected, are metaphors for all forms as studied in philosophy, all forms are those of mathematical objects: philosophy sees them directly, in themselves, mathematics approaches them indirectly. The part of the simile concerning mathematics must presuppose only the forms that mathematics studies indirectly if they do not exhaust the range of forms: similarly, the part of the simile about philosophy must presuppose the entire range of forms, but the metaphors for the entire range of forms can be put into one-to-one correspondence with the metaphors for the range of forms of mathematical objects, hence all forms are forms of mathematical objects (cf. Intro. on *R.* 7, 537b7–c8).

If so, however, there arises a problem: what is to be done with the forms explicitly mentioned in *Republic* 5, the forms of beauty and ugliness, of justice and injustice, of the good and the bad? If the range of forms contains only forms of mathematical objects, then it seems to have no place for the forms named in *Republic* 5, as well as for the indefinitely many other forms which are assumed to also exist apart from them and those of mathematical objects but are unnamed, if these anonymous, non-mathematical forms are posited in accordance to the principle laid down in *Republic* 10: each word applied to a multitude of distinct things such as *bed* and *table*, hence the name of any other artifact, is the name of a form (596a5–b3).[25] This principle yields the forms of mathematical objects, at least of those known at any given time to mathematics, and the forms mentioned in *Republic* 5, but also many others.[26]

---

25 For an alternative but unconvincing construal of the sentence see Smith (1917) 70–71.
26 Cf. the one-over-many argument for the existence of forms from Aristotle's *On forms* (Alex. Aphr. *In metaph.* 80.8–15 Hayduck).

1.2 The problem of the range of forms

1.2.1 The evidence

That in the cave simile forms of mathematical objects seem to be the only existing forms is a facet of the well-known problem raised in the *Parmenides* about the range of forms. In the first part of this dialogue Socrates posits forms of similarity and dissimilarity, multitude and oneness, changelessness/rest and change/motion and all suchlike. Parmenides asks whether he thinks that there are also forms of justice, beauty, the good and all similar things:[27] to this question Socrates answers positively without hesitation, but when Parmenides next asks if he also posits forms of things such as man, fire and water, he admits that he is often puzzled about whether he ought to posit such forms or not. And when Parmenides next asks if he is also puzzled about the possibility of forms of laughable things such as hair, mud and filth, at first he denies that there can be such forms and then confesses that he is often troubled by the possibility that all kinds of forms exist but is averse to entertain it seriously, fearing that he might drown in nonsense. Plato has Parmenides answer that Socrates is still young and does not yet philosophize as he will when he will mature and, disregarding the prejudices of people, will not despise anything (129d6–130e4). Here Plato perhaps endorses implicitly the unrestricted application of the principle laid down in *Republic* 10 so as to widen the range of forms to the greatest possible extent;[28] alternatively, he might endorse a quite narrower range of forms and warn that the principle in *Republic* 10 yields not only forms but also many other things that may look like forms but are not, for reasons, though, that have nothing to do with the prejudices of those who would pour scorn on a philosopher's worry about the possibility that hair, mud and filth can exist apart from those on dirty bodies or clothes.[29]

In the *Statesman* Plato seems to restrict the strength of the form-generating principle laid down in *Republic* 10. He has the Eleatic Stranger warn that humans cannot be correctly divided into Greeks and barbarians, for the word *barbarian* is not applied to things that have something essential in common, which is probably the case with the word *Greek* too; nor can numbers be split into ten thousand, which in Greek is denoted by a single word, and the rest if we decide to call all of

---

27 Answering to incomplete predicates, concealed comparatives such as *beautiful* as well as relatives such as *equal*, these forms are the only ones whose existence is posited in the middle dialogues, except in *R*. 10, according to Owen (1957) and others.
28 See Ross (1951) 85.
29 Cf. Fine (1995) 110–113.

them by a certain name. If the divisions will be correct, they will be made according to those parts which are also forms, not mere parts: humans will be split into males and females, numbers into odd and even numbers (262c8–263a1).[30] Here Plato either rejects the principle "one form for each word applied to many things", to which he subscribed at the time he wrote *Republic* 10, or just finds an opportunity to make it clear that, as he also might suggest in the *Parmenides*, he never intended this principle as generator only of forms in the sense in which this term is employed to describe what is really studied in mathematics and philosophy.

Aristotle notes in *Metaph.* A 9, 990b8–15, that some of the arguments for the existence of forms are inflationary, for they yield forms not assumed to exist such as the forms of negations, presumably the forms of the not-beautiful, not-just, not-good etc., and a few lines below remarks that there are no Platonic forms of artifacts (991b6–7). In *EN* A 4, 1096a10–18, he reports that Plato did not posit a form of number since he did not posit a form over many things in serial order. But the division of numbers in the *Statesman* according to the forms of oddness and evenness, which are also posited in the *Phaedo* (see 1.1.2), seems to assume the articulation of the form of number into these two forms and other parts, which are clearly not forms, such as those defined by e.g. 10,000. As seen above, moreover, the form of dissimilarity, a negation, appears in the *Parmenides*.

1.2.2 The forms of negations, of similarity and dissimilarity and of opposites

The existence of the forms of number, even and odd number, negations and all artifacts is guaranteed by the principle of *Republic* 10. It is unlikely that Plato countenances forms of negations.[31] But a negation cannot be understood independently of the thing whose name is negated: if this thing is Platonically conceived as a form, its complement comprises all other forms than the one whose name is negated, and this complement could be called form of this negation in a derivative sense of the term, insofar as it is objectively determined by a true form.[32] The form of dissimilarity in the *Parmenides* can be understood in this manner: not as one of the infinitely many true forms in which things participate in order to take on the aspect of dissimilarity but as all true forms other than a given one in which participation would mark the participants as similar and which thus

---

30 Cf. *Phdr.* 265d2–e3 and Arist. *Metaph.* Λ 3, 1070a18–19.
31 See Fine (1995) 108–110 and 113–116.
32 Cf. Fine (1995) 108–110 and 113–115 with n. 61 and 62.

can be called form of similarity, an alias for any true form. If so, in *Metaph*. A 9, 990b8–15, Aristotle simply points out what Plato himself might hint in the *Parmenides* and the *Statesman*: the principle in *Republic* 10 (and its underlying argument; cf. n. 26) does not generate only forms in the par excellence sense of the term, in which it denotes the abstract entities endowing aspects of the sensible world with derivative properties, but a hodgepodge of forms and form-like entities.

Even if Plato does not admit forms of negations, he countenances forms of opposites:[33] the forms of even and odd number(s) are said to be opposite in the *Phaedo* (see 1.1.2).[34] This need not mean, however, that he also posits forms of e.g. ugliness, injustice and badness. These forms are mentioned in *Republic* 5 and their existence, like that of forms of even and odd number(s), is guaranteed by the principle of *Republic* 10. However, it is difficult to see why Plato would need to introduce the forms of ugliness, injustice and the bad if the forms of beauty, justice and the good help explain why various things around us are, and are thus called, beautiful, just and good: things that are ugly, unjust and bad must be such simply because they do not participate, directly or indirectly, in the forms of beauty, justice and the good, though they should, or because they do so but very defectively, not because they participate in opposite forms.[35] One's actions and activities are defined in *Republic* 4 as just only if they preserve and promote that condition of the soul which is defined as justice and, as will turn out, results from the soul's direct participation in the form of justice, in which all just actions and activities thus participate indirectly: one's actions and activities are unjust if, on the contrary, damage that condition of the soul, provided, of course, that it exists, i.e. if they are incompatible with it, hence with the participation of the soul in the relevant form of justice (443b9–444a9). As with injustice and being unjust, so with ugliness and being ugly or badness and being bad. Again, however, all unjust, ugly, and bad things fall into kinds as well defined by the failure to participate in the relevant forms of beauty, justice and the good as are the kinds of beautiful, just and good things which are informed by the forms of beauty, justice and the good: Plato might have thus mentioned in certain contexts all things that fail to resemble a form, though they should, as a form, one bearing the name of the

---

33 See Fine (1995) 113 n. 53 and 191 n. 28.
34 Other forms of opposites are e.g. the forms of large and small, on which see 1.3.2, and of equality and inequality, on which see 1.3.3.
35 For another reason for denying that Plato posits forms of all opposites see Fine (1995) 191 n. 28.

property which is the opposite to that after which the true form is named, without intending to introduce the form of e.g. ugliness next to that of beauty.

1.2.3 The forms of artifacts

As for artifacts, what must be known in order to construct them can be paralleled with the objects of mathematical and philosophical knowledge, the forms, insofar as it is intersubjective, can be learned with difficulty in many cases and is a paradigm for the relevant articles that instantiate it and resemble it in varying degrees (cf. *R.* 6, 500b8–d10, and *Lg.* 12, 965b7–c8): thus, since the content of this knowledge, though manmade, unlike forms, shares a lot with forms, Plato can refer to it as the form of the relevant artifact and again Aristotle can report its lack of formhood as usually understood.[36] Similar to the forms of artifacts as understood here seem to be the mathematical objects, or intermediates, which, according to Aristotle, Plato wedged between forms and sensibles as a third kind of existents. Although these are similar to forms in two respects, they are similar to sensibles in another respect: they are like forms insofar as they are eternal and unchangeable, but also resemble sensibles in that each of them is not single but comes in many copies (*Metaph.* A 6, 987b14–18). They can be plausibly understood as the indefinitely large multitude of non-sensible 'shadows' of each form of a mathematical object in the discipline of mathematics, a product of human intellectual and social activity transcending any individual intelligent soul, though it cannot exist apart from souls. Nor thus can its purported objects do so, unlike the forms, the true objects of mathematics, whose 'shadowy copies' they are. Yet they are like the forms in that they are non-material and, as long as there is mathematics, enjoy a stable and very long objective existence, though they are certainly not eternal, or unchangeable in the same sense as the forms. Plato could have stressed the similarity between the forms of mathematical objects and the indefinitely many 'copies' of each as defined in contemporary mathematics only for Aristotle to argue polemically that the latter must also be as eternal and unchangeable as the former and accuse Plato of ontological inflation.[37]

---

[36] Cf. Fine (1995) 81–88 and 101–102.
[37] There is no hint in Plato's works that he introduced the distinction between intermediates and forms; nothing in e.g. *R.* 6, 509d6–511e5, hints that his example of an object studied in mathematics, the square itself with the diagonal itself, is not a form but an intermediate (it is an intermediate according to e.g. Yang [1999], a form according to Franklin [2012] 494–497). Not unreasonably, scholars have doubted that Plato had put forth this distinction even in his discussions with members of the Academy. For references see Arsen (2012) 201, who argues in

1.2.4 The form of number

1.2.4.1 The Good

The context of Aristotle's testimony in *EN* A 4, 1096a10–18, on the form of number is a criticism of the Good: whereas Plato correctly did not assume the existence of the form of number, he assumed erroneously the existence of the Good, a form whose existence should not have been posited, for there is not a single goodness over and above what is good in each category of beings, just as there cannot be a form of number over and above the supposed individual form-numbers. Just as there is no doubt that Plato assumes the existence and the paramount importance of the Good, however, there is every reason to think that he would not object to the existence of the form of number. The Good seems to be nothing other than all forms as a unified whole structured by their interrelationships (see 1.1.2). This whole is described in the *Sophist* as the bright land of being to which the philosopher belongs and, as a consequence, it is not easy to see him, for the eyes of the soul of the many cannot stand this divine light (254a8–b2). This allusion to the sun as symbol of the Good in the sixth and seventh books of the *Republic*, and to a passage in the latter where the point about the eyes of the soul is repeated (518a1–b6), suggests that the Good is the structure of the domain of forms (cf. 1.3.8). As Socrates puts it in the *Gorgias*, what is good, in a particular field of expertise and in the human soul, is the arrangement of various distinct elements into a well-ordered, harmonious whole (503d6–504a5): so the Good as the highest object of philosophy, the paradigm of what is good anywhere, must be the harmony of the interrelationships among the other objects studied in philosophy, all the other forms.[38]

---

favor of intermediates (for references to proponents of intermediates see Cleary [2013b] 422 n. 17). For a survey of older literature against the inclusion of intermediates in Plato's ontology see Brentlinger (1963). He suggests that as intermediates, in a weaker sense than that in which the term is employed by Aristotle, Plato must have viewed the objects of definitions in arithmetic and geometry. In *Ep.* 7, 342a7–344d2, definitions are one of the means by which everything can be known, so their objects, which are different from both sensibles and forms whose representations they actually are, are indispensable to mathematical knowledge, which is actually of forms: mathematicians fail to realize this crucial fact, thus ending up treating erroneously as objects of mathematical knowledge what are only means to it. Cf. Pritchard (1995) 156–160. Blyth (2000) attempts to save the distinction between intermediate or mathematical numbers and form-numbers by arguing on the basis of the so-called generation of numbers in the *Parmenides* (on which see below 1.2.4.3) that form-numbers are ordinals whereas intermediate numbers are cardinals; see, though, Cleary (2013b) 423–424 (and cf. 422–423 on Annas [1975]).

38 Cf. Fine (1999) 226–229 and Seel (2007) 185 and 193. Schindler (2008) 107–117 offers a helpful survey of views on the Good. On the metaphor of the sun see 2.1.

In the *Republic* Plato notoriously presents Socrates as very reluctant to expatiate on the nature of the Good: Socrates says that this form is not sufficiently known and then that about it he has only opinions, which he reveals with images (6, 504e6–505b3 and 506d5–e1). But a crucial passage suggests that the Good is simply the orderly interconnectedness of all forms into a system. Expert craftsmen of temperance, justice and all virtue or goodness, the philosophers are said in *Republic* 6 to have their minds fixed on the rational order of always unchangeable beings, the forms, seeing them neither wronging nor being wronged by one another and thus trying to imitate their order as much as possible (500b8–d10): this order, the relations of mutual support binding together all other forms into a system, seems to be the highest form of them all, the Good, and the paradigm whose 'images' are all virtues, the human good. In a relevant passage of the *Philebus*, moreover, Plato has Socrates say that in order to try to understand what is the good for man and for everything else, or at the level of the entire cosmos, and get an idea about the nature of this form, one must look at the most beautiful and undisturbed, literally free from factional strife, blend or union (63e7–64a3). This union is of reason, on the one hand, and true or pure pleasures (cf. 51b1–52b9), health and virtues, on the other, and seems to hint at the nature of the Good as the unifying communion of forms into the structure illustrated earlier by the analogy of the elements of speech and harmony and their sets (see 1.1.2): the cognate verbs of the nouns translated here as "blend" or "union" (μεῖξις καὶ κρᾶσις) are used in the *Sophist* for the communion of forms (252e9–253d4).

1.2.4.2 The Good-like form of number

If this is how Plato thinks of the Good in his dialogues, it is hard to believe that he rejected the existence of the form of number, as Aristotle reports. For he could easily think of this form, by analogy with the Good, as the unified arrangement of all sets into which the individual form-numbers belong and which are forms unto themselves: the sets of odd and even form-numbers, the forms of even and odd number(s) or of evenness and oddness, are two of them (see 1.1.2). To use the analogies of forms with elements of speech and musical notes (see again 1.1.2), each individual form-number is like an element of speech or a note, the sets in which these forms belong, such as those of even and odd form-numbers, answering to the sets of the elements of speech and to the intervals composed by many notes. As it is, if Plato grants the status of form on sets of form-numbers such as those of the even and odd form-numbers but not on those of e.g. all form-numbers up to and including any given form-number and of all the remaining form-numbers, there is no reason why we should not ascribe to him the notion of the unified structure of these sets as a Good-like form, the form of number.³⁹

1.2.4.3 The 'generation' of numbers in the *Parmenides*

Plato's interest in the sets into which numbers are naturally organized, disregarding the sets into which their totality can be divided as if badly carved by an inexperienced cook (cf. *Phdr.* 265d2–e3), is evident in the so-called generation of numbers in the second hypothesis of the *Parmenides*.⁴⁰ Actually, Plato does not generate the numbers but assumes their existence and the truths of arithmetic:⁴¹ by so doing, he attempts to show that the subject of the hypothesis "if the one is" (ἓν εἰ ἔστιν), considered in itself, independently of the being of which it partakes, has been broken down into the largest possible, infinitely large multitude of the smallest and largest possible parts, as many as those into which being is itself divided.

An earlier argument has established that, insofar as it participates in being, the subject of the hypothesis has infinitely many parts: the one is different from the being of which it has a share and which is said of the one; and, since each part of the composite one-being, the one and the being, must both share in being and be one itself, the doubleness of the initial one-being is doubled, which goes on ad infinitum (142b1–143a3).⁴² Having introduced the difference of the one from the being in which the one participates, Plato points out next that we can refer to the difference and the one or to the difference and being or to the one and being as "both", and to the difference or the one or being as "each", which means that we can refer to them as "two" and "one" respectively; but two plus one make three, which are odd, just as two are even, and two are two times one, just as three are three times one, so we can also form the products two times two, three times three, two times three and three times two: we have thus obtained the even times even numbers like two times two, the odd times odd numbers like three times

---

39 *Plt.* 262c8–263a1 suggests that e.g. form-numbers up to and including 10,000 and all the rest are mere parts of the form of number which are not themselves forms; cf., though, 1.3.2.
40 The second hypothesis in the second part of *Prm.* can be plausibly assumed to be a general study of any Platonic form as "one that is", as one-being, which analyzes its subject into two parts, i.e. oneness and being, indissolubly related to both it and to each other but logically separable and conceived as forms in which each form must participate to be what it is in virtue of itself and to be exactly one in virtue of itself; see Silverman (2002) 105–121.
41 Cf. Allen (1970) and Schofield (1972) 102–103.
42 This passage is often assumed to be the first part of the 'generation' of numbers; see e.g. Turnbull (1998) 75–82 and Annas (1976) 48–51. But is seems to be a different argument.

three, the odd times even numbers like three times two and, finally, the even times odd numbers, which are not different from the last ones, like two times three; this means that we have got all numbers; as it is, the hypothesis entails the existence of numbers but, if there are numbers, it follows that there is an infinitely large multitude of beings, that of numbers which comes to be by participation in being, just as each part of an number also comes to be (143a4–144a9). Being has thus been divided up as much as possible into an infinitely large multitude of parts, into the smallest and largest possible beings, i.e. not only into numbers but presumably also into each constituent part of a number which Euclid calls "unit" when he defines in *El.* 7 Def. 2 number as a multitude of units, and into infinitely large sets of numbers such as those that so prominently appear in the argument (it is unlikely that as largest possible beings or largest possible parts of being Plato here hypothesizes infinitely large numbers); however, there is no way in which a part of being can fail to be one part, so not only being but also the one itself necessarily has been completely fragmented, isomorphically with being (144b1–e9).

The argument that the hypothesis "if the one is" entails the existence of numbers seems to be an application to the analysis of the hypothesis at hand of the principle in *R.* 7, 522c1–9, that all knowledge and all thought presuppose the concepts of one, two, three and, in general, number: as turns out from the words we use when talking about the one-being, thinking about it presupposes the concepts of one, two and three, thus evenness and oddness, multiplication and all species of numbers mentioned in the argument. These species are neither exhaustive nor mutually exclusive, for the odd times even numbers are not different and the even times odd ones, the even times even ones overlap with them, and a most important and interesting class of odd numbers, the primes, are missing, odd times odd numbers being non-prime odds.[43] But if the odd primes are implicitly present as all odd numbers such as 3, their addition to the other number species makes the list exhaustive. All kinds of number are thus presupposed, and the next step in the argument, the infinity of numbers, can be explained as a tacit importation from arithmetic, which assumes infinitely many numbers of each kind as well as infinitely many units combinable in infinitely many ways into the multitudes numbers are defined to be. The next step in the argument, the identification of units, their multitudes, i.e. the numbers, and the multitudes of these multitudes, such as odd numbers, with beings can follow from the tacit application of the Parmenidean principle to numbers, the only entities the logical

---

43 Cf. Heath (1981) vol. 1, 71–72.

investigation of one-being presupposes: only being can be spoken of, thought of and known (cf. 142a1–8).

The argument cleaves closely to the mathematics of Plato's day, at least to the extent that Euclid's *Elements* can be considered a safe indicator of it.[44] The arithmetical books of the *Elements* do not begin with an ancestor of the modern approach to the natural, as we call them, numbers, whereby one lists a handful of axioms which capture our intuitive notion of the series of these numbers and also guarantee that there are no other natural numbers than those produced as consequences of these axioms. The definitions with which they begin are a definition of number, which is mathematically useless and captures the common-sense notion of number as a multitude of individuals (Def. 1–2), and definitions of relations between numbers and, mainly, various categories of number: after the definition of number are given those of the number which is a part of another number and of the number which is "parts" of another number (Def. 3–4), of the number which is a multiple of another one (Def. 5), of even and odd numbers and of their kinds Plato mentions in the *Parmenides* (Def. 6–10);[45] next come the definitions of prime and composite numbers as well as of those numbers which are prime and composite to one another (Def. 11–14), the definition of the product of two numbers and the definitions of plane, solid, square and cubic numbers (Def. 15–19), the definitions of proportional and similar (plane or solid) numbers (Def. 20–21) and the list ends with the definition of perfect numbers (Def. 22). Numbers are conceived as coming naturally organized into various families.

It is quite likely that in the second hypothesis of the *Parmenides* Plato also presupposes tacitly the kinds of plane, solid, square and cubic numbers: for, having first concluded that, if the one is, then all numbers must exist too, he goes on to argue from the finitude of the parts of being, which can only be the numbers, that being shares in shape (144e8–145b5). The actual wording of this conclusion seems to rule out a connection with the sets of 'geometrical' numbers since the shape in which being shares is described as rectilinear or round or a mixture of rectilinear and round shape (145b3–5). But here Plato might very well presuppose tacitly the conception of plane and solid numbers not only as products of two or

---

44 There is no reason to assume, as Scolnicov (2003) 101–106 does, that Plato operates in the *Parmenides* with a novel conception of number foreign to contemporary mathematics. Although he seems to have believed that future mathematics would bear a vague resemblance to the mathematics of his day (see 1.2.4.9), nothing hints that he boldly thought himself capable of going beyond the contemporary conception of number (see 1.2.4.6–8), though the realization of the logical priority of ordinals over cardinals can be attributed to him; see Cleary (2013b) 438–439.

45 The definition of odd times even number given after Def. 9 of the even times odd number is considered an interpolation; see Heath (1956) vol. 2, 283–284.

three equal or unequal numbers but also as figurate:⁴⁶ that is, as sets of points which form a geometrical figure on the plane and are thus the numbers called triangular, square, pentagonal and so; or which form a geometrical figure in space and are thus the numbers called pyramidal, whose bases are triangular, square, pentagonal and so on, and cubic.⁴⁷ If so, polygonal numbers with the indefinitely increasing multitude of their 'sides' and pyramidal numbers with the similarly indefinitely increasing multitude of their 'faces' can be plausibly described as having shapes which are mixtures of rectilinearity and roundness. By saying that the shape in which being shares is rectilinear or round or a mixture of both Plato does not offer three alternatives but with the third member of the disjunction explains that roundness should not be literally understood.⁴⁸

1.2.4.4 Aristotle's testimony in *EE* A 8, 1218a15–28

Aristotle's testimony in *EN* A 4, 1096a10–18, that Plato did not posit a form of number is contradicted by what he says in *EE* A 8, 1218a15–28: "The right way, moreover, of demonstrating that the Good exists is the contrary of the one now chosen. It is from things not admitted to possess goodness that they now derive the goodness of the things admitted to be good: they prove from numbers that justice and health are good because they are arrangements and numbers on the assumption that goodness belongs to numbers and their unities since the Good is unity. The right way, however, is to start from the things which are admitted to be good, e.g. health, strength, temperance, and prove that beauty is present to an even greater degree in what is unchanging;⁴⁹ for all these admitted goods consist in order and rest and, if this is so, the unchanging things are good to an even greater degree, for they possess order and rest to a greater degree. Proving, moreover, that the Good is unity with the claim that numbers aim at unity is an act of despair. For it is not clearly explained how they aim at unity but it is just said that

---

46 On these two notions of plane and solid numbers see Heath (1956) vol. 2, 287–291.
47 Speusippus discussed figurate numbers and the five regular solids of Plato's *Timaeus* in his treatise *On Pythagorean numbers* (122 I.P.). On figurate numbers see Deza & Deza (2012).
48 The second hypothesis in the second part of the *Parmenides* seems to offer numbers and geometrical objects as the only candidates for Platonic one-beings, forms: for, if numbers are beings, since there are figurate numbers named after some geometrical objects, then these geometrical objects themselves cannot but also qualify as beings on the same grounds on which numbers do so, and this must hold for all geometrical objects. Numbers as beings seem to be conceived in the *Parmenides* as defined in contemporary mathematics; cf. 1.1.3 and 1.2.4.6–8.
49 Cf. *Metaph.* M 3, 1078a31–b6.

they do so, and, at any rate, how can one think that lifeless things can have desire?"⁵⁰

Before these interesting lines Aristotle in effect repeats what he says in connection with the form of number in *EN* A 4, 1096a10–18: there is nothing common to, and separate from, a multitude of things each one of which is the successor of another, which means that there is no form of number (*EE* A 8, 1218a1–8). Here, too, Aristotle intends to argue against the existence of the Good by an analogy of individual goods with individual numbers, though the analogy and the conclusion of the argument are both missing due to a lacuna in the text. The passage just translated, however, suggests that Plato posited the existence of the form of number as unqualifiedly as he posited that of the Good. Aristotle leaves no doubt that the numbers, which here can only be form-numbers, are either those things whose unity constitutes the Good or, of all things whose unity is the Good, those which exemplify this unity in the most paradigmatic way. If the first, however, how and why would Plato have wanted to avoid not only positing the existence of the form of number but also identifying this form with the Good? If the unity of form-numbers is the Good, then how and why could it not be the form of number too? If the second, how and why would Plato have wanted to deny the existence of the form of number as a unity among others, all of which are linked into the maximal unity of the Good which the form of number exemplifies paradigmatically? It is plausible to assume, as argued above, that Plato conceived of this form as the structure of all sets into which the numbers are naturally arranged such as those of evens, odds, primes etc. It is also plausible to assume that the many unities of numbers to which Aristotle refers when he reports that "goodness belongs to numbers and their unities since the Good is unity" are these sets, and that, if Plato spoke of form-numbers as aiming at unity, he spoke metaphorically of their natural organization into these sets. The word translated as "unities" (μονάδες) can be translated as "units", but the context shows that Aristotle here speaks of what in numbers is analogous to the various unifying arrangements in things exhibiting derivative goodness, and the suitable translation of the word here seems

---

50 ἀνάπαλιν δὲ καὶ δεικτέον ἢ ὡς νῦν δεικνύουσι τὸ ἀγαθὸν αὐτό. νῦν μὲν γὰρ ἐκ τῶν ἀνομολογουμένων ἔχειν τὸ ἀγαθόν, ἐξ ἐκείνων τὰ ὁμολογούμενα εἶναι ἀγαθὰ δεικνύουσιν, ἐξ ἀριθμῶν, ὅτι ἡ δικαιοσύνη καὶ ἡ ὑγίεια ἀγαθόν· τάξεις γὰρ καὶ ἀριθμοί, ὡς τοῖς ἀριθμοῖς καὶ ταῖς μονάσιν ἀγαθὸν ὑπάρχον διὰ τὸ εἶναι τὸ ἓν αὐτὸ ἀγαθόν. δεῖ δ' ἐκ τῶν ὁμολογουμένων, οἷον ὑγιείας ἰσχύος σωφροσύνης, ὅτι καὶ ἐν τοῖς ἀκινήτοις μᾶλλον τὸ καλόν. πάντα γὰρ τάδε τάξις καὶ ἠρεμία· εἰ ἄρα, ἐκεῖνα μᾶλλον· ἐκείνοις γὰρ ὑπάρχει ταῦτα μᾶλλον. – παράβολος δὲ καὶ ἡ ἀπόδειξις ὅτι τὸ ἓν αὐτὸ τὸ ἀγαθόν, ὅτι οἱ ἀριθμοὶ ἐφίενται· οὔτε γὰρ ὡς ἐφίενται λέγονται φανερῶς, ἀλλὰ λίαν ἁπλῶς τοῦτό φασι, καὶ ὄρεξιν εἶναι πῶς ἄν τις ὑπολάβοι ἐν οἷς ζωὴ μὴ ὑπάρχει;

to be "unities".⁵¹ Plato employs it for the unitariness of forms in the *Philebus* (15a1–b8) before he suggest that a form can be a class of individuals, set of classes of individuals and so on (see 1.1.2).

1.2.4.5 Aristotle's testimony in *EN* A 4, 1096a10–18

Although it is almost certain that in *EN* A 4, 1096a10–18, Aristotle talks about Plato himself, the view that there is nothing common to, and separate from, many things each one of which is the successor of another is not attributed to Plato in *EE* A 8, 1218a1–8, though the mention of separation might be thought to suggest otherwise, and it seems that Aristotle himself denied the existence of something common to all things which come in serial order, whether or not this view was also espoused by Plato or other Academics.⁵² In *EN* A 4, 1096a10–18, Aristotle can be understood as saying merely that Plato did not posit the form of number anywhere in his dialogues, just as nowhere in his works he assumed, correctly by Aristotle's own lights, the existence of a form over many things in serial order: as pointed out above (1.2.1), the form of number is probably presupposed in the *Statesman*, but a single implicit mention of the form at issue does not invalidate Aristotle's report, which thus does not conflict with the hint at this form in *EE* A 8, 1218a15–28. If so, Aristotle's tacit point in *EN* A 4, 1096a10–18, against the existence of the Good is that, although in his writings Plato never talks about the supposed form of number, which should not have been posited to begin with, just as he correctly does not posit any form over things in serial order, he places much emphasis in his dialogues on the Good: this form should not have been posited either, however, for there is not a single goodness over and above what is good in each category of beings, just as there cannot be a form of number over the individual numbers.

Aristotle's antipathy towards the Platonic form of number does not arise only from his view that members of a series do not have something in common which is over them as a universal and could thus be platonically conceived as a form. He reports that, as we expect, a number platonically conceived as a form is not a heap of units piled together but an individual unity (*Metaph.* M 8, 1084b22–23). He raises, however, the issue of how this can be so in connection not only with form-numbers but all forms of mathematical objects: unlike the things that are

---

51 Even if Aristotle talks about units as unified into numbers in the passage under discussion, he undoubtedly locates goodness as unity in both units and numbers, and thus he also talks implicitly about the numbers themselves as unified: but this can only mean that numbers are naturally organized into sets such as those of evens, odds, primes etc.
52 See Ross (1951) 181–182 and Cleary (2013b) 437.

here around us, mathematical objects as denizens of the Platonic world of forms cannot be assumed to owe their unity and coherence to soul, a part of soul or something else and, since they are divisible quantities, no account of their unity and coherence can be plausibly forthcoming (*Metaph.* M 2, 1077a20–24). However, if he is unwilling to countenance the unitariness of individual form-numbers, he would be dead set against the view of finite or infinite sets of form-numbers as forms in themselves and thus as real unitary wholes: to consider a collection of individuals a unity, assuming that each item in the collection is somehow an individual and leaving aside the issue of a collection's actually infinite size, would be a nonstarter by his lights, for what would turn the collection from a heap into a unitary whole? The same problem plagues the conception of the entire structure of all these sets as a higher form overarching all of them, that of number.

1.2.4.6 Aristotle and Plato's conception of the forms of mathematical objects

Whether justified or not, Aristotle's objection to the unitariness of the Platonic forms of mathematical objects shows the gulf separating his and Plato's conception of mathematical objects, irrespective of the form of number. Aristotle clearly assumes that Plato's forms of geometrical objects are divisible, and thus extended, magnitudes like the homonymous objects which are studied in geometry, and that form-numbers are sets of units like the numbers studied in arithmetic. As seen above (1.1.3), however, Plato's *Phaedrus* leaves no doubt that he conceives the forms of geometrical objects as lacking shape, which can only mean that they are not extended and divisible unlike their 'images' which are studied in geometry not for their own sake but only in order to access their forms, the true objects of this discipline; the proximate subject matter of geometry corresponds to what Aristotle calls intermediates (see 1.2.3). For better or worse Plato took these forms to be as different from all their participants, both physical and mental, as the form of beauty is powerfully described in the *Symposium* to be from its 'images'. It is Aristotle who thinks that what in Plato's own view are mere 'images' of forms of geometrical objects and just homonymous with them are the true subject matter of geometry. In opposition to Plato he believes that geometers do actually study nothing but points, lines, plane and solid figures and, on top of that, he takes them to be nothing but the points, lines, plane and solid figures of physical bodies studied in isolation from these bodies from which they can be separated in thought with no resulting falsity (*Ph.* B 2, 193b22–194a12).[53]

The situation with numbers is similar. In reporting that a form-number is not a heap of units but a unitary entity Aristotle adds that a form-number is assumed to owe its unity to the fact that it is made up by its own special units which are different from those making up any other form-number. He distinguishes "mathematical" numbers, each of which contains its predecessor plus one unit, from numbers which do not each contain their predecessors; the former are made up of undifferentiated and combinable units, whereas each number of the other type has its own special units which cannot be combined with those contained in any other number (*Metaph.* M 6, 1080a12–35). Units in both kinds of number lack magnitude, are partless and indivisible (cf. *Metaph.* M 6, 1080b16–20, and 8, 1083b8–17). Aristotle calls numbers which are sets of indivisible units "monadic" (from μονάς, "unit"). Numbers with combinable units are intermediates since he says that for each one of them there are infinitely many alike (*Metaph.* M 7, 1081a5–12); numbers with non-combinable units are said to be forms since a form is unique (*Metaph.* M 7, 1082b24–28).

It is likely that the numbers with combinable units had indeed been posited by Plato himself (whether he called them and their geometrical analogues "intermediates" or the term was used only by Aristotle) as mental 'shadows' of form-numbers studied in contemporary arithmetic instead of these forms themselves. Leaving form-numbers aside, if Plato did conceive the subject matter of contemporary arithmetic in this way, he described accurately the implicit ontology of this arithmetic as we know it from the arithmetical books of Euclid's *Elements*. The definition of number as a multitude made up of units (*El.* 7 Def. 2) and the accompanying, mathematically useless, definition of the unit as that in accordance with which each thing is called one (*El.* 7 Def. 1) can be understood as positing in effect infinitely many idealized, undifferentiated units and at the same time infinitely many combinations of them into multitudes:[54] there is no number 1, the unit being not a multitude, and no unique 2, 3, 4… but an infinity of each of these multitudes.[55]

Form-numbers are clearly not intermediates. Indeed, as noted above (1.1.3) irrespective of the distinction between forms of mathematical objects and intermediates, Plato would not have conceived of form-numbers as multitudes of

---

53 On whether in Aristotle's view physical objects have perfect geometrical properties which are separable in thought see Mueller (1970), Lear (1982) and Kouremenos (2003).
54 These definitions seem to be presupposed by Plato; see 1.2.4.8.
55 See Mueller (2006) 58–59. On the number 1 see Pritchard (1995) ch. 5.

idealized units indistinguishable in all form-numbers, i.e. as Aristotle's first type of monadic numbers and as numbers can be thought to be defined in Euclid's *El.* 7. As just said, moreover, this view of number does not count 1 as a number but as the unit, whose multitudes are the numbers; this is clear from Aristotle's own conception of number in *Metaph.* N 1, 1087b33–1088a14, as a multitude of measures and of the unit as the measure, the designation e.g. 'finger' or 'animal', under which things are counted as ones. Plato, however, seems to assume the existence of the form-number 1. For the unit and the dyad mentioned in the *Phaedo* as beings, by participating in which a thing is one and two things are two (101b9–c9), can be best understood as the form-numbers 1 and 2 (unless one is willing to attribute to Plato the view that, leaving aside 1 as form-number for a moment, apart from the form-numbers 2, 3 etc., there are also the forms of twoness, threeness etc. as universals, the entities at issue in the *Phaedo* passage): since two things are assumed here to be two not because they have been added together but instead because they participate in the form-number 2, to think that a form-number, e.g. 2 or 3, irrespective of its unity, exhibits itself this very characteristic, combination of units, be they combinable with the units of other numbers or only with themselves, seems to be implausible; if so, though, there is no need to think that the form of unit in the *Phaedo* cannot be the form-number 1. Indeed, in the *Sophist* it is agreed that, since all numbers are beings if anything is to count as being, of numbers neither multitude(s) nor the one should be attached to non-being (238b2–3: μὴ τοίνυν ἐπιχειρῶμεν ἀριθμοῦ μήτε πλῆθος μήτε ἓν πρὸς τὸ μὴ ὂν προσφέρειν): the structure of the sentence suggests that form-numbers include not only what is called "multitudes of units" in Euclid's *El.* 7 but also what is called "unit" there.[56] That each form-number has its own units which are incombinable with those of any other, i.e. that form-numbers had been conceived by Plato as Aristotle's other kind of monadic numbers, can be ruled out in view of the *Phaedo*, as already seen. It would be very strange if Plato believed that such slight tinkering with the hypotheses of arithmetic as making the units of a number different from the units of all other numbers could reveal the nature of form-numbers.[57] This was perhaps just an image he used to illustrate concretely the

---

56 Cf. *Tht.* 185d1: ἕν τε καὶ τὸν ἄλλον ἀριθμόν. The indefinite pronoun ἄλλος, though, might mean not "other" but "besides" (Smyth [1956] §1272), in which case the one or the unit is distinguished from, and thus not included among, the numbers. Pritchard (1995) 71–78, who denies that Plato and Aristotle conceive of the unit as a number, does not discuss these passages.

57 Wedberg (1955) 66, 80–84 and 120 denies that form-numbers can be monadic since forms are simple; he also cites van der Wielen (1941) ch. 7, esp. 87–89, according to whom Aristotle misrepresented Plato's form-numbers (van der Wielen [1941] is extensively reviewed in Cherniss [1947] 235–251). See also Findlay (1974) 56–57, Tarán (1981) 13–29 and Tarán (1991) 206–224. The

radical difference of form-numbers from the infinitely many 'shadows' of each form-number in the arithmetic of his day.⁵⁸

1.2.4.7 The philosophical arithmetic of the *Philebus*

In the *Philebus* (56d4–e6) Plato recognizes two kinds of arithmetic: one is the vulgar arithmetic, whose numbers are units different from one another, the other is the arithmetic of the philosophers, whose units are completely undifferentiated from one another. The examples of numbers from vulgar arithmetic (two unequal camps and oxen) give the impression that he is concerned with the units of each number, not of all numbers, as regards the arithmetic of the philosophers too: but if the numbers of this arithmetic are form-numbers, then Aristotle seems to be right in attributing to Plato the conception of each form-number as made up by its own peculiar units, different from those of any other form-number. The distinction between two kinds of numbers in the *Philebus* appears also in *Republic* 7, however, in the discussion of arithmetic as one of the indispensible propedeutics to philosophy: a careful reading of this part of *Republic* 7 suggests that monadic numbers, made up of indivisible units undifferentiated in all of them, are numbers as studied in the field of mathematics called arithmetic, not form-numbers but their mathematical 'shadows', form-numbers approached indirectly, through hypotheses, or the numbers Aristotle calls mathematical and views as intermediates (cf. 1.2.3). In *Republic* 7 it seems to be a brief dialectical examination of the relevant hypotheses, the definitions of unit and number in the arithmetic of the

---

self-predication of forms need not suggest that form-numbers are monadic, sets of two, three etc. members, as Cleary (2013b) 417–419 thinks; see Fine (1995) 52–54. Pritchard (1995) 150–155 agrees that form-numbers as conceived in *Phd.* 101b9–c9 are incomposite; he thinks, though, that the numbers whose units are incombinable according to Aristotle's testimony are numbers of forms, those forms into which other forms can be divided as is explained in *Phlb.* 16c5–18c6 (see above 1.1.2), and that Plato's later theory of forms substituted monadic numbers of forms for the original, non-monadic form-numbers, which are not mentioned by Aristotle (for similar views see Becker [1931] and Stenzel [1933²], discussed and criticized in Ross [1951] 194–198, and Klein [1968] 79–99). If so, however, the numbers of the parts of the denizens of the realm of forms ought to be infinitely many in order to take the place of form-numbers, an implausible assumption. Form-numbers cannot be simple if they are viewed as structures (see Scolnicov [2003] 101–106 on the so-called generation of numbers in the *Parmenides*, who calls Plato's form-numbers "the prototypes of structured pluralities"), for any structure must have elements and relations defined on them, or if they are conceived as ratios (see Toeplitz [1929] discussed in Ross [1951] 198–199), which cannot but have terms. Trying to explain how arithmetical propositions can be understood in terms of form-numbers is a pointless exercise; cf. Mendell (2008) 127–128 with n. 3 on Moravcsik (2000).

58 Cf. van der Wielen (1941) in Cherniss (1947) 235.

dramatic time and long afterwards, that leads to this view of the proximate objects of arithmetic, which can explain why numbers so conceived are said in the *Philebus* to be studied in the arithmetic of the philosophers: they are numbers as understood by the mathematicians aided slightly by the philosophers, not form-numbers but their 'shadows'.[59]

1.2.4.8 Numbers in *Republic* 7

The discussion of the arithmetic in *Republic* 7[60] aims only at establishing the intelligibility of its objects: its numbers are forms, not collection of sensible objects.[61] A first argument for the intelligibility of numbers concludes that, since any collection of sensible objects such as three fingers, a number of what the *Philebus* calls vulgar arithmetic, can be also regarded as arbitrarily many other multitudes of sensible objects, e.g. as nine phalanges etc., no collection of sensible objects can be any number itself, which implicitly must be just what it is and not also something incompatible (522c5–525b8): the intelligibility of numbers is established by a cursory reference probably to the argument implicit in *R.* 5, 478e7–480a13, that, since everything sensible and beautiful is ugly too, nothing sensible and beautiful can possibly be identified with beauty itself, which must be intelligible, i.e. a form. Numbers as intelligible beings are not said to be forms, but this can be plausibly assumed to be implicit. Should we conclude that they are like the numbers of what is called in the *Philebus* arithmetic of the philosophers, in other words that they consist of units which are indivisible and also completely undifferentiated but, as Aristotle specifies, only in each form-number?

---

59 Cf. Pritchard (1995) ch. 7.
60 This section is based on Kouremenos (2015) 1.5.2.
61 The first topic (μάθημα) in the curriculum of the future philosopher-rulers is described in various ways, first as τὸ ἕν τε καὶ τὰ δύο καὶ τὰ τρία διαγιγνώσκειν...ἐν κεφαλαίῳ ἀριθμόν τε καὶ λογισμόν (522c5–7), then as λογίζεσθαι τε καὶ ἀριθμεῖν δύνασθαι (522e2), as λογιστική τε καὶ ἀριθμητική (525a10) and, finally, as simply λογιστική (525c1) and τὸ περὶ τοὺς λογισμοὺς μάθημα (525c8–d1). I assume that in this context logistic and arithmetic are not only the art of calculating and counting respectively, whose rudiments are acquired in childhood, but also their theoretical and closely related counterparts, the theory of ratio and proportion, whose terms are numbers, and what we would call number theory, i.e. the subject or Euclid's *El.* 7–9; see the discussion in Klein (1968) 17–25 where, though, Euclid is not mentioned (for logistic as the theory of ratio and proportion see also Fowler [1990] 108–111 who, though, proposes a speculative reconstruction of the mathematics of Plato's time). For another Euclidean approach to logistic and arithmetic in *R.* 7 see Pritchard (1995) 14–15; for an opposite approach that explicitly downplays *El.* 7–9 and treats Plato's logistic and arithmetic as mere calculating and counting see Mendell (2008), esp. 157.

Plato closes his argument for the intelligibility of numbers by having the main codiscussant, Socrates, point out that the future philosopher-rulers ought to study arithmetic for the sake of turning round their souls from becoming to being and truth until they arrive αὐτῇ τῇ νοήσει at viewing the nature of numbers (525b9–c7). νόησις, as the context clearly suggests, is used here in the technical sense established in the divided-line simile at the end of *Republic* 6 for the dialectical approach to forms, which relies only on the forms themselves, and the resulting cognitive condition (511c2–e5). It is, therefore, the cognitive condition of those who have managed to see form-numbers in themselves: not at the end of their prolonged study of all fields of an advanced mathematics not yet existent, at both the dramatic time and the time of composition, but rather at the end of their study of an advanced philosophy also not yet existent since it must build on a mathematics not yet available as its foundation (see 1.2.4.9). How plausible is it that in the first argument for the intelligibility of numbers Plato would have really wanted to hint at any conception of form-numbers, let alone one which is closely patterned on the numbers of vulgar arithmetic, turning their units into indivisible and indistinguishable in each form-number but completely different from those in any other?

The conception of numbers as composed of indivisible and completely indistinguishable units, evidently throughout the number series, is explicitly formulated by Socrates in the second argument for the intelligibility of numbers (525c8–526b3). It is attributed to certain people who at first think of their monadic numbers as sensible and balk when someone points out to them that what they take to be an indivisible unit, e.g. a finger, is in fact made up of smaller parts, e.g. three phalanges: in order to save the indivisible unitariness of the unit they counter that these are not in fact a finger's parts but other units, also lacking parts. They are groping towards Aristotle's conception in *Metaph*. N 1, 1087b33–1088a14, of the unit as an indivisible measure, such as 'finger' or 'phalanx', used to measure and count things, a number being a multitude of such measures, irrespectively of how the things at issue can be divided into parts. Presupposing these people's view of monadic numbers as sensible and the novel view of numbers as intelligible, Socrates tries to help them out. He invites Glaucon to imagine what they would answer if one asked them "what are those numbers you're talking about in which the unit is as you demand it, equal to any other and without even the slightest difference and has no parts?", to which question Glaucon unhesitatingly replies "they would say, I believe, that they're talking about those numbers which only thought can approach and cannot be grasped in any other way"; Socrates finally reinstates the conclusion of their previous argument using once again the dative αὐτῇ τῇ νοήσει (526a1–b4).[62]

The identity of those who would be so easily won over to Socrates' view of numbers as intelligible is suggested by the infinitive διανοηθῆναι which Glaucon uses to express the intelligibility of numbers in his reply to Socrates on behalf of these people. If the noun νόησις is used here too in the technical sense established in the divided-line simile for the direct, dialectical, approach to forms and the resulting cognitive condition, this infinitive can only contrast it sharply with διάνοια in the technical sense of this term again already established in the divided-line simile: διάνοια is the indirect, solely mathematical, approach to forms and the resultant cognitive condition of mathematicians who see forms not in themselves but indirectly, as if in a dream. Thus the people who think of numbers as monadic and would easily come to believe that these monadic numbers are not sensible but intelligible must be mathematicians;[63] their intelligible and monadic numbers must be not form-numbers[64] but their 'shadows' studied in the mathematics of the time.

According to the divided-line simile, mathematics approaches forms indirectly in that it relies on their sensible 'images', in the case of arithmetic collections of sensibles, and on their problematic definitions or hypotheses (510c3–511b1). The mathematicians Socrates asks to clarify the nature of numbers, apparently as studied in arithmetic, tacitly presuppose a definition of number similar to that found in Euclid's *Elements*:[65] "a number is a multitude composed of units" (*El.* 7, Def. 2: ἀριθμὸς δὲ τὸ ἐκ μονάδων συγκείμενον πλῆθος), where the unit is defined as "that in accordance with which each thing is called one" (*El.* 7, Def. 1: μονάς ἐστιν, καθ' ἣν ἕκαστον τῶν ὄντων ἓν λέγεται).[66] "Each thing" cannot be anything other than each thing around us, a sensible. These definitions formalize

---

62 Τί οὖν οἴει, ὦ Γλαύκων, εἴ τις ἔροιτο αὐτούς· "Ὦ θαυμάσιοι, περὶ ποίων ἀριθμῶν διαλέγεσθε, ἐν οἷς τὸ ἓν οἷον ὑμεῖς ἀξιοῦτέ ἐστιν, ἴσον τε ἕκαστον πᾶν παντὶ καὶ οὐδὲ σμικρὸν διαφέρον, μόριόν τε ἔχον ἐν ἑαυτῷ οὐδέν;" τί ἂν οἴει αὐτοὺς ἀποκρίνασθαι;

Τοῦτο ἔγωγε, ὅτι περὶ τούτων λέγουσιν ὧν διανοηθῆναι μόνον ἐγχωρεῖ, ἄλλως δ' οὐδαμῶς μεταχειρίζεσθαι δυνατόν.

Ὁρᾷς οὖν, ἦν δ' ἐγώ, ὦ φίλε, ὅτι τῷ ὄντι ἀναγκαῖον ἡμῖν κινδυνεύει εἶναι τὸ μάθημα, ἐπειδὴ φαίνεταί γε προσαναγκάζον αὐτῇ τῇ νοήσει χρῆσθαι τὴν ψυχὴν ἐπ' αὐτὴν τὴν ἀλήθειαν;

Καὶ μὲν δή, ἔφη, σφόδρα γε ποιεῖ αὐτό.

63 Cf. Pritchard (1995) 14–15 and 121–122. Mendell (2008) 151–152 assumes that they are "expert calculators"; cf. above n. 61.

64 See Cherniss (1944) 518 and Cherniss (1947) 239 n. 79; cf., though, Pritchard (1995) 120–125.

65 Cf. Pritchard (1995) 23–31 on the pre-Euclidean notion of number; cf. Cleary (2013b) 416–417.

66 On the translation of καθ' ἥν see Pritchard (1995) 13–14.

the common-sense conception of number which is shown to be untenable in Socrates' first argument that numbers must be intelligible, forms, on the strength of the general argument in *Republic* 5 for the existence of some forms.[67] If Plato has Socrates next turn his sights on the formalization in mathematics of a conception of number which has already been rejected, his point in so doing is in all probability to stress that mathematicians, far from being discomfited by the view of the numbers they study as intelligible objects, ought to welcome it.

In the immediately following discussion of geometry, Plato will present Socrates introducing a view of what geometry really does which even those who know only basic geometry, hence geometers too, would easily adopt (527a1–b11). Similarly, here he has Socrates point out that mathematicians would not find it particularly difficult to concede the intelligibility of numbers; at the same time, he finds an opportunity to illustrate some of the points he has Socrates make in the simile of the divided line, the problematic way in which mathematics defines the objects of its study, which are in fact forms, and philosophy's aim to transcend these problems and see the forms in themselves, an aim called in *Republic* 7 "destruction" of the hypotheses (533c9): the conclusion to which the mathematicians jump that arithmetic studies not sensible but intelligible numbers follows from a brief dialectical examination of the definitions of unit and number in contemporary arithmetic. But it is not a full-blown one that could "destroy" these hypotheses so as to reach the intelligible objects at issue in themselves and thus be able to view them clearly as forms, for it does not transcend the hypotheses of arithmetic but only clarifies them. Its objective is restricted to demonstrating that, as currently defined in arithmetic, numbers can only be intelligible.[68]

At the end of the discussion of all branches of mathematics, before he passes on to dialectic, Socrates says that mathematicians are not dialecticians, capable of giving and receiving an account, and Glaucon comments that he has met very few dialectically capable mathematicians (531d6–e5). The mathematicians with whom Socrates is portrayed having a conversation about numbers are certainly not dialectically gifted: it is, therefore, completely implausible that Plato intended to reveal the nature of form-numbers in the account of numbers as monadic and intelligible which these mathematicians would partly give of their own

---

[67] On these definitions see Pritchard (1995) 9–18.
[68] Pritchard (1995) 14–15, who also thinks that Plato operates here with a notion of number current in contemporary mathematics and later formalized by Euclid in his *El.* 7 Def. 1–2, assumes that in this context only the view of arithmetic as part of the education of future philosopher-rulers is peculiar to Plato. Mendell (2008) 149–156 assumes that those he calls expert calculators (cf. above n. 61) presuppose explicitly even the intelligibility of their numbers.

accord and partly receive unhesitatingly from a philosopher like Socrates; nor is it less implausible that Plato intended this imaginary conversation between Socrates and some mathematicians to be read as implying a notion as useless to mathematics as the undifferentiatedness of units only in each intelligible and monadic number. In Plato's view, at the dramatic time of the *Republic* and at the time of the work's composition even those few mathematicians who were philosophically gifted could not have possibly been able, as argued above, to see the form-numbers directly, in themselves, and give an account of them.

Form-numbers are thus presupposed in *Republic* 7 but, since not a word is said about their nature, it can be plausibly assumed that Plato did not think of form-numbers as monadic, just as he did not think of the forms of geometrical objects as geometrical and of beauty itself as akin in any way to its 'shadowy copies'. It is, of course, conceivable that he changed his mind at some point and decided that form-numbers ought to be regarded as monadic and that the forms of the mathematical objects studied in geometry ought to be similarly regarded as having shape and extension themselves. But nothing suggests that Plato abandoned his denial of shape to all forms and thus the consequent denial of monadic composition to form-numbers, though his brief discussion of arithmetic in the *Philebus* and the longer one in *Republic* 7 could suggest a visualizable conception of form-numbers as monadic to those who for some reason felt dissatisfied with Plato's purely negative description of forms and thus form-numbers.[69]

1.2.4.9 Plato and Aristotle on mathematics

Plato seems to have denied that form-numbers are made up of completely undifferentiated units, a historically important conception of numbers as studied in mathematics that could be attributed to him on the evidence of *R.* 7 and the *Philebus*, though he did not take it to be revelatory of the nature of form-numbers, which was perhaps only illustrated by a variation of it. But Aristotle would have had no truck at all with the notion that the objects studied in arithmetic, which for Plato are actually the form-numbers, are completely different from their definition in this field. Consider what he says in *Cael.* Γ 1, 299a3–6, about those who take all physical bodies to be made up of planes, i.e. Plato in his *Timaeus* and others who adopted the cosmology of the *Timaeus* wholesale or in part: they "happen to contradict mathematics in many other ways, which are easy to see, though it is right either not to subvert mathematics or to do so only if arguments more compelling than its propositions are available". The word translated by

---

[69] Cf. the conclusion of 1.2.4.6.

"propositions" (ὑποθέσεις) is also used by Plato for the definitions of mathematical objects in *Republic* 6 (see 1.1.3). Although in the passage Aristotle is not interested only in definitions, his point about Plato's conception of physical bodies in the *Timaeus* vis-à-vis the propositions of mathematics also applies to Plato's conception of form-numbers and the forms of geometrical objects as totally different from their definitions in mathematics. The view of physical bodies in the *Timaeus* subverts mathematics since it conflicts with the propositions of mathematics and is thus inadmissible because in Aristotle's view it entails the existence of indivisible lines. Much worse is the situation with the conception of the true objects of mathematics as form-numbers and forms of geometrical objects, both of which are assumed to be fundamentally unlike their definitions in current arithmetic and geometry: these definitions are denigrated by Plato himself in *Republic* 6 sparing Aristotle the trouble of detecting a conflict with propositions of mathematics. Here too Aristotle could have easily objected that "it is right either not to subvert mathematics or to do so only if arguments more compelling than its propositions are available". Plato would not of course have offered any reasons for his belief that forms do not bear any resemblance to their participants, and that the definitions of mathematical objects describe not form-numbers and forms of geometrical objects which are the true objects of mathematics but only their mental 'shadows' as if these realities were seen in a dream. Aristotle's own conception of number evidently sticks to the letter of the definitions of the unit and number in Euclid's *Elements* (see 1.2.4.8), although the view of numbers studied in arithmetic as what Aristotle calls Plato's monadic mathematical numbers captures nicely the implicit ontology of Euclidean arithmetic (see 1.2.4.6); in his criticism in *Metaph.* A 9, 992a19–24, of Plato's rejection of points as fictions of the geometers, moreover, Aristotle takes the Euclidean definition of the extremities of lines as points (*El.* 1 Def. 3) self-evidently for granted, although Plato or anyone for that matter could have appropriately questioned such definitions of elementary geometrical objects independently of philosophical concerns.

It seems that Plato and Aristotle had very different views about the maturity of the mathematics of their day. In *Republic* 7 Plato singles out three branches of contemporary mathematics as undeveloped, solid geometry (528a6–c7), astronomy (530b6–c4) and harmonics (531b2–c5). But it is unlikely that he regarded that other two, arithmetic and plane geometry, as having already been developed as much as possible since he places great emphasis on the unity of mathematics (see 531c9–d5 and 537b7–c8).[70] Growth in a part of a unified whole can only induce growth in the rest of the system. At any rate, Plato relates the future growth of

---

[70] On Plato's conception of the unity of mathematics in *R.* 7 see Kouremenos (2015) ch. 2.

astronomy to solving construction problems, like those in solid and plane geometry, beyond those already solved in contemporary geometry;[71] similarly, he boldly proposes that, if harmonics is to grow, it ought to turn its attention to numbers, as if it were arithmetic, but the numbers that will be of interest to it are described by an adjective that does not point to any category of numbers recognized in contemporary arithmetic. The growth of astronomy and harmonics entails their exit from the cave, their abandonment of a strict observational approach to their empirical subject matter and their mathematization, their search for forms which, being visibly manifested in the heavens and audibly in melody, will provide explanatory accounts of astronomical and harmonic phenomena. Geometry, both plane and solid, will thus also grow thanks to its interaction with astronomy, which will ask it to effect novel constructions thereby adding to its already investigated objects new interesting ones (all "true figures" mentioned in 529c6–d5) and widening the range of known forms of mathematical objects. The problems about numbers, which in Plato's view harmonics must turn to, concern the investigation of numbers called "concordant" (σύμφωνοι, 531c2–3): he seems to imply that the interest of contemporary harmonics in those numbers whose ratios are the pitch-relations forming the basis of musical scales might eventually evolve into the recognition and study of one or more new types, hence forms, of number other than those of odd, even, prime and composite numbers known to contemporary arithmetic, whose growth will thus be promoted by the explanatory needs of harmonics.[72] This is probably not a prescription but rather an exempli gratia illustration of the close ties that, as Plato hopes, will develop between arithmetic and harmonics. His so-called concordant numbers can very well be numbers such as 6, 8, 9 and 12, called "harmonic" centuries later by Gersonides.[73]

These four numbers express in simplest form the structure of a tetrachord divided into two fourths which are joined together by a tone (see 1.1.2): all of them are products of the numbers 2 or 3 and 3 or the square of 2, the numbers which together with 1 express in simplest form the intervals of the octave, the fourth and the fifth. Plato's interest in the powers of 2 and 3 is evident from his description of the harmonic construction of the cosmic soul in the *Timaeus* (35b4–c2). If his concordant numbers are Gersonides' harmonic numbers 1, 2, 3, 4, 6, 8, 9, 12... , i.e. those numbers that can be expressed as products of a power of 2 and a power of 3, a question about the concordant numbers that Plato might have had in mind

---

[71] On astronomy and its relation to geometry in *R*. 7 see 2.9–12 and Kouremenos (2015) ch. 1.
[72] Cf. Barker (1978).
[73] In his *De numeris harmonicis*, recently translated in Katz et al. (2016) 277–283; for a French translation see Meyer & Vicker (2000).

while writing the relevant lines in *Republic* 7 could well be the one Gersonides eventually addressed: apart from 1 and 2, 2 and 3, 3 and 4 and 8 and 9, are there other pairs of concordant numbers differing by 1? These pairs express all basic harmonic intervals, so a proof that there are no other such pairs, which was provided by Gersonides, would have interested Plato. It would have offered an abstract, number-theoretic reason why sounds forming these intervals if their pitches stand to the ratios between the members of the pairs at issue are pleasantly perceived as a unified blend (the reason would be that these are the only pairs of concordant numbers differing by 1, the smallest possible difference between two numbers).

Be that as it may, Plato seems to have firmly believed that mathematics should and would evolve considerably in the future, near or not, at least insofar as it would overcome its fragmentation into barely communicating branches in his day and would recognize a greater variety of objects thus revealing new forms. His comments on solid geometry show that he is optimistic about the future of mathematics.[74] Perhaps he also believed that those very few mathematicians said in *Republic* 7 to be philosophically capable (531d6–e5) would make a transformational contribution to this evolution, and thus to philosophy itself, in that it would be they who at some point would start the "destruction" of the hypotheses of contemporary mathematics (533c9): the process of trying to resolve the issues arising from the problematic definitions on which mathematics rested, in a desire to view the forms, which this discipline is really about, not in a dream, defectively, as they were defined at the time, but in full awakeness, as philosophy aims to do (cf. 1.1.3). It is unlikely that in Plato's view the elucidation of the foundations of mathematics would be carried out exclusively within philosophy and then handed over to mathematics. He could have envisaged this process to unfold along the lines of the search for beings from hypotheses needing an account, which he describes in *Phd.* 101c9–102a2: that is, as a diachronic series of progressively superior hypotheses, the formation of each of which will probably be motivated by the continual accumulation of results, both enriching each field of mathematics and bridging different fields, with the purpose of giving an account of its predecessor(s), slightly shaking off the distorting shackles of dream and reaching "something adequate" at the time, an account of a form or forms as close to full wakefulness as possible at the time. If so, Plato could have imagined that future mathematics would bear a faint resemblance to the mathematics of his day, for it would approach even the forms studied in its benighted ancestor under a light much more like the true daylight shining in the realm of forms (cf. *R.* 7,

---

74 On solid geometry in *R.* 7 see Kouremenos (2015) 1.7.

521c5–8). It is thus not surprising at all if he refused to take the contemporary definitions of number and geometrical objects to be the last word on the subject.

There is evidence leading to the suspicion that Aristotle, on the other hand, believed that in his day both mathematics and philosophy not only had made immense advances in a very short period but had almost completed their work. If so, again it is not surprising at all if, in stark contrast to Plato, Aristotle took the contemporary definitions of number and geometrical objects to be the very last word on the subject. Fr. 53 Rose bears a marked similarity to the discussion of solid geometry in Plato's *R.* 7, 528a6–c7, because it too celebrates the advancement of mathematics despite not only the lack of societal support but also the discouragement from its study. But, whereas Plato celebrates the growth of mathematics in order to affirm his belief that currently immature branches of mathematics will grow in the future and solve open problems, Aristotle simply puts all his emphasis on the great advancement of contemporary mathematics and philosophy in a very short timespan, and he seems to also have believed that the great advances in contemporary philosophy heralded its imminent completion, which suggests that in all probability he took contemporary mathematics too to have virtually completed its work. He leaves open the possibility of future advances in astronomy in *Metaph.* Λ 8, 1073b8–17, before he outlines the theory of homocentric spheres of Eudoxus with Callippus' modifications, but he might mean that they will be just minor tidying up. Indeed, in *APr.* A 39, 46a17–27, he refers to astronomy as a completed science when he illustrates the relation between empirical research and the principles of sciences by pointing out using the aorist that the astronomical proofs have been discovered after the sufficiently accurate description of astronomical phenomena.

It is conceivable that in this context he talks about not all of astronomy but rather its elementary branches of spherical astronomy and the fixed-star phases, which are presented in the surviving works of his almost contemporary Autolycus of Pitane and about which his comment is apposite; on the other hand, he can very well talk about all of astronomy since he believes that our empirical starting points for the study of the heavens are by necessity very few (*PA* A 5, 644b22–31), which seems to imply that almost all we can observe in the heavens has already been observed with sufficient accuracy. At the end of his *Sophistical Refutations* Aristotle states that rhetoric and the other arts, which most probably include mathematics, have undergone tremendous growth in his age by a continuous process of addition to their humble beginnings and, although he does not say that this signals their imminent completion, he might very well intend it: in the *Poetics* he uses language strongly reminiscent of this passage to say that tragedy developed by small increments after its beginning and then it stopped growing, having acquired its own nature (4, 1449a9–15). The perfection of tragedy is clearly assumed to have occurred at the time of Sophocles, and thus it is not farfetched to assume that Aristotle did believe in the imminent completion of all mathematics and philosophy. His concluding remarks in the *Sophistical Refutations* extoll his own contribution to dialectic and, though he acknowledges the incompleteness of his work in this field, he boasts that he both laid down the first beginning of the discipline, the nucleus of all subsequent growth whose establishment is as important as it is difficult, and brought the discipline singlehandedly to a state of advancement comparable to that of fields which have grown to maturity in his time after a long series of incremental improvements by many contributors (34, 183b15–184b8).

If Plato believed that contemporary mathematics was primitive and would certainly be transformed beyond recognition in the future, whereas Aristotle thought that mathematics had been virtually completed in his day, we can explain why Plato also believed in the organic unity of mathematics, though the mathematics of his day could provide scant support for this view, divided as it broadly was into arithmetic, which studied discontinuous numbers, and geometry, which dealt with continuous magnitudes, whereas Aristotle took for granted the contemporary division of mathematics into distinct branches communicating not at all or in a very limited sense. There can be no doubt that Plato's belief in the unity of mathematics was motivated primarily by his belief in the unity of all forms (see 1.2.4.1). The true objects of mathematics are forms, so the harmonious interrelationships among them cannot but be reflected in mathematics; his demand, moreover, for the growth of mathematics through the pursuit of the links between its branches can also be most convincingly related to the profound importance he places on the unity of all forms. As said above, he envisages the unity of mathematics as at least the mutually beneficial interaction between seemingly distinct branches such as astronomy and geometry or harmonics and arithmetic: one branch raises issues opening new vistas in the other, which reciprocates by illuminating the original problems. Developments in contemporary mathematics, which can be plausibly thought to be presupposed in *Republic* 7 (cf. 2.12), could have inspired this view of the unity of mathematics. Aristotle, unlike Plato, speaks not of the kinship (συγγένεια and οἰκειότης) of distinct branches of mathematics and of their communing with one another (κοινωνία) but of a proof from one fitting, or being accommodated by, the other or the objects studied in it. A proof concerning the properties of the kind of objects studied in a branch of mathematics does not cross over to, or fit, a different kind of objects studied in another branch, unless the objects in the second kind are or can be understood to be the objects belonging to the first kind: arithmetic e.g. crosses over to harmonics insofar as pitches can be understood to be numbers (*APo.* A 7, 75a38–b20). Aristotle pioneered the formalist view of each branch of mathematics as a distinct axiomatic system which on its own is unable to capture the mutually beneficial interaction Plato seems to envisage in *Republic* 7 between e.g. arithmetic and harmonics. Nevertheless this conception of mathematics is closer to the situation in the mathematics of his time than the Platonic view of mathematics as a unity, which is more appropriate to modern mathematics and was barely noticeable in his time, testifying to the power of his vision.

1.2.4.10 Forms galore
It thus seems that, no matter what other forms might be studied in philosophy apart from those really studied in mathematics, the principle in *Republic* 10 yields them together with a great number of form-like entities such as those whose formhood is reported by Aristotle to have been rejected, though Plato does not refrain from mentioning them as forms in his works, probably meaning that they are merely form-like. Entities such as the forms of ugliness and artifacts are essentially unlike proper forms and can thus be assumed to interest philosophy indirectly, insofar as they depend on true forms or are sufficiently like them to be mentioned occasionally alongside them or serve as illustrative examples of them. Plato could have also mentioned even the forms of Greek and barbarian in a certain context since the words *Greek* and *barbarian* have a certain meaning fixed objectively for the speakers of a language and describe many individuals, though they are not names of real forms studied in philosophy or mathematics. He could also have spoken of the form of number less than or equal to e.g. one thousand and of number greater than one thousand, assuming e.g. that speakers of a language agreed among themselves to name both sets of numbers for some reason and used the agreed upon names consistently, though these two forms would be much unlike the forms of e.g. even and odd numbers as referents of the words *even* and *odd*.[75] He could have spoken of forms of the ridiculous things listed in the *Parmenides*, where he may warn us that they should not be considered true forms. If only some of the embarrassment of riches yielded by the principle in *Republic* 10 are forms in the sense in which this word is used to label the objects of philosophy and mathematics, as entities existing outside space and time but informing all aspects of the sensible world independently of our necessarily limited mind, which only attempts to understand them, could all forms be forms of mathematical objects, as the simile of the cave in *Republic* 7 hints?

---

75 Cf., though, 1.3.2 on the forms of large and small.

The very term *form* (ἰδέα or εἶδος) Plato uses to describe beings seems to point to a conception of beings as geometrical objects since one of its original meanings is 'shape of a thing', e.g. someone's figure. Platonic beings are neither sensible nor spatial and they are called forms insofar as they inform sensibles from outside, as it were, and not because they belong to formed sensibles as their figures. But if Plato did posit his forms as mathematical objects conceived in the peculiar manner named after him, he could be plausibly said to have brought to a conclusion a pronounced fifth-century-BC tendency to conceive beings in mathematical, both geometrical and arithmetical, terms. Aristotle acknowledges two influences on Plato's concept of forms: on the one hand, Socrates' attempt to define the virtues in a way that captures what is common to the many manifestations of a virtue and, on the other, the view of the Heraclitean Cratylus that all sensibles are ever-changing; whence it follows that, if Socratic definitions and knowledge, both of which demand stable objects, are possible, no sensible can serve as referent of a Socratic definition but there must be some other entities that do so, non-sensible, unchanging and existing apart or separately from the sensibles to which Socratic definitions apply and which are accordingly named after these entities; these entities, Aristotelian universals whose ontological separation from sensibles is attributed by Aristotle to Plato in explicit contrast to Socrates, were graced by Plato with the name *forms* (see *Metaph.* A 6, 987a29–b9, and M 4, 1078b9–36). This term could have been used by Socrates himself for the commonality he sought in the diverse manifestations of the virtues (cf. *Euthyphro* 5d1–5 and 6d9–e1, assuming that the early dialogues to which it belongs depict roughly the historical Socrates).

Democritus, however, had also employed the term *form* to describe Parmenidean beings conceived as Abderite atoms, shape being one of their very few properties and apparently so important that it could be used as metonym for the beings themselves (for the term see DK 68 A 57, 67, 102 and B 141); more importantly, he seems to have used the term *form* for a being with one of the infinitely many geometrical shapes atoms have and for that which all infinitely many beings with a given shape have in common (see DK 68 B 141; cf. B 124).[76] Abderite forms are, of course, just bodies, for nothing hints that Democritus might have thought that form as what is common to many individuals is immaterial, in contrast to the individuals the term *form* also refers to in his usage. But they presuppose no less than Socratic forms might have done the conceptual separation of what it is common to a multitude from what this is common to, the prerequisite

---

76 Cf. Mourelatos (2006) 70.

for its ontological separation by Plato.⁷⁷ Moreover, insofar as they are explicitly posited as non-sensible unchanging beings approachable by the intellect alone, although this is due to their microscopic bodily size and not to their immateriality and non-spatiality, Abderite forms look like inchoate Platonic forms more than Socratic forms do. Despite his focus on Socrates, Aristotle might suggest a possible Abderite influence on the Platonic concept of form where he says in the historical note on this concept that, apart from Socrates who restricted himself to ethics, among natural philosophers only Democritus had some interest in definitions and gives as examples his definitions of hot and cold (*Metaph*. M 4, 1078b19–21 = DK 68 A 36). These definitions had referred to beings as three-dimensional mathematical objects that are also the indivisible corpuscles making everything else up (Arist. *de An*. A 2, 405a8–13 = DK 68 A 101), Abderite forms that provide a plausible parallel to Plato's possible view of all beings as mathematical objects, conceived after his own fashion, and could have influenced him in its development.⁷⁸

The conception of a category of beings, the most important ones from an epistemological point of view, as mathematical objects is also found in Philolaus of Croton, in whose view the cosmos and everything in it are made up of two kinds of beings joined together into a harmony in each case: what is unlimited and what is limiting (DK 44 B 1 and 2). If there had existed only what is unlimited, we could not have known anything (DK 44 B 3), so what is limiting is implicitly exalted by Philolaus from an epistemological point of view and, since he says that nothing can be object of our thought or knowledge without number (DK 44 B 4), the beings thanks to which knowledge and thought are possible and which are limiting what is unlimited seem to be numbers. Philolaus seems to have believed that numbers too cannot be known to us independently of what is unlimited with which they are joined together since he contrasted our limited knowledge of beings with a divine knowledge of them and "nature itself" (DK 44 B 6), presumably the nature of beings in themselves independently of their harmonies. Whatever he might have meant by that, it is too farfetched to attribute to him the Platonic conception of numbers, although he too spoke of their sets as forms (ἴδια εἴδη; DK 44 B 5).⁷⁹

---

77 See also Mourelatos (2006) 67–73 on Democritus and the development of the concept of universal.
78 On Democritus and Plato see also Mourelatos (2006) 72–73.
79 See also Mourelatos (2006) 65–67 on Philolaus and the development of the concept of universal.

1.3 Are all forms only forms of mathematical objects?

1.3.1 The forms of oneness and multitude(s)

At least some of the forms mentioned in Plato's works apart from the forms of mathematical objects can easily be identified with forms of such objects. As seen above (1.2.4.6), Plato seems to have assumed the existence of the form-number 1 in contrast to contemporary mathematics, according to which numbers were only those greater than 1, which was defined to be the unit, since number was defined to be a multitude of units, a position also adopted by Aristotle: if so, however the form of oneness mentioned in the *Parmenides* can only be the form-number 1, by participation in which a sensible thing is one according to *Phd*. 101b4–c9, for it would be explanatorily otiose to posit both a form of oneness and the form-number 1.[80] Moreover, since in this passage it is also said that e.g. a sensible decad is more than an octet due to the form of multitude but a sensible decad is what it is only due to its participation in the form-number 10, if its participation in the form-number 10 can make it to be more than an octet because this form-number stands in what could be called a certain order relative to the form-number 8, then here the form of multitude is actually the form of *a* multitude, the form-number 10: that is, there is not a single form of multitude but infinitely many forms *of multitudes*, the form-numbers after the form-number 1, each of which can be naturally called form of *a* multitude. In *Republic* 7 Glaucon says "we see the same thing as one and at the same time as indefinitely many multitudes" and Socrates notes "if this applies to one, it applies to all numbers" (525a5–8), presumably because a number is assumed to be defined mathematically as a multitude of ones or units, as in contemporary mathematics: any form-number after the form-number 1 can, therefore, be also called the form of (a) multitude, which, unlike its arithmetical 'shadows', cannot itself be a multitude of any units in a certain order relative to the other form-numbers, as the form of a geometrical object is not itself geometrical and the form of beauty is unlike any of its blurry 'images' (see 1.1.3 and, for extensive discussion, 1.2.4.6–9).

---

80 In *Prm*. 129d6–e1 what is called here the form of oneness and is included among αὐτὰ καθ' αὑτὰ τὰ εἴδη is τὸ ἕν, whereas in *Phd*. 101b4–c9 is ἡ μονάς, in which things each of which are one, not two, participate, and which is also described as ἰδία οὐσία τῆς μονάδος, in which each thing that is one participates. I assume that the form of oneness mentioned next to that of multitude in *Prm*. 129d6–e1, in the first part of the dialogue, is not the metaform of oneness introduced in the second hypothesis of the second part of the dialogue (see above n. 40) but the entity mentioned in *Phd*. 101b4–c9.

1.3.2 The forms of half and double, third and triple etc., small and large

The forms of half and double, and thus of third and triple etc., and of small and large are presupposed in *Republic* 5 (478e7–479b7) and each can be understood to be a form in the sense in which the formhood of oddness and evenness can be understood (1.2.1). The form of half can be conceived as consisting of all form-numbers $n = k/2$, that of double, inversely, of all form-numbers $k = 2n$, and so on for the forms of third, triple etc. (the infinitely many forms of half, third etc. are "joined together" [see 1.1.2], as are the form of double and the form of even number, and the form of multitude and the form of any number greater than 1; we will see more forms called by more than one name). The forms of half, third etc. comprise all form-numbers which 'measure' one of their 'successors' a given number of times, that of double, triple etc. all form-numbers 'measured' by one of their 'predecessors' a given number of times (see Euc. *El.* 7 Def. 3 and 5), so any two opposite forms such as those of half and double are extensionally distinct. We can, therefore, go on and define similarly the form of all form-numbers which are certain "parts" of other form-numbers, a proper fraction (see Euc. *El.* 7 Def. 4) and, inversely, the form consisting of all these other form-numbers.

Any sensible, therefore, which is e.g. half or double another sensible, is half because the multitude of units it measures on a certain scale participates in a form-number $n = k/2$, whereas the multitude of units the other sensible measures on this scale participates in the form-number k; or it is double if the multitude of units it measures on a scale partakes of a form-number $k = 2n$ and the multitude of units the other sensible measures on this scale participates in the form-number n (cf. *Prm.* 140b7–c4). A number of units can measure what in one context is e.g. half but in another double, and thus can itself be viewed as half and double (*R.* 5, 478e7–479b7); but, as defined above, the form of half cannot be the form of double and vice versa (cf. *R.* 7, 523c10–524c14, and *Phd.* 74a9–c3). It must be emphasized that the notation used here, or any verbal equivalent Plato would have used, does not capture the true relations of the form-numbers constituting the forms of half, double etc.: this is just how the relations at issue must appear in the dream in which mathematics sees form-numbers since these beings cannot yet be seen in full wakefulness, so philosophy must be contented with at best a clearer view of their 'shadows' studied in arithmetic (see 1.2.4.9 for extensive discussion).

The infinitely large set each member of which is the set of the form-numbers 'before' a given form-number (or of both the form-numbers 'before' a given form-number and the latter itself) can be called the form of small; the set each member of which is the set comprising a given form-number and those 'after' it (or only those 'after' it) can thus be called the form of large, provided that the comparison of sensible things which are small and large because they participate each in form-numbers belonging to one of these two forms can be expressed as a ratio of whole numbers.[81] A sensible thing which is large is large because the multitude of units it measures on a scale participates in a form-number $k \geq n$ (or $k > n$), whereas the multitudes of units that all the other sensibles with which it is compared in a certain context measure on this scale participate in the form-number $l < n$ (or $l \leq n$).[82]

A number of units can measure what in one context turns out to be large but in another small, and thus the length etc. it measures can be viewed as both large and small (see again *R.* 5, 478e7–479b7); but the form of large cannot be the small itself and vice versa (cf. again *R.* 7, 523c10–524c14, and *Phd.* 74a9–c3). The comparison of two or more things cannot be always expressed as ratios of whole numbers. If it cannot, as in the case of the side and diagonal of the square, the forms of large and small in which compared things participate can be identified with the properties which belong to forms of geometrical objects, e.g. to the square itself, and can be instantiated, in a mathematician's mind or in material objects, as a larger and a smaller length, area or volume respectively, whatever these properties might be which can be somehow geometrically instantiated, though they do not belong to objects that are themselves geometrical.[83] This problem

---

[81] These infinitely many sets of form-numbers with which the opposite forms of large and small are identified here are strictly speaking parts of the form of number which, unlike the sets of even and odd form-numbers, are not themselves forms; cf. 1.2.1. Since Plato has no problem speaking of forms of e.g. artifacts, however, he would have no problem speaking of these sets too as forms, of the large and the small, all the more so since they are much more form-like than what he in all probability calls forms of artifacts (on which see 1.2.3).

[82] The form of large or that of small can also be called the form of inequality; see next section.

[83] In *R.* 6, 509d6–511e5, Plato gives as example of an object really studied in mathematics the square itself with the diagonal itself, which he contrasts with any sensible square with its sensible diagonal. If the object called the square itself is a form, as is suggested by the context, and not an intermediate (cf. above n. 37), in view of the description of forms in *Phdr.* 247c6–8 as lacking shape, the diagonal itself is not even remotely similar to the diagonal of any sensible or mentally visualized square: it is whatever 'in' a non-spatial, non-geometrical entity like a form might be manifested geometrically as the diagonal of this form's spatial or mental instantiations. The introduction of space in *Ti.* 48e2–53c3, esp. 52a8–b5, leaves no doubt about the non-spatiality of all forms which are thus non-extended and non-geometrical, including those of the geometrical objects which inform formless space by being 'impressed' or 'stamped' onto it, as if it were a soft material, thereby endowing it with shape (on space and these forms see 1.3.4): the manner of this informing is said to be inexplicable and marvelous probably because the non-spatial 'signets' lack shape but somehow produce a geometrical impression, a difficulty whose

with the forms of the mathematical objects studied in geometry is similar to that raised above for form-numbers.

1.3.3 The forms of equality and inequality

Another form which seems to be a form of a mathematical object is that of equality. It is mentioned in the *Phaedo* (74a9–76e7 and 78d1–9; cf. Alex. Aphr. *In metaph.* 83.6–16 Hayduck) and can be any form-number in which the multitudes of the members of different groups, or of the units that some things measure on a given scale, participate; or, as in the case of the forms of large and small (see 1.3.2), it can be the property of some form of a geometrical object that is multiply manifested as the irrational length, area or volume of the things which turn out to be equal under comparison in these respects.[84] The form of inequality, also presupposed in the *Phaedo*, can be understood in the arithmetical case as the form of large, of small or as the forms comprising all ordered pairs, triplets etc. of form-numbers; or it can be any pair, triplet etc. of properties of forms of geometrical objects instantiable as unequal incommensurable lengths, areas or volumes. All sensible measurements and counts are equal (to others) in one context and unequal (to others) in another, but the equal itself is not the unequal itself and vice versa (see *Phd.* 74a9–c3).

1.3.4 The forms of the elements: fire, air, water, and earth

Although Plato presents Socrates in the *Parmenides* as unsure about the existence of forms of fire and water, in the *Timaeus* the forms of fire, air, water, and earth, the four elements of all material things, are posited unhesitatingly (51b7–52b5). These four forms can be easily accommodated if the range of forms is restricted to those of mathematical objects because in the *Timaeus* the four forms of fire, air, water, and earth seem to be nothing other than the forms of four of the five regular solids, the regular tetrahedron, octahedron, icosahedron and cube respectively (on the fifth, the dodecahedron, see n. 87). The identification is not

---

implicit acknowledgement is tellingly accompanied by the unfulfilled promise to tackle it later (50a5–c6).

84 The expression αὐτὰ τὰ ἴσα Plato uses in *Phd.* 74c1–5 next to αὐτὸ τὸ ἴσον and ἰσότης for the form at issue might suggest a plurality of forms, each of which can make any number of participants to be equal to one another. On αὐτὰ τὰ ἴσα see Pritchard (1995) 147–148 n. 33.

explicitly stated. However, Plato seems to have viewed space as possessing a quantized geometrical structure, whose elements are two-dimensional and triangular but not atomic, and elementary matter as emerging from these spatial quanta being glued together into larger geometrical structures by participating in certain forms, the forms of the four elements, or from these forms being projected onto spatial quanta. He seems to have conceived the atoms of the four elements as microscopic tetrahedral, octahedral, icosahedral and cubic regions of space bounded by triangular elements of its two-dimensional structure (53c4–56c7). He hypothesizes that the faces of the atoms of the four elements are made up by two different types of triangular quanta, isosceles and scalene, the latter having hypotenuses double their shorter sides, and these quanta can be economically assumed to be simply the two-dimensional quanta of space itself, probably products of projection of the form of the relevant geometrical object.[85] The planar elements of atoms of fire, air and water are of the same kind, so quantities of each of these stuffs can turn into another, and amounts of any two of them can turn into the third stuff; none can turn into earth and vice versa, though. Empedocles had introduced the four elements named after him as Parmenidean beings exempt from coming into existence and going out of existence (DK 31 B 17.30–35), but Plato accords the status of beings to the forms of the four elements which can be economically assumed to be the forms of the regular tetrahedron, octahedron, icosahedron and cube.[86]

---

[85] On the polyhedra as configurations in space see Harte (2002) 250. Space is introduced in *Ti.* 48e2–53c3 before the introduction of the triangles making up the polyhedral atoms of the elements. Geometrical forms, whether of the triangle or the four regular solids, are not participated in by space in the sense that thereby what is not in itself space turns into space. Space is said to lack all forms it receives in that it does not acquire its nature from any forms in which it participates. For views on the nature of the triangles see Miller (2003) 173–178.

[86] Silverman (2002) ch. 7 distinguishes the forms of the triangles and the polyhedra, the geometrical forms, from the forms of the four elements which he calls "forms of the traditional sort". By his lights, Plato relies on the geometrical forms to generate out of space in one fell swoop place and body as the scaffolding in which he then locates the 'copies' projected by the forms of the four elements. Silverman points out the ad hoc-ness of the coincidence of form-'copies' and the right sort of body, and as a plausible, in part at least, way out he suggests that the arrangement of the spatial triangular elements into the right sort of polyhedron to house the 'copies' of a form of an element is somehow guided by the form of the element itself. But it seems preferable to go all the way and do away with the distinction between the forms of the polyhedra and those of the elements, identifying them and thus identifying the regions of space bounded into places and bodies with the 'copies' of the forms of the elements: in other words, if form of a polyhedron, which, as non-spatial, is itself not geometrical, somehow informs space geometrically by 'guiding' the arrangement of its planar elements, space turns into both place and body endowed with certain properties. Cf. Harte (2002) 262 n. 189 on Silverman (1991); she thinks that geometrically

We have thus four forms of mathematical objects doubling as forms of the elements. One of them can be referred to either as e.g. the tetrahedron itself, which is the object a geometrical theorem is really about, just as at the end of *Republic* 6 a theorem about squares is said to actually pertain to the square itself, or as the form of fire, fire itself (*Ti.* 51b8). One and the same form, of a mathematical object, bears two names, one mathematical, which can be called its proper name, and one physical, and can be called by one or the other name in the appropriate context, or even by both of them in the same context, in which case we might be led to the wrong conclusion that we are dealing with two distinct forms: in a mathematical context such as that of *Republic* 6 it can be called the tetrahedron itself, whereas in a cosmological context such as that of the *Timaeus* it can be called the fire itself, and in either context both of its names can appear next to each other, referring to a single entity in different senses.[87]

---

configured portions of space are particles of the elements, but also warns that this is not to suggest that "the forms of fire and earth are themselves (the type) regular solids". Kahn (2013) 6.6 also distinguishes the forms of the four polyhedra from those of the four elements since he thinks that appropriate mathematical structures, both as geometrically informed parts of space and as geometrical forms over them, function as a "middle term" between the forms of the elements and their occurrences, which implies that the forms of the polyhedra and those of the elements are different: on Kahn's account, the form of an element is imitated by its sensible instantiations necessarily through imitating the right mathematical structure so as for a species type to be determined, which anticipates Aristotle's notion of enmattered form. He concludes that "Plato's conception of mathematics as the link between Forms and their sensible images suggests that the Forms themselves will have something like mathematical structure. But how exactly Plato understood this quasi-mathematical character of the Forms we can scarcely guess. Our written sources do not allow us to recover the line of reasoning that Plato presented in his public lecture on the Good, or in his private discussions in the Academy" (Kahn [2013] 205–206). The outright identification of forms as forms of mathematical objects seems preferable on all counts to the notion of forms having "something like mathematical structure" and a "quasi-mathematical character".

87 Given the status of the *Timaeus* cosmology as a "likely story" (29c4–d3), Plato need not be committed to the details of his theory of elementary matter such as the specific quantization of the geometrical structure of space in two dimensions, the specific geometrical structure of volumes of space arising out of it as elementary material corpuscles and the identification of the stuffs these corpuscles are corpuscles of with the four Empedoclean elements. This might very well be an illustration of his firm belief that, no matter how many and what the elements of matter are, they arise out of the geometry of space, as forms of exquisitely symmetrical and beautiful mathematical objects (cf. *Ti.* 53d7–e8) are projected onto it, all of them being tightly knit into a family, a higher form whose example is the form of regular polyhedron (see next section) and which 'encodes' all kinds of matter, both elementary and composite, their properties and interactions. Plato seems to have envisaged this form as also 'encoding' at least some, if not all, structural features of the cosmos at its largest scale. The role of regular dodecahedron in the *Timaeus*

Referring to a form of a mathematical object as the form of a material element cannot but presuppose implicit reference to a particular mode of its instantiation in order for the causal powers of this element to be produced, without reference to which the element cannot be meaningfully spoken of (in the *Timaeus* it is thanks to the specific medium onto which the form of a polyhedron is projected that this form can be called form of an element). Speaking of the form of a regular solid as the form of an element forces us to regard this form not in itself but, let us say, impurely, i.e. in the preferred frame of some of its instantiations (the adverb is borrowed from *Phlb.* 61d10–62d3, where the human circle and sphere in the impure arts such as building are contrasted with the divine circle and sphere themselves, forms studied in philosophical geometry [55c4–57e5], in whose impure counterpart, building, they are instanced as the specific human circles and spheres this art requires for its needs);[88] Plato might want to draw attention to this when he presents Socrates in the *Parmenides* as being quite unsure about the forms of the elements.

Each of the four natural kinds defined by the forms of the regular polyhedra comes in different varieties, depending on the size of the spatial triangular elements making up the faces of the polyhedral regions of space shaped by each form into corpuscles (*Ti.* 57c7–d3), i.e. on the size of the corpuscles, as well as on

---

can be understood in this light. It is vaguely associated with the cosmos (55c4–6), whereas the other four regular polyhedra are each associated with a particle of an element: since in three-dimensional Euclidean space there are no other regular solids, the related forms of these symmetrical and beautiful mathematical structures determine the kinds of matter existing in the cosmos at its microscopic scales and somehow describe a feature of its largest scale, thereby uniting these two seemingly opposed scales. The regular dodecahedron can be associated with the cosmos because its face, the regular pentagon, is used in the construction of a regular pentadecagon, whose side subtends an angle which is approximately equal to an important cosmological parameter, the obliquity of the ecliptic; see Euc. *El.* 4.16 and Procl. *in Euc.* 269.8–21 (Friedlein). If Plato does suggest that an important structural feature of the cosmos at its largest scale is 'encoded' in the form of a mathematical object that encapsulates all kinds of matter making up the cosmos and their interactions, he thinks that it is partly thanks to this form that the Good is channeled down to the physical realm of motion and change from that of forms (see also 1.3.7); on the Good as unifying interrelationships between all forms into a beautiful whole, such as the form of the regular solid into which the individual forms of the five regular solids are united, see 1.2.4.1 and 1.3.8–9.

88 Physics is thus not fully reducible to mathematics, no matter how heavily mathematized it might become, just as the knowledge of the human circles and spheres used in various technical disciplines is not reducible to that of their divine counterparts according to *Phlb.* 61d10–62d3. The two types of knowledge are distinct but, despite the priority of the former over the latter, both are needed for one to possess philosophical knowledge, whose mark according to *R.* 7, 537b7–c8, is comprehensiveness; cf. Intro. and 1.1.2.

the interstices between them (*Ti.* 58d4–61c2): in physical contexts each of these forms can be referred to by the name denoting a variety of fire, air etc., provided that the variety is not anonymous, as is often the case (*Ti.* 58c5–d4). Each variety of fire, air etc. is made up of particles that are variously sized and spaced 'images' of the same form in each case, and their names thus refer to one and the same form impurely, i.e. with respect to how this form is instantiable in a specific medium. Plato treats snow as a variety of water (*Ti.* 59d4–e5), so the form of snow, whose existence seems to be assumed in the *Phaedo* (103c10–e8), can also be understood as a form of a mathematical object.

1.3.5 The forms of compound material substances

Apart from pure varieties of each element, in the *Timaeus* Plato recognizes two other types of material substances, mixtures of varieties of an element and of varieties of two or more elements (57d3–5). As with the form of each of the many varieties of an element, so with the form of a mixture of any number of them: the form of one of the four regular polyhedra can be referred to impurely by the name of a mixture of many varieties of the same element. In the case of material substances that are mixtures of varieties of different elements there seems to arise a serious difficulty, however. How can each of the names of substances of this sort be said to refer impurely to a single form, one of a mathematical object, which would thus be the form named after this substance too? The makeup of these substances presupposes two, three or four of the forms of the regular solids, not one, as in the previous cases, which is also the form referred to by the name of a substance: however, if there are going to be forms of the substances in question too, then the names of these substances must refer each to what is somehow a single form. Given the forms of two, three or four regular solids that are forms of varieties of two, three or all four material elements, can each group be considered a single form, one to which the name of a substance composed by varieties of the material elements at issue refers to impurely?

As far as the forms of all regular polyhedra are concerned, i.e. the forms of regular tetrahedron, octahedron, icosahedron, cube and dodecahedron, they are the forms into which a single form is ultimately 'divided', that of regular polyhedron (cf. 1.1.2). This form is like the form of number and the form of the good (see 1.2.4.1–2): it is similarly 'composed' by other forms, of all existing regular solids, which are five. The tetrahedron, the octahedron and the cube are the only three regular polyhedra whose sides have certain rational ratios to one another: the icosahedron and the dodecahedron have sides that stand in certain irrational ratios to each other and to the sides of the other three polyhedra.[89] Thus the form of regular solid 'divides' naturally into two forms, each of which is 'composite' just like the superordinate form of regular polyhedron: one is the form of those regular polyhedra whose sides stand in rational ratios to one another, whatever 'in' a form might be that which is geometrically manifested as side (cf. 1.3.2); the other is the form of regular solids with sides having irrational ratios to each other and to the sides of the other three regular solids. But before the final level of the five 'atomic' forms of the regular tetrahedron, octahedron, icosahedron, cube and dodecahedron is reached, there are also those 'compound' forms that are determined by the ratios between the sides of any four, three and two of the polyhedra. Thus, if a substance consists of varieties of the three elements whose forms are regular solids with sides having rational ratios to one another, the name of the substance can be said to refer impurely to a form: if a substance is composed by varieties of any two of these three elements, or of any one or two of them and the fourth or of all four elements, its name can again be said to refer impurely to a form.[90]

In the *Timaeus* Plato discusses in some detail a number of substances other than the elements, reducing them to the shapes of the particles of all or some of the elements making them up, to the sizes of these particles and the interstices between them, i.e. to the specific modes in which the forms of the elements are instantiated in space and in which their various instantiations are spatially related (58d4–61c2): the name of each of these substances, and by implication of many others like them, most of which are anonymous, though certainly namable, can be the name of a form, a part of the form of regular polyhedron, referred to impurely, i.e. not as a mathematical object however instantiable but as one instantiable in a specific medium and way. This can apply to compound substances such as copper that have no biological role but also to those that have such a role: marrow, bone, flesh, sinew, skin and hair, whose mention as name of a form disturbs Socrates in the *Parmenides*. Plato devotes a section of the *Timaeus* to the discussion of all these biological compounds of the four elements (73b1–76e6),

---

[89] Euc. *El*. 13.18.
[90] It is conceivable that Plato imagined the form of regular polyhedron not as the set of all regular polyhedra into which, as well as into whose combinations, the set 'divides' but instead as an individual form, like a form-number, instantiable, though, in five distinct ways (irrespective of the variability among manifestations of each type) which would correspond to what we could call its distinct aspects or features. The latter could be described as forms, since whatever 'in' the form of the square is spatially or mentally manifested as a square's diagonal is described in *R*. 6 as if it were a form unto itself; cf. n. 83. The account of the forms of compound substances is easily recast in these terms.

and their names can be thought to be names of forms of mathematical objects impurely referred to as instantiable in a specific medium and way in order for certain biological functions to be served. The principle in *Republic* 10 which posits a form for each name attributable to many distinct things can thus be true of the samples of all existing material substances, and the forms it generates need not require a range of forms beyond the forms of mathematical objects (cf. above n. 87).

1.3.6 The forms of properties of matter

The same conclusion can be reached for the properties of all these material substances: the names of the properties that adjectivally describe material substances possessing these properties can also be considered names of forms of mathematical objects. Plato seems to presuppose in *Republic* 7 the existence of forms of two pairs of such properties: weight and lightness, hardness and softness (523c10–524c14). In the *Timaeus* he assumes that a quantity of each of the four elements is heavy if it is surrounded by unlike particles of a different element, in which case it tends to move towards what Aristotle calls its natural place in the cosmos, where it concentrates in its greatest abundance in the cosmos and its particles are surrounded by their likes: the larger of two unequal quantities of an element is heavier and the smaller lighter (62c3–63e7), and when quantities of fire, air and water are in question, the one made up of larger particles, bounded by more triangular elements of space, is heavier, the other or others lighter (55d7–56c7). Thus, if there are forms of weight and lightness, both can be any part of the form of regular polyhedron discussed above that 'comprises' two forms of regular solids. All these parts can be impurely referred to as forms of compound material substances in a 'chemical' context. But any of these can be referred to impurely as the form of weight, or as the form of lightness, in another context: this context, in which a part of the form of regular solid can be referred to impurely as the form of weight or lightness, must concern a region of space as simply configured partially into an element by one 'constituent' form but to a lesser extent than it is shaped into another element, irrespective of whether it is free or bound with the first element, by the second 'constituent' form (by substituting the part of the form of regular polyhedron which comprises the forms doubling as those of fire, air and water, we can obtain the form of weight and lightness for these elements defined as functions of the size of their particles and the number of two-dimensional parts of their faces).

As for the properties of hardness and softness, in the *Timaeus* they are briefly defined in terms, first, of the size of the faces of the polyhedral particles of the elements and, second, of the density of the particles (62b6–c2): if there are forms of hardness and softness, both can once again be identified naturally with any part of the form of regular polyhedron discussed above which comprises two, three or all four forms of the regular solids doubling as forms of the material elements and is, of course, impurely referred to in the appropriate context. The forms of two other properties of material substances, namely heat and coldness, are mentioned in the *Phaedo* (103c10–e8) and, in view of the *Timaeus* (61d5–62b6), they can also be understood as forms of mathematical objects.[91] Plato's brief mention of heat and coldness in the *Timaeus* seems to hint that the corresponding forms could be whatever 'in' the forms of the regular tetrahedron and icosahedron respectively are manifested as those geometrical aspects of spatial regular tetrahedra and icosahedra, the corpuscles of fire and water, that endow these three-dimensionally informed regions of space with the causal powers called heat and coldness (cf. again *Phd.* 103c10–e8 and above n. 87).[92]

1.3.7 The forms of living things

The form of man, whose existence is doubted by the young Socrates in the *Parmenides* but is assumed in the *Statesman* and follows from the principle in *Republic* 10, as does also the existence of a form of any animal, can also be a form of a mathematical object if the form of life, in which souls that make matter alive participate, is assumed to be the form of a mathematical object whose 'images' are souls. If this form is further assumed to be like the form of regular solid in that it 'divides' into a large number of 'atomic' forms as the form of regular solid 'divides' into the regular tetrahedron, octahedron etc., the names of all living things can be the names of these individual forms, each impurely referred to by the name of a species of living things as instantiable in a specific complex arrangement of matter which is alive thanks to this instantiation in that it performs certain functions in a way characteristic of a species (cf., though, n. 90). The form of life is presupposed in the final proof of the immortality of the soul in the *Phaedo*

---

91 The hot and the cold are discussed in the *Timaeus* as sensations, not as properties of material substances per se. However, there is no reason to deny that the latter can be hot and cold in themselves and, as such, can bring about certain effects when they act on other insensate pieces of matter.
92 For aspects of forms referred to as forms unto themselves see above n. 83.

(106d5–7), where it is implicitly assumed that souls are its participants, and a conception of the rational soul, the soul par excellence, as 'image' of a form of a mathematical object seems to be presupposed in the *Timaeus*.

The soul of the cosmos, a living being, is presented in the *Timaeus* as having been formed from a mixture of intelligible being and sensible matter with their prior mixture into a third substance, which was intermediate between its two pure components: then the second mixture was divided into a number of circular bands according to a complex mathematical formula and, finally, these bands were implanted concentrically into the cosmos and began to rotate (34b10–36d7). Plato refers to them as circles and motions and seems to think of these components of the cosmic soul as circular and uniform motions of space: they enliven the whole cosmos and the celestial objects, bring about the diurnal rotation of the cosmos and all the other celestial motions (37c6–40e2), and also endow the cosmos itself and all celestial objects with paradigmatically supreme, divine rationality (47a1–c4). This soul is not only motive and endowed with reason, whose intelligible objects must be forms, but is also able to perceive sensibles (36d8–37c5), despite the fact that the body it enlivens, the cosmos, lacks sensory organs (33c1–4).[93] Now, an analogue of the cosmic soul in all animals, which must be responsible for their locomotion and sense perception and is rational potentially only in humans, is presented as having been formed from second- and third-rate leftovers of the mixture from which the cosmic soul had been made (39e3–40a2, 41a7–42e4): its constituent motions, which in all animals with head take place in the brain (44d3–8, 73b1–d1), lack the full uniformity and orderliness of its cosmic analogues and only in the case of man can become similar to them with learning and hard thinking (42e5–44d2, 90b6–d7).[94]

The two other parts of the human soul in the *Republic* are also thought in the *Timaeus* to have counterparts in other animals (41a7–d7, 76e7–77c5) and are

---

93 The forms that must be the objects of the cosmic soul's thought and knowledge seem to be the forms of mathematical objects by knowing which this soul brings about celestial motions: in other words, the mathematical structure of the laws determining celestial motions (cf. ch. 2, n. 69). They can be identified with the forms of the "true figures" that are mentioned in *R.* 7, 529c6–d5, and are implicitly contrasted with the visible paths of enmattered celestial motions whose intelligible paradigms they are and in which they cannot but be imperfectly manifested, just as everything intelligible is in matter. On *R.* 7, 529c6–d5, see 2.9–11 and Kouremenos (2015) 1.6 –7. In *Lg.* 10, 898c1–10, all motion in the heavens is said to be produced by one or more rational and good souls.

94 According to *Ti.* 47a1–c4, to assimilate our mind to the cosmic mind we must observe its revolutions in the heavens–obviously indirectly, since souls are not sensibles, by observing the visible celestial motions it causes–learn and understand them; cf. 2.5.

sharply contrasted with the part that is akin to the purely rational cosmic soul, though at the same time they are closely related to it since they are assumed to be somehow connected with the marrow, of both the spine and the bones, which is considered the same stuff as brain matter (73b1–e1; the seat of the spirited part is located in the area of the heart according to 69a6–70d6, and the seat of the desire for sustenance in the organs of the belly according to 70d7–73a8, sexual desire being assumed in 90e1–91d5 to reside in the genitals, but the connection of the marrow with these organs is not explained, with the exception of male genitals in 91a1–b7). No matter how the counterpart to the cosmic soul in all animals is precisely related to the two other parts of their souls, both it and its cosmic paradigm seem to be conceived as the 'images' of a form, that of a mathematical object.

Since in the *Timaeus* Plato describes as intermediate between forms and matter the 'images' of the former in the latter (50c7–e1), the 'stuff' out of which the cosmic soul and its analogues in animals have been fashioned can be plausibly understood as a metaphor for their nature: they connect forms and matter as intermediate between the two, being 'images' of a form in matter, not, though, as some sensible bodies but as non-sensible motions enlivening complex arrangements of various kinds of compound matter.[95] This form seems to be what is called, at the beginning of the cosmological part of the *Timaeus*, the intelligible or complete living thing: it 'contains' all intelligible animals, as species and as individuals, and its 'image' is the living cosmos with all its species of animals and their individuals (30c2–31b3; plants are included among living things in 76e7–c5, where they are said to be enlivened only by the desire for sustenance and the sense of pleasure and pain and to have no share whatsoever in reason, though they must have some if they are to count as living creatures since the nutritive soul in animals is somehow related to the rational, as is also their spirited soul). The form of living thing is probably identical with the form of life mentioned in the *Phaedo*.[96] If it is a form like the form of the regular polyhedron, each of the 'atomic' forms it 'contains' can be referred to as form of a species of animal and of its individuals, as an intelligible animal, in connection with the specific complex arrangements of matter it enlivens thereby endowing them with certain functions performed in a way peculiar to this species of animal.[97]

---

[95] For souls as a special kind of form-'copies' see Silverman (2014) 222–223.
[96] Cf. Kahn (2013) 184 n. 11 who, though, thinks that the intelligible living thing Plato mentions in the *Timaeus* is not one form among the many but the entire network of forms, the Good.
[97] Cf. Mohr (1985) 30–31.

The form of living thing seems to be a form of a mathematical object since its 'image' on the cosmic level is metaphorically presented by Plato as having been made according to a mathematical formula, i.e. as being a 'copy' of a form of a mathematical object which is symbolized by the formula and concretized in the cosmic soul. This formula is a sequence of ratios implicitly describing the relations between the pitches of successive notes forming a musical scale, as if the cosmic soul were a musical instrument woven into the cosmos, its strings producing tones having these pitch-relations to one another. But in *Laws* 10 circular motion is explicitly said to be a mere metaphor for the nature of rational soul which is unknown (896d5–898d5):[98] the scale seems thus to be a metaphor too, for a mathematical object itself, a form, whose 'image' is any rational soul. Belonging to harmonics, one of the branches of mathematics discussed in *Republic* 7, the concept of the scale is not as intriguing mathematically as the regular polyhedra from solid geometry whose forms double as forms of the elements in the *Timaeus*. It is, however, aptly chosen as a metaphor for the form of a mathematical object, whatever that may be, whose 'copy' is any rational soul and which is the form of living thing: a scale is an abstract mathematical pattern serving as basis for an indefinitely large variety of melodies whose musicality depends on it and in which it becomes concretized, just as a form of a mathematical object is the principle of life for all the different living things in which it is manifested as soul. At issue here is in all probability a mathematical object unknown to the mathematics of Plato's day (see 1.2.4.9 and cf. n. 87).

If the form of all living things, the principle of life, can be assumed to have been conceived by Plato as the form of a mathematical object, can we also assume that each of the moral forms, the Good and the form of justice or any other virtue, is also the form of a mathematical object, known or unknown to the mathematics of his day? The moral forms, the iconic Platonic forms, are among the few forms that have yet to be accommodated if the range of forms could have been plausibly restricted by Plato himself only to forms of mathematical objects.

1.3.8 The Good and the forms of virtues

As seen above (1.2.4.1), the Good as highest object of philosophy and paradigm of what is good anywhere seems to be the relationships among all other objects of philosophy, all other forms, that harmoniously unify them. All virtues, the human good, must thus be 'images' of the relationships unifying all other forms into

---

98 See 2.5 and Kouremenos (2015) 3.3.2.

a system, which is the highest form. Temperance is defined in *Republic* 4 as harmony among the parts of the soul and agreement that reason must rule, as the unity of the soul; justice is defined as each part's doing its own job and the other two civic virtues, wisdom and bravery, are defined as the agreed-upon job of reason and the spirited part respectively (441d11–442d7; cf. 430d3–432b2). Each part of the soul cannot do its proper job, however, unless there is agreement to that effect among them: as it is, the definitions of justice and temperance collapse these two virtues, and the other two which they implicitly define, into one another, and it is not surprising that only a few lines below in the same book justice is described first as each part of the soul doing its own job and then as the unity of all three parts and their harmonious agreement (443c9–444a2), the imitation in the human soul of the supra-human harmony among all forms that is the Good. It is thus only this form that is manifested in the human soul as the virtues, not as many distinct forms as there are virtues. Considered impurely as instantiable in the human soul, the Good can be called the form of temperance if the focus is on the soul as the whole which the soul becomes due to this instantiation; it can also be called the form of justice if wholeness is viewed as the specific relations structuring the parts of the whole into this whole, and it can be called the form of bravery or wisdom if the focus is restricted to the place of a specific part in this whole. The reduction of the moral forms, those of justice and the other virtues, to the Good and the conception of the latter as the system into which all other forms are unifyingly ordered by the relations among them could allow Plato to talk about moral forms while assuming that all forms are forms of mathematical objects without positing that a moral form is a form of a mathematical object known or unknown to contemporary mathematics.[99]

---

99 That Plato identified the Good with the unity of the forms that are the real objects studied in mathematics is supported by Aristoxenus' famous report of Aristotle's oral testimony about a public lecture Plato delivered on the Good (*Harm.* 39.8–40.4 da Rios). To the surprise of the audience, who waited to hear about what is commonly thought to be good, e.g. wealth, health and power, Plato lectured on mathematics, numbers, geometry and astronomy, and at the end he declared that the Good is unity: καὶ τὸ πέρας ὅτι ἀγαθόν ἐστιν ἕν. At issue here is presumably the unity not of all branches of mathematics such as geometry and astronomy, but rather the deeper ontological unity that is adumbrated by the unity of mathematics, i.e. the unity of the intelligible beings mathematics studies (cf. 1.2.4.9). τὸ πέρας can be taken as part of what Plato said, not as an adverbial expression meaning "at the end", as understood above. If so, τὸ πέρας ὅτι ἀγαθόν ἐστιν ἕν identifies the Good with a unifying limit: Sedley (2007) 270 translates this clause "the Good is a unification of limit" and rejects the view that the Good is unity arguing that it is to be understood as "an ideal proportionality, intelligible only through the conceptual framework of a high-level mathematics" (for a similar view cf. Burnyeat [2000] 74–81, in whose view the Good is unity generated as well as sustained by concord, attunement and proportion, all of which are

The highest object of philosophy, the Good, will be mirrored in the studies propedeutic to philosophy. The goal of the preparatory mathematical studies, if they will really help in the subsequent approach to the Good and the form of beauty, will be to produce understanding of the affinity and kinship of (a) the different branches of mathematics and (b) the nature of beings: to make one see how all branches of mathematics are related to one another forming a good and beautiful system which reflects the connections among all objects really studied in mathematics, among the natures of a form and any other form, into what philosophy will show to be the model of goodness and beauty (*R.* 7, 531c5–d5 and 537b7–c8; cf. 1.2.4.9). If it adumbrates epistemically the interconnectedness of the forms of mathematical objects, the unity of mathematics in its close link with the Good makes it unlikely that the forms of mathematical objects are a subset of the totality of forms: as is suggested in the allegory of the cave, these forms seem to be all existing forms, considered purely. Although it is philosophy that describes beings as forms and also identifies them as the objects really studied in mathematics, their range will be explored by mathematics, and philosophy's job will be to examine their nature as forms and their manifestations in the sensible world, considering them impurely as forms of material substances, life virtues etc. (cf. Intro. and 1.1.2).

The parts of a well-ordered whole share with one another the benefit that each can offer to the whole, and each one of them serves to bind all of them into the whole insofar as it contributes to their mutual benefit, the good truly binding them into a system. In *Republic* 7 it is the common benefit of all citizens that confers upon the city the unity that is its greatest good (519e1–520a5; cf. *R.* 5, 462a2–b3).[100] In Socrates' autobiography in the *Phaedo* answers in terms of the good to questions about the celestial bodies and their phenomena are thought to refer not only to what is good in each particular case but also to the common good, the true binder and unifier (97b8–98b6, 99b6–c6). What binds mathematics together seems thus to be the mutual benefit of its branches, the help one can offer to the others. As propedeutic to philosophy, Plato demands in *Republic* 7 not just learning but, more importantly, doing mathematics and advancing it: he emphasizes

---

fundamental to aesthetics and mathematics). If it is only through such a framework that the Good is intelligible, however, since in the *Republic* this framework cannot be anything other than the unity of mathematics, on which see below, the Good is a unity, and there is no reason to think that this unity is only manifested as, or in, proportionality. In *Ti.* 31c2–32a7 Plato does declare that the best bond is proportion, for it effects in the best way the fullest unification of the things that are bound together, but he probably means that it is the best example of a unifying bond, not unity itself.

100 Cf. *Phlb.* 63b7–c4, *Plt.* 310e5–311c8, *Lg.* 5, 739b8–e7, and 7, 793a9–d5.

the importance of finding solutions to outstanding problems with an example of a problem which, in view of his call in the same context for the geometrization of astronomy and the arithmetization of harmonics, hints at his wish for major advancements in geometry and arithmetic motivated by astronomy and harmonics respectively. He believes that mathematics is not just a jumble of four diverse fields, two of which, arithmetic and geometry, are largely independent of each other and are applied to the rest, harmonics and astronomy, but that it will grow into a system in which each part will be brought to bear fruitfully upon the others: the kinship between the branches of the mature mathematics of the future will lie in their mutually beneficial interrelations which will be grasped only through a prolonged active immersion in all fields of mathematics. This will be a very difficult task, as Plato has Glaucon note when Socrates outlines his view on the goal of studying mathematics as propedeutic to philosophy (*R.* 7, 531c9–d5), and in Plato's time it was certainly unachievable given the undeveloped state of contemporary mathematics, as a result of which its branches were unrelated or only tangentially related (cf. 1.2.4.9). The difficulty of this task matches the difficulty of philosophizing, for which it will prepare the mind, and its unachievability in Plato's time explains plausibly his unwillingness to talk in concrete terms about the methods of philosophy (*R.* 7, 532d2–533a9).

Plato has Socrates claim in *Republic* 6 that each of the other forms, a being, owes its being to the Good and that it can be known thanks to the Good (509b5–c2), which is why the highest object studied in philosophy is the Good. This is so because each of them is part of a system. Since a form is a being in the sense that it is the object referred to in the answer to the question "what is…?", whose subject is the name primarily of that form and secondarily of everything which partakes in it, its interconnections with the other forms in the system, all of them considered both purely and impurely, must determine what it is, and thus it can be fully understood only in their light (cf. 1.1.2). A theorem cannot be fully understood independently of the proofs of all those theorems on which its proof depends, nor can any branch of mathematics be really understood independently of all the other branches with which it interconnects in all possible ways. Similarly, in philosophy a form cannot be really understood independently of all other forms with which it builds a system, unless, that is, it is considered as a part of this system. A true philosopher, according to *Republic* 7, will be a comprehensive viewer in the sense that s/he will study the forms, considered both purely and impurely, not in isolation but as a system, a task for which s/he will have prepared during the preliminary mathematical studies which will have led to a synoptic view of the kinship of the diverse fields of mathematics and of the nature of beings (537b7–c8). The branches of mathematics will be first approached independently in these preparatory studies, with no emphasis on their kinship, but the final goal will be to bring all of them together paving the way for philosophy. The Good, the kinship of all other forms, will be the intelligible illumination in which they will be viewed synoptically: the interconnections which bind all forms together and radiate everywhere in the intelligible realm can be allegorically likened to bright sunlight which diffuses everywhere in the sensible realm allowing its contents to be viewed synoptically.

In *Republic* 5, 6 and 7 Plato calls the Good a form and describes it as a single entity (476a5–9, 507b4–7, 517b7–9), but in *Republic* 6 he also denies that the Good is a being (509b5–c2), i.e. a form, probably hinting in a striking manner at its fundamental difference from all other forms, at its unique unhypotheticalness (see 1.1.2). However, their interconnections, can be viewed globally, in their structuring totality which transcends all its particular elements, as a single source from which mutually illuminating relationships of all kinds spread out everywhere between them, just as bright sunlight radiates everywhere from the sun to which the Good is likened in the allegory of the cave.[101]

1.3.9 The form of beauty

In *R.* 7, 531c5–d5, the goal of the propedeutic mathematical studies is to facilitate the approach to the Good and the form of beauty through the understanding they foster of the affinity and kinship of all branches of mathematics. In *R.* 7, 526d6–e5, only the Good is explicitly mentioned as the highest object of philosophy for the approach to which the prolonged study of mathematics will pave the way, not the form of beauty too. But the two forms seem to be one and the same form, referred to not much below by two names again in connection with the goal of the study of mathematics. In *Republic* 6 the Good is said to be the cause of knowledge and truth, both of which are beautiful, but also to be by far superior to both in beauty, for its beauty is something extraordinary (508d10–509a8): what else can this marvelous beauty derive from to surpass even that of knowledge and truth if not from a most privileged relationship of the Good to the form of beauty, from their identicalness, since the form of beauty is sharply distinguished in the *Symposium* too from knowledge, one of its participants (209e5–211b5)? Indeed, in *Republic* 7 the Good is explicitly said to cause all beauty (517b7–c4), which in the

---

[101] Cf. Fine (1999) 228. On the metaphor of the sun see 2.1.

Phaedo is said of beauty itself (100c10–e3).[102] Thus, if we do not need for the Good a special form unrelated to those of mathematical objects, the same holds for the form of beauty as well.[103]

1.4 The equation of forms with form-numbers, and their principles

1.4.1 The equation of forms with form-numbers

If, as is suggested in the *Republic*, all forms are forms of mathematical objects, Aristotle need not have in mind only Plato's successors, Speusippus and Xenocrates, and Plato's purportedly late "unwritten doctrines" when he deplores in *Metaph.* A 9, 992a32–b1, the reduction of philosophy to mathematics by those who believe in forms: he can very well presuppose a view hinted at in the cave allegory in the *Republic*.[104] We can also explain why Aristotle often attributes to Plato the paradoxical view that forms are numbers, i.e. that form-numbers exhaust the range of forms (see e.g. *Metaph.* A 9, 991b9).[105] This attribution need not be in its entirety another example of Aristotle's tactic of reducing justly or unjustly a position under criticism, in this case Plato's theory of forms, to another he can easily reject as absurd (he explains this tactic himself, in *Cael.* Γ 4, 303a8–10, where he attributes to the atomists the view that all things are made up of numbers, noting that this is not explicitly espoused by them but it is what they mean when they posit atoms as the elements of all things; not much earlier, in Γ 1, 299b23–300a19, he argues that Plato too in the *Timaeus* is committed to the Pythagorean view that all things are made up of numbers). If Plato thought that the only forms are those of mathematical objects, Aristotle could attribute to him the view that the only forms are in fact form-numbers simply because the forms, since they are assumed to be principles, must be forms only of the primary mathematical objects, which for Aristotle are the numbers (cf. *Metaph.* A 2, 982a19–28, M 3, 1078a9–12, and *APo.* A 27). He attributes the identification of forms with

---

102 Cf. *Phlb.* 64e5–65a5. Plato's identification of the Good and the form of beauty seems to be presupposed in Aristotle's *EE* A 8, 1218a15–28 (translated in 1.2.4.4). Beauty and goodness are distinct for Aristotle, but he too thinks that beauty is profoundly manifested in mathematics, in its proofs and thus most probably in its objects too; see *Metaph.* M 3, 1078a31–b6.
103 As does also for the five greatest forms in *Sph.* 254b7–255e7; see Silverman (2002) ch. 5.
104 Plato's "unwritten doctrines" are mentioned by Aristotle in *Ph.* Δ 2, 209b14–15. For a useful recent survey of scholarly attitudes toward them see Nikulin (2013).
105 In *Metaph.* M 4, 1078b7–12, he says that originally forms had nothing to do with numbers.

numbers to Speusippus and Xenocrates too, both of whom, he says, collapsed Plato's supposed distinction between form-numbers and mathematical numbers (see 1.2.3), Speusippus by conceiving of Plato's exotic form-numbers as plain mathematical numbers and Xenocrates by absurdly considering mathematical numbers to be forms (*Metaph.* M 1, 1076a19–22 = Speus. fr. 74 I.P., Xenocr. fr. 107 I.P.). This need not suggest that Speusippus and Xenocrates abandoned the forms of geometrical objects. They seem to have retained them but as dependent on form-numbers, no matter how each had conceived form-numbers.[106] They could have argued, moreover, that this dependence was genuinely Platonic. For Aristotle, however, the assumed dependence of the forms of geometrical objects on form-numbers would have entailed that form-numbers are the only existing forms (cf. *Metaph.* N 3, 1090b20–26).[107]

To credit Plato with the attribution of priority to form-numbers one could have pointed to passages in his dialogues such as *Prm.* 144a4–7, from the second hypothesis, where it is concluded that, "if the one is", then there must be numbers and thus an infinite multitude of beings: whatever the purpose of the hypotheses in the second part of the *Parmenides* might be, the beings mentioned here can be assumed to be forms, which are thus numbers, all other mathematical objects being secondary to them since next it is shown that the hypothesis entails the existence of geometrical objects too (144e8–145b5). *Sph.* 238a10–b1, where it is assumed that all numbers are among the beings if anything else is a being, is another relevant passage. The belief that Plato somehow privileged numbers over the other mathematical objects, and thus might have even restricted forms to form-numbers, could have been further supported by his possible use of the form of number to illustrate the Good (see 1.2.4.2). To make sense, however, this restriction would have required a reduction of the objects of geometry to numbers but, given Plato's strong interest in incommensurability, it is best to think that he retained the two fundamentally irreducible classes of objects recognized in contemporary mathematics, numbers and geometrical objects, and thus that, if he took all forms to be forms of mathematical objects only, he did not restrict them to form-numbers.

---

106 Cf. Dillon (2003) 45 (on Speusippus) and 108–109 (on Xenocrates).
107 For other attempts to explain Plato's mysterious identification of forms with numbers often reported by Aristotle see Robin (1908) 268–269 and 450–468, Ross (1951) ch. XV (he discusses the views of Stenzel [1933²], Toeplitz [1929] and Becker [1931] in ch. XII on form-numbers and their principles), Findlay (1971) 54–66, Annas (1976) 62–73 and Gerson (2013) 113–125.

1.4.2 The principles of form-numbers

A related view attributed by Aristotle to Plato is that the form-numbers have principles, one formal, "the one", and one material, which is dyadic, "the great and the small". These are the ultimate principles or elements of all things if the principles of all things are forms which are assumed to be form-numbers (*Metaph.* A 6, 987b18–21). Varieties of "the great and the small" in one, two and three dimensions are mentioned as dependent dyadic principles of forms, presumably, of geometrical objects, though the relation of these dimensional dyadic principles to their dimensionless arithmetical correlate is left obscure: they are "the long and the short", "the broad and the narrow", "the deep and the shallow". As one expects, in this scheme there are also geometrical counterparts to the first principle of form-numbers, the dimensionless "one", which are derived from it: the form-numbers 2, 3 and 4 for forms of lines, planes and solids respectively but, Aristotle adds without providing any further specification, other form-numbers too (*Metaph.* A 9, 992a10–18, and N 3, 1090b20–26). The dimensional varieties of "the great and the small" are treated by Aristotle as kinds of material substratum, infinite extension in one, two and three dimensions, which become finitized and determinate as lines, plane and solid figures by the imposition of a form-number on them: 2 in the case of lines that are bounded by two points, 3 in the case of the "first" plane figure, the triangle, 4 in the case of the "first" solid figure, the tetrahedral pyramid, and the infinitely many other form-numbers apparently in the cases of the infinitely many other polygonal and polyhedral plane and solid figures. This reduction of polygonal and polyhedral geometrical objects to ultimate principles is also referred to by Aristotle as a generation of these geometrical objects. There is no evidence as to how it could have been applied to plane and solid figures such as the circle, the sphere or the cylinder, and its context might have mentioned the so-called figurate numbers, which are perhaps implicit, at least in part, in the second hypothesis of the *Parmenides*, where Plato shows that "if the one is", there must be numbers and geometrical shapes (cf. 1.2.4.3). In *Ph.* Γ 6, 206b27–33, Aristotle describes "the great and the small" posited by Plato as principle in forms (see 203a1–16) not as infinite extension in one, two and three dimensions but as infinite divisibility: Plato, he says, posited a double infinitary principle because the partial sums of an infinite series of decreasing terms in constant ratio, considered as parts of a magnitude, grow continually, though they cannot become arbitrarily large but all are less than the limit, in a counterintuitive contrast to the continually diminishing terms of the corresponding infinite

The equation of forms with form-numbers, and their principles — 71

sequence which can exceed any assigned bound.[108] Aristotle goes on to object, in view of the connection of "the great and the small" with form-numbers, that in numbers there is no infinite decrease but only infinite increase which, nevertheless, Plato does not need since he stops the numbers, which in this context must be form-numbers, at the decad.

In attributing to Plato a mystifying pair of principles of form-numbers and thus all other things Aristotle also mentions a generation of numbers (*Metaph.* A 6, 987b33–988a1). This was probably an attempt to generate the numbers from the fewest possible logical starting points.[109] Since the dyadic principle produces doubling (*Metaph.* M 7, 1081b21–22),[110] these starting points seem to have been derived from the fact that every number is even, having the form $2k$, or odd, having the form $2k+1$, except the number 1, which without the concept of number 0 cannot be thought to have the form $2k+1$. It is clear that every number after 1, the first number, is either a multiple of 2, starting from 2 itself, or 1 doubled, the smallest multiple of 2, and becoming arbitrarily large, and can thus be plausibly called "the great and the small"; or it is a sum of a multiple of 2 and 1, the latter, unlike the multiples of 2, being ever the same. The entire series of numbers can thus be generated with just 1 and two simple operations, doubling, which can be plausibly called "the great and the small", and the addition of 1, "the one", which was perhaps assumed to be applied first to simply generate the first number: doubling it generates 2 and adding 1 to 2 generates 3;[111] doubling the product of the first doubling generates 4 and adding 1 to it generates 5; doubling the outcome of the first addition of 1 to a number generates 6 and adding 1 to it generates 7;[112]

---

108 Cf. Simp. *in Ph.* 453.25–454.16 (Diels) based on Porphyry.
109 Cf. Annas (1976) 42–43.
110 See Alex. Aphr. *in Metaph.* 56.33–57.11 (Hayduck) based on Aristotle's lost *On the Good*, an account of Plato's lecture mentioned above in n. 104.
111 For the number 2 as 1 doubled see Alex. Aphr. *in Metaph.* 57.9–10 (Hayduck).
112 This seems to be the three-step process mentioned in Arist. *Metaph.* M 8, 1084a3–7: ἡ δὲ γένεσις τῶν ἀριθμῶν ἢ περιττοῦ ἀριθμοῦ ἢ ἀρτίου ἀεί ἐστιν· ὡδὶ μὲν τοῦ ἑνὸς εἰς τὸν ἄρτιον πίπτοντος περιττός, ὡδὶ δὲ τῆς μὲν δυάδος ἐμπιπτούσης ὁ ἀφ' ἑνὸς διπλασιαζόμενος, ὡδὶ δὲ τῶν περιττῶν ὁ ἄλλος ἄρτιος ("The generation on numbers is always or an even or odd number. When the one applies here to an even number, an odd number [is generated], when the two [i.e. the process of doubling] applies here, the numbers doubled from one [are generated] and then, when the odd numbers [apply] here, the other even numbers [are generated]"). Two kinds of even numbers are clearly presupposed by the expression ὁ ἄλλος ἄρτιος, which denotes one kind, and the second kind can only be ὁ ἀφ' ἑνὸς διπλασιαζόμενος: these even numbers can be plausibly taken to be the powers of the number 2 produced by the application of doubling to its smaller powers, "the other even numbers" $2k$ being those for odd k. It is strange that the generation of "the other even numbers" is described by the phrase ὡδὶ δὲ τῶν περιττῶν, sc.

doubling the product of the second doubling generates 8 and adding 1 to it generates 9; doubling the outcome of the second addition of 1 to a number generates 10 and adding 1 to it generates 11 and so on.[113]

A simple generation of numbers via repeated addition of 1 was perhaps not opted for in order for the oddness and evenness of each number to be emphasized since Aristotle informs us that numbers were produced as even or odd (*Metaph.* M 8, 1084a3–4). But Plato could have hinted at it by representing each even and odd number his two-step process yields as the parts of a bisected line segment whose half is bisected and so on continually;[114] this could explain why Aristotle associates doubling or "the great and the small" in numbers with the diminishing terms of an infinite sequence in constant ratio ("the small") and their increasing partial sums ("the great").[115] The context of Plato's generation of numbers is unknown. It could have been a simple and vivid illustration of the ultimate, though inaccessible, at least in his time, simplicity underlying the Good, which he could have likened in its complexity to the form of number, its immensely rich and mysterious part, though the number series itself is easy to build (cf. 1.2.4.2). But it is

---

ἐμπιπτόντων εἰς τὴν δυάδα, ὁ ἄλλος ἄρτιος instead of ὡδὶ δὲ εἰς τοὺς περιττούς, sc. τῆς δυάδος ἐμπιπτούσης, ὁ ἄλλος ἄρτιος.

113 This generation of numbers is C in Ross (1951) 191–194. He offers it as a more plausible variation of the two generations of numbers up to 10 in Robin (1908) 278–286 and 442–450, but rejects it on the ground that Plato never gave a mathematical generation of numbers, having posited "the great and the small" as simply indefinite manyness and fewness and "the one" as the successive possible degrees of definiteness imposed on it, the number 2 having the first degree of possible manyness and fewness, the number 3 having the next possible degree and so on ad infinitum (see Ross [1951] 202–205). Annas (1976) 52–54 outlines the same generation of numbers but assumes that the numbers "came out in a bizarre order" (because "the great and the small" alone can only generate the powers of 2 and, in order for the other even numbers to be generated, "the one" is presupposed to have first generated the odd numbers). This, however, is not required, nor is there any evidence that the numbers had been generated out of order.
114 Cf. again the passage from Simplicius referred to above in n. 108.
115 Aristotle's evidence and the passage from Simplicius cited above in n. 108 need not be assumed to imply that Plato generated the numbers as ratios of lengths; such an account of the Platonic generation of numbers has been put forth by van der Wielen (1941) 118–137, a work reviewed extensively in Cherniss (1947) 235–251 (the generation of numbers proposed by van der Wielen is discussed in Ross [1951] 200–202 who argues against objections raised by its author). For another attempt at reconstructing Plato's generation of numbers as ratios arising from a geometrical construction see Gaiser (1963) 115–125; but cf. Ilting (1965) and Annas (1976) 53 n. 67. That the concept of number had been reduced to that of ratio in the Platonic generation of numbers has also been assumed by Toeplitz (1929) without prioritizing geometry; cf. Ross (1951) 198–199. A natural outcome of such views is to credit Plato with an inchoate conception of rational and irrational numbers; cf. Taylor (1955[6]) ch. 19 and Popper (2002) 122 n. 55.

unlikely that in this mental process he saw a path to the ultimate principles of both form-numbers and the forms of geometrical objects. However, in assuming that Plato did see such a way, Aristotle once again seems to have subscribed to an understanding of Plato's thought current in the Academy after some point.

That mental generation can uncover principles of what is ungenerated is not a problem in itself. It might have been none other than Plato himself who had presented the creation of the cosmos in his *Timaeus* as merely a mental process, one which aimed, though, at imparting an understanding of the metaphysical principles of the eternal cosmos and was like a geometrical proof: what is proven is always or timelessly true, just as the cosmos is eternal, but in order to understand it we carry out or study its proof and mentally see it coming to be true at a certain time (Arist. *Cael.* A 10, 279b32–280a10 = Speus. fr. 94 I.P., Xenocr. fr. 153 I.P.). This mathematical analogy might have incited an Academic interpretation of Plato's generation of numbers as another case of the *Timaeus* strategy, as a mental process which brings out the principles of form-numbers. Both Speusippus and Xenocrates thought that the cosmogony of the *Timaeus* was non-literal, and in their own 'generation' of form-numbers they posited the pair of principles as Plato himself had supposedly posited in his own 'generation' of these entities (Arist. *Metaph.* N 1, 1087b4–9 = Speus. fr. 82a I.P., Xenocr. fr. 99 I.P.): it can hardly be accidental that Xenocrates (fr. 188 I.P.) saw the 'generation' of numbers from the one and the dyad in the elaborate creation of the cosmic soul in the *Timaeus*. The second hypothesis in the *Parmenides* could have been adduced again as supporting evidence: for "if the one is" is shown to entail the existence of numbers because it entails, first, an infinite doubling, since its two parts, "the one" and "being" are said of each other infinitely often, and, second, the difference between these two parts as a unit element, whence follow all different varieties of even and odd numbers (142b1–144a9, discussed above in 1.2.4.3). If form-numbers were assumed to be at issue here, then in the light of the *Timaeus* their 'generation' could have been easily understood as a mental process that brought out their supposedly ultimate principles, "the one" and "the great and the small" in Plato's more precise 'generation' of numbers in some of his discussions with members of the Academy.[116] The two principles could have also been assumed to correspond to "the limit" and "the unlimited" of the Philebean metaphysics (23c9–d1), their "mixture" being here the form-numbers, though "the limit" in the *Philebus* is described as number or ratio of numbers, neither of which seem to

---

116 Cf. Annas (1976) 48–49.

be itself a "mixture" of the principles, and "the unlimited" is a pair of completely unquantified intensities of opposites, e.g. the hot and the cold (24b10–25b4).[117]

Whatever, moreover, might have been the point of Plato's unwritten analysis of geometrical objects into a dimensional substratum and numbers, the next argument in the second hypothesis of the *Parmenides* that, "if the one is" and there are numbers, geometrical figures must be too could have suggested an interpretation of this analysis as a reduction of the forms of geometrical objects to form-numbers and, necessarily, to three dimensional varieties of "the great and the small". In the *Timaeus* Plato says that three-dimensional parts of space, informed tetrahedrally, octahedrally, icosahedrally and cubically into particles of the four elements of matter by the forms of only four of the five regular solids, have higher principles than the two-dimensional elements of space making up their faces (53c4–d7): these could have been understood as non-dimensional principles of the four forms of geometrical objects at issue, as the four forms of the synonymous figurate numbers that 'make up' the geometrical forms named after them by being imposed on a purely geometrical indeterminate extension in three dimensions, just as the geometrical forms in their turn make up particles of the material elements by being imposed on the indeterminate extension of physical space in three dimensions. This idea could have then been easily extended in an analogous manner to plane figures and lines. If so, physical space, the receptacle of the *Timaeus*, would have been understood as a fourth variety of "the great and the small" in numbers. Indeed, pushing to extremes his complaint that the relations between "the great and the small" and its dimensional varieties was obscure, Aristotle goes so far as to say in *Ph.* Γ 2 that in his so-called unwritten doctrines Plato used a different name for *Timaeus*' receptacle (209b11–16), and then he objects parenthetically that Plato ought to have explained why forms and numbers are not in a place if he calls *Timaeus*' receptacle "the great and the small" (209b33–210a2): the objection presupposes an interpretation of *Timaeus*' receptacle as a fourth variety of "the great and the small" in numbers, which is taken to be absurdly identical with its physical variety since their relation was left obscure.

If the concept of figurate numbers did play a role in attributing to Plato the reduction of the forms of geometrical objects to form-numbers and varieties of one of their principles, "the great and the small", this reduction might have originated in Speusippus' work *On Pythagorean numbers* (fr. 122 I.P.). In it Speusippus discussed figurate numbers alongside the five regular solids of Plato's *Timaeus*, and, as the title suggests, this Academic work might have partly initiated the

---

[117] Cf. Annas (1976) 43–44.

long-lived link of Plato with what is called Pythagoreanism, which is prominent even in Aristotle's account of Plato's thought in *Metaph*. A 6 and *Ph*. Γ 6.[118] The dyad played a role in both Speusippus' and Xenocrates' account of the forms of geometrical objects (Speus. fr. 87 I.P. = Xenocr. fr. 100 I.P.), though the details are unclear,[119] and in *On Pythagorean numbers* Speusippus had also discussed the decad, the sum 1+2+3+4 revered by the Pythagoreans as the sacred *tetraktys* whose last three summands as form-numbers are associated by Aristotle with Plato's forms of geometrical objects. Speusippus had posited a single unitary principle of all forms of geometrical objects, the point which corresponded to the form-number 1 (Arist. *Metaph*. M 9, 1085a31–34 = Speus. fr. 84 I.P.): although it is unclear what role he might have assigned to the other form-numbers in the decad, all four of them had been considered forms of geometrical objects by Xenocrates (fr. 260 I.P.), 1 of points, 2 of lines, 3 of triangle, the first plane figure, and 4 of the pyramid, the first solid figure.[120] Xenocrates, who wrote *On things Pythagorean* (fr. 2 I.P.), seems to also have been interested in the *tetraktys*, and it might be the case that Aristotle accuses Plato of absurdly stopping the form-numbers at the decad in the light of a projection of Academic Pythagoreanizing onto Plato: this is certainly a polemical point since Aristotle himself also associates Plato with a far greater range of numbers in connection with the forms of geometrical objects.[121]

Aristotle, however, seems to doubt that the geometrical objects Plato reduced to the principles after the form-numbers were forms (*Metaph*. N 3, 1090b24–25). Although this might be interpreted as a polemical point that they could not actually be forms as they were assumed to be, it is indeed very unlikely that they were. There is no reason to assume that the conception of forms as shapeless, and thus extensionless, in the *Phaedrus* (see 1.1.3) was ever discarded by Plato, as it ought to have been if he had posited one-, two- and three-dimensional infinite extension as principles of the forms of geometrical objects. If he never abandoned the view that the form of a geometrical object is not itself geometrical, just as the form of beauty is totally unlike its 'shadowy images', it is clear why in the late *Timaeus* he says that parts of space informed tetrahedrally, octahedrally, icosahedrally and cubically into atoms of the four material elements have higher principles than the two-dimensional spatial elements making up their faces: these principles are just the forms of the geometrical objects which inform space

---

118 On the origins of Neopythagoreanism in the Old Academy see Dillon (2014) 250–260.
119 See Dillon (2003) 45–47 on Speusippus and 108–109 on Xenocrates.
120 See also Dillon (2003) 108–109.
121 Cf. *Metaph*. N 3, 1090b20–26. On Plato and the decad, see also Annas (1976) 54–55.

geometrically without being themselves geometrical, hence do not admit of the analysis appropriate to their 'shadowy images' into an indeterminate extension and a number of its infinitely many points which finitizes this extension. The higher principles at issue, Plato says, are known to god and those who are beloved of god, apparently because, as he says elsewhere in the *Timaeus*, only gods and few men have access to forms which constitutes knowledge (51d3–e6). He would have hardly said this, even if he had counted himself among those lucky few who had access to forms, to what god knows, in order to hint at a facile conception of forms of geometrical objects as just idealized figurate numbers: he is best understood to hint at the shapelessness and extensionlessness of the forms of geometrical objects, to whose true nature even those beloved of god have no access at all. If Plato was interested in figurate numbers, they most probably interested him as example of the connections between geometry and arithmetic (cf. 1.2.4.9) and as expression of the complexity of the number series and thus of the form of number, not as a means of reducing the forms of geometrical objects to form-numbers.

The problem with the two principles of form-numbers is similar. If Plato did ever posit them, he must have thought of form-numbers as made up of units. As seen above (1.2.4.6), in his *Metaphysics* Aristotle ascribes to Plato a view of a form-number as composed by its own units, as indivisible as are the units making up any other form-number but different from all of them so that a form-number, unlike all of its 'shadows' studied in mathematics, the mathematical numbers, as Aristotle calls them, does not contain its predecessor plus another unit. It is form-numbers supposedly conceived in this manner as principles of which Plato is said to have posited "the one" and "the great and the small", no matter precisely how the operations in a rather clunky algorithm for the generation of the number series could be plausibly turned into metaphysical constituents of form-numbers so conceived. As argued above, however, Plato would not have regarded a form-number as "monadic", as a group of units of any kind, like its 'shadows' in mathematics, just as for him the form of a geometrical object is not itself geometrical and the form of beauty is unlike all its 'blurry images' (see 1.2.4.6–8). If he ever spoke of each form-number as made up of its own units, he probably did so only to illustrate the independence of form-numbers from one another and their fundamental difference from the infinitely many 'shadows' of each one in mathematics, not to explain their nature.

2 Plato on Astronomy and Philosophy

2.1 Astronomy in the cave

Let us go back to the cave simile with which *Republic* 7 opens. At first the forcefully freed prisoner can bear looking only at shadows of people etc. around him and their reflections in surfaces of water. Plato has Socrates distinguish looking at shadows from looking at reflections: the former prisoner is able to look only at shadows at first and then can turn his eyes to reflections. What he could see inside the cave, at first shadows and then what cast them, replicas of things outside the cave, answers to the two segments of the divided line in the homonymous simile at the end of *Republic* 6: they stand for sensibles, approached first indirectly and then directly. What the freed prisoner sees outside the cave answers to the two other segments of the divided line representing forms, as they are approached first in mathematics, indirectly, and then in philosophy, directly. By analogy, therefore, the freed prisoner must see some things first indirectly, metaphor for forms as approached indirectly in mathematics, and then in themselves, metaphor for forms as approached directly in philosophy. Plato has Socrates suggest that the indirect approach to forms unfolds in two successive stages, the former prisoner's being able at first to look only at the shadows of things and then at their reflections in water, perhaps in order to hint at a crucial element to be introduced in the course of *Republic* 7. There are two clear stages in the long study of all branches of mathematics required of all future philosopher-rulers before they take up the study of philosophy: an elementary introduction to mathematics until the age of twenty is to be followed by a decade-long immersion in all branches of mathematics aiming at the realization of their unity (537b7–c8; cf. 531c5–d5). The direct approach to forms unfolds in successive stages too, not two, though, but four. The freed prisoner can first look directly at people and other things like them around him. These are clearly things in his immediate surroundings, for Plato has Socrates explain that, having been able to look directly at these things, the former prisoner can then look directly at the night sky itself and its celestial objects because it is much easier to look directly at the moon and the other celestial objects in the night sky than at the bright sun in the day sky. He can then dare look at the sun itself in its own place, not at its reflection in water or through other indirect means as he could do till then; before being able to look directly at the night sky and its celestial objects, he presumably used to look indirectly at them too. At long last the freed prisoner realizes that the sun causes the seasons and the years, governs everything in the sensible realm and is somehow also responsible for what the prisoners inside the cave.

The sun has been introduced as a bold metaphor for the Good in *Republic* 6 before the simile of the divided line, to which the solar metaphor for the Good serves as an elaborate introduction (505a2–509d5). There too it is emphasized that the sun causes everything in the sensible realm, in the heavens, the universe or the cosmos (οὐρανός, a word Plato connects paretymologically with ὁρατός, "visible", in 509d1–4): for it is the sun that makes sight possible and brings about generation, the other main feature of the cosmos beside its being sensible, as well as growth and sustenance of what is generated, certainly plants and animals, the contents of the cosmos Plato has here in mind as beneficiaries of the sun (509b1–4). After the simile of the cave, in *Republic* 7 the solar metaphor for the Good recurs in the discussion of the last stage of the training of the philosopher-rulers. Having completed their long studies in mathematics and a five-year-long first course in philosophy, and having also spent the next fifteen years in various administrative posts, at the age of fifty the best among them must fulfill the goal of their efforts: they have to raise the eye of their souls, for which Plato uses a poetic word (αὐγή) that also means "sunlight", to the very source of light for all and, having seen the good itself, for the rest of their lives they must use it as a paradigm to arrange the state, the citizens and themselves, each of them spending most of his or her time in philosophy but, when the time comes, taking up office for the state's sake, not because ruling is good in itself but because it is necessary (540a4–c2). If we want to relate this discursive account of the last state in the education of the future philosopher-rulers to its metaphorical depiction in the cave simile, the five-year-long first course in philosophy can be plausibly assumed to correspond to the freed prisoner's looking directly at other people and the other things in his immediate surroundings. His looking directly at the night sky and the celestial objects in it is in all probability to be grouped together with his looking directly at the sun and realizing its power into a metaphor for the second and final stage of his philosophical education. There can be no doubt that looking directly at the sun and grasping its power in the cosmos is a metaphor for the final state in the philosophical education and, since the sun is more closely related to the other celestial objects than to people and the other things in our immediate surroundings, it is natural to consider looking directly at the night sky and the celestial objects in it as a metaphor for the first phase of the second and last stage in the philosophical education.

The description of the Good as the template for arranging the state, the citizens and oneself harks back to the justification in *Republic* 6 of the thesis in *Republic* 5 that only philosophers should rule (473c11–e4) and presupposes that the

Good is the orderly arrangement of the forms into a unified whole.[1] Socrates and his codiscussant agree at the beginning of *Republic* 6 that in fact only philosophers can rule because they possess knowledge of each being, have in their souls a clear exemplar and, like painters, can always look up at what is most true and, beholding it as accurately as possible, legislate here in accordance with it about what is beautiful, just and good and also preserve already existing legislation (484b4–d9). Beings, i.e. forms, seem to be considered here as isolated from one another, the Good being just one among them, though the highest. But, if the Good is to be the exemplar for the arrangement of the state, the citizens and oneself, it can only be itself an arrangement and, since it is the highest object of philosophy, the only things it can be an arrangement of are the other objects of philosophy, the other forms. Indeed, not much below the philosopher is described as one whose mind is truly fixed on beings and has no time to look downwards at the affairs of people and be filled with envy and ill-will in his disputes with them: always directing his gaze towards things, i.e. forms, that are well-arranged and always unchangeable, seeing them neither wronging nor being wronged by one another but forming a rational order without exception, he strives to imitate them as much as possible and assimilate himself to them. Since he is related to what is divine and orderly, he becomes orderly and divine himself to the extent this is possible for humans and, if for some reason he is compelled to apply what he sees there to human customs, bringing it to both private and public affairs and not only molding himself to it, he cannot turn out to be a bad craftsman of temperance, justice and all civic virtue (500b8–d10). The template for the orderly arrangement of oneself and, through appropriate legislation, of the other citizens and of the entire state, the Good, is thus not one being, the highest, among the many beings but the rational order of all other beings which is prior to them all in that it transcends them all.

The expression in this passage translated by "rational" (κατὰ λόγον) likens implicitly the relationships among the elements of the eternal and stable order of forms to those among the sounds constituting a musical scale, i.e. to the ratios of their pitches, thanks to which the sounds, though distinct, are arranged into a coherent whole and are thus susceptible to rational analysis via the branch of mathematics called harmonics.[2] The harmonic metaphor, as one expects, figures

---

[1] See 1.2.4.1 and 1.3.8.
[2] See 1.1.2 with n. 13. κόσμῳ...καὶ κατὰ λόγον ἔχοντα in *R.* 6, 500c5, can be translated as "being ordered by proportions", but the emphasis is on the rationality of a unifying order exemplified in proportion. According to *Ti.* 31c2–4 the best bond is proportion, for it effects in the best way the fullest unification of the things which are bound together.

notably in what is molded from the Good. It is as the orderly organization of oneself, as the harmony among the parts of the soul and their agreement, that temperance is defined in *Republic* 4, justice being defined as each part's doing its own job within this system and the other two civic virtues, bravery and wisdom, as the specific jobs of two of these three parts (441d11–442d7; cf. 430d3–432b2): not much below, however, justice is first defined as each part of the soul doing its own job and then redefined as temperance, as the unity of all three parts and their harmonious agreement (443c9–444a2). As with the orderly arrangement of oneself, so with the ordering of the citizens and the state through appropriate legislation. To explain the willingness of philosophers who have been freed from the cave and have seen the luminous Good to go back inside the dark cave and rule the state, Plato has Socrates say that the founding law of the state that has made it possible for such individuals to exist, and thus any other law instituted by the philosophers ruling in the state, is not concerned with how one class in the city will be better off than the others: it contrives to impart well-being to the whole city, uniting harmoniously the citizens by various means and making them share with one another the benefit each one of them might be able to offer to the community. The law produces for the city people with this ability not in order for each one of them to be free to go in whatever direction they please but in order to use them to bind the city together (*R.* 7, 519e1–520a5). We can easily guess Plato's answer to the question of the highest good legislators should aim at and the worst evil they should avoid: there is no worse evil for a city than what breaks it into a multitude, he has Socrates say in Republic 5, and no greater good than what binds the city together and makes it a unity (462a2–b3). In both the state and the soul, be it of the philosopher-legislator or another citizen, the good is thus a harmonious ordering of distinct elements into a unified whole reflecting the Good, the highest object of philosophy, which thus can only be the unifying harmony of all other objects of philosophy, all other forms. The sun is a truly fitting metaphor for the Good in that sunlight suffuses the sensible realm, just as the relationships among all other forms ordering them into a unified whole permeate the intelligible realm as harmonious structure: considered in its totality, apart from the interrelationships radiating locally among other forms and structuring them, it can be likened to the sun, the source of all-suffusing visible light.

There seems to be another, astronomical, reason for Plato's having chosen the sun as a metaphor for the Good. In the intelligible realm each of the other forms can be known only in the intelligible light of the Good (*R.* 6, 509b5–c2), through the web, that is, of its multiple interrelationships with other forms. Similarly, in the heavens each of certain main aspects of them can be easily known only in the visible and all-suffusing light of the sun through its links with all other kindred aspects of the heavens into a system revealed by the sun. The sun is described in the *Timaeus* as a bright light kindled in the second revolution about the earth to light up the whole heavens and serve as a conspicuous measure of the relative fastness and slowness of all eight celestial revolutions: the diurnal revolution of the fixed stars and the zodiacal motions of the five planets, the sun and the moon (39b2–c1). The diurnal motion of the sun determines a fundamental unit of time-measurement, the solar day; it is very close to the period of the diurnal rotation, the revolution of the so-called fixed stars about the axis of the cosmos (equivalently, the rotation of the whole cosmos). This unit is used to compare the periods of all eight celestial revolutions with one another. Plato mentions next the synodic month and the tropical year, and complains that most people do not know the periods of the five planets, perhaps both the zodiacal and the synodic ones, have no names for them and do not measure one against another with numbers nor do they even realize that the wanderings of these celestial objects, amazing in number and marvelous in complexity though they are, do constitute time, which means that they are periodic (39c2–d2). Grasping all periodicities of these apparent wanderings, however, and thus coming to fully understand each one of them, is made possible by measuring both each one of them against the fundamental unit of measuring time and against all the others, by seeing how each fits with the rest to form a coherent and arithmetically describable system, all of which is made easy by the sun and its light. It is not farfetched to think of the sun as an image of the harmonious structure itself that sunlight helps reveal in the heavens, standing metaphorically as pars pro toto for the heavens as knowable ordering, and then to transfer this image from the visible to the intelligible realm, to the harmonious relationships among all forms that make each one and all of them fully known.[3]

The celestial periodicities appear also in *Republic* 7. Plato has Socrates mention the relation of nighttime to daytime, that of nighttime and daytime to the synodic month and the tropical year and, finally, the relations of the other celestial objects, i.e. of the planetary periods, to the synodic month and the tropical year (530a4–b5). Night- and daytime make a solar day (νυχθήμερον) and their relation can be plausibly understood as the variation of their lengths in the course of the year. It is unlikely that in Plato's time there was any attempt to calculate the length of daytime and nighttime at any given time of the year (for a given

---

[3] Cf. Johansen (2013) 102–103. Plato gives implicitly but unambiguously the values of the zodiacal periods of Venus and Mercury (*R*. 10, 617b1–2; *Ti*. 38d1–3). He does not report a value of the synodic period of any planet, however. Simplicius attributes a list of values of planetary synodic periods to Plato's contemporary Eudoxus of Cnidus (*in Cael*. 496.4–9 [Heiberg]).

latitude); the first known attempt to tackle the problem is Hypsicles' *Anaphorikos* from the first half of the second century BC, but the problem could have been posed quite earlier. The relation of the tropical year to the synodic month, which does not measure exactly the tropical year, is clearly a lunisolar cycle, a number of tropical years containing almost a whole number of synodic months.[4] It is easy to determine how many years of the cycle must have a thirteenth month added so that a lunar calendar, such as those used by Greek cities, does not get noticeably out of step with the seasons, as well as how many months of the cycle are full months of 30 days and hollow months of 29 days (as the month does not measure exactly the year, so the day does not measure exactly the month). In our sources Euctemon or Meton or both are credited with the introduction of the 19-year or Metonic cycle in Athens, beginning at the summer solstice of 432 BC. 19 tropical years are almost 235 synodic months; thus in a period of 19 years 12 years must have each 12 months (144 months in total), whereas each of the remaining 7 years must have 13 months (91 months in total), and of the total number of months 125 must be 30-day months and 110 must be 29-day months. As for the reference to the relations of the periods of the planets to the year and the month, these relations might be the lengths in months and years of the tropical and synodic periods of the planets or also the relations between numbers of a planet's tropical and synodic periods and a number of years; the latter were known to Babylonian astronomers most probably already by Plato's time,[5] but it is unlikely that Plato was aware of much more than their mere existence if there is indeed an allusion to them here and in the *Timaeus*.[6] The *Timaeus* is generally considered to have been written after the *Republic*.[7] Although Plato's mention of the celestial periodicities and their relations in the *Republic* does not refer to the sun and its light as serving the goal of making them easily graspable, his interest in the phenomenon when

---

4 Cf. *R.* 7, 527c10–d3: Socrates suggests that he and Glaucon consider astronomy to be the third subject after arithmetic and geometry to which philosopher-rulers in the making must apply themselves before taking up the study of philosophy, and Glaucon readily agrees, pointing out the importance that better awareness of the seasons, months and years has not only for agriculture and sailing but also for generalship. "Better awareness of months and years" is another reference to lunisolar cycles; see also Kouremenos (2015) 1.3.1.

5 See Evans (1998) 304–305 and 312–315.

6 In *R.* 7, 530a4–b5, Plato has Socrates mention not only the relations of the planetary periods to the synodic month and the tropical year but also their relations to one another. This is perhaps a grand generalization of the Metonic cycle and the Babylonian cycles of a planet's tropical and synodic period and the year. It would relate all celestial periodicities: after this period of years would have elapsed, the sun, the moon and the planets would be found in the relative positions they had occupied at the beginning of the period. Cf. *R.* 8, 546b4–5, and *Ti.* 39d2–7.

7 Owen (1965) dates it to the same period as the *Republic*; cf., though, Cherniss (1965).

he was writing the *Republic* could have decidedly influenced, as he seems to suggest in the *Timaeus*, his choice of the sun as a metaphor for the Good in *Republic* 6–7.

In view of the simile of the divided line, as said above, in the simile of the cave the shadows and the reflections of things symbolize the forms as approached indirectly in mathematics, whereas the things themselves stand for the forms as approached directly in philosophy. As argued in 1.1.4, the fact that the same things are metaphors both for those forms that are studied indirectly in mathematics and whose 'shadows' or 'reflections' are the mathematical objects and for those that are approached directly in philosophy suggests that all forms are forms of mathematical objects. Thus the night sky and its celestial objects seen directly by the freed prisoner stand for forms of mathematical objects instantiated in the heavens and studied indirectly in astronomy but directly in philosophy: more exactly, in an astronomy pursued not merely as a branch of mathematics propedeutic to philosophy (nothing hints that Plato envisaged an eventual demathematicization of astronomy) but also, and more importantly, as part of philosophy whose study marks the beginning of the last stage in the education of future philosopher-rulers, metaphor for which is the former prisoner's looking directly at the night sky and all the celestial objects in it. Plato thinks that seeing how all diverse branches of mathematics are related to one another into a tightly knit family paves the way to the highest object of philosophy, the Good or the unifying relations that tie together all forms indirectly studied in mathematics and directly in philosophy and are reflected in the unity of mathematics (R. 7, 531c5–d5 and 537b7–c8).[8] But his imagery in the simile of the cave hints that he accords a special role within this family to astronomy, and to the forms this branch of mathematics really studies, for paving the way to the Good. If this special role has something to do with the manifestation of the Good in the heavens as the relations among the periodicities in celestial motions, among which is that of the bright sun, thanks to which the system of these relations can be easily accessed and which can thus symbolize it, Plato might have also chosen the visible sun as an image for the intelligible Good with this special role in mind. This special role can also be seen in the unmistakable image of the Good he uses in the eschatological myth of Er, at the end of the *Republic*, a straight column of bright and pure light running through the heavens and earth (616b2–6): the extremities of the fastenings of the heavens stretch to the middle of this column, the binder

---

8 On Plato and the unity of mathematics in *R.* 7 see 1.2.4.9 and Kouremenos (2015) ch. 2.

of the heavens that holds together the celestial revolutions functioning like the celestial trireme's hogging truss (616b6–c4).[9]

Interestingly, astronomy is placed very high in Aristotle's tripartite division of theoretical philosophy into physics, mathematics and theology. In *Metaph.* Λ 8 Aristotle shows that an unmoved mover causes the eternal rotation of the spherical shell in the mass of which the stars are fixed. But this rotation is not the only eternal motion in the heavens: eternal are the motions of the five planets, the sun and the moon as well. Unmoved movers, therefore, must bring about these motions too (1073a23–b1). How many such movers there might be in the heavens, however, must hinge on the analysis of the complex motion of each of these celestial objects, and astronomy, the branch of mathematics that is most akin to philosophy, is the discipline one must turn to (1073b1–8).[10] Astronomy, according to Aristotle, can contribute immensely to the highest part of theoretical philosophy: the celestial unmoved movers are the highest causal principles and the

---

9 The column of light stretches throughout the heavens (616b4–5: διὰ παντὸς τοῦ οὐρανοῦ καὶ γῆς τεταμένον φῶς εὐθύ, οἷον κίονα) and the extremities of the bonds of the heavens stretch from the limits of the heavens to the middle of this column (616b7–c2: κατὰ μέσον τὸ φῶς ἐκ τοῦ οὐρανοῦ τὰ ἄκρα αὐτοῦ τῶν δεσμῶν τεταμένα), just like temperance (or justice) in a community, the human good, stretches throughout the city making the strongest and the weakest citizens and those in the middle literally singing together in unison through all notes (*R.* 4, 432a2–7: δι' ὅλης ἀτεχνῶς τέταται διὰ πασῶν παρεχομένη συνᾴδοντας τούς τε ἀσθενεστάτους ταὐτὸν καὶ τοὺς ἰσχυροτάτους καὶ τοὺς μέσους, εἰ μὲν βούλει, φρονήσει, εἰ δὲ βούλει, ἰσχύι, εἰ δέ, καὶ πλήθει ἢ χρήμασιν ἢ ἄλλῳ ὁτῳοῦν τῶν τοιούτων· ὥστε ὀρθότατ' ἂν φαῖμεν ταύτην τὴν ὁμόνοιαν σωφροσύνην εἶναι). For the harmonic metaphor cf. *R.* 4, 443c9–444a2. The harmonic metaphor is strikingly present in the elaborate myth of Er too. The celestial column of bright and pure light is re-described as the spindle of Necessity, which is made of steel (616c4–7) and whose circular whorl is made up of eight circular, close-fitting parts like the bearing rings or races of rolling bearings, each corresponding to a celestial revolution (616d1–e3): the diurnal rotation and then the zodiacal motions of the planets Saturn, Jupiter, Mars, Mercury, Venus followed by those of the sun and the moon close to the Earth. On each part of the whorl perches a Siren riding with it and singing a single pitch, all eight of them making up a consonant whole, a harmony (617b6–8: ἐπὶ δὲ τῶν κύκλων αὐτοῦ ἄνωθεν ἐφ' ἑκάστου βεβηκέναι Σειρῆνα συμπεριφερομένην, φωνὴν μίαν ἱεῖσαν, ἕνα τόνον· ἐκ πασῶν δὲ ὀκτὼ οὐσῶν μίαν ἁρμονίαν συμφωνεῖν).
10 ὅτι μὲν οὖν εἰσὶν οὐσίαι, καὶ τούτων τις πρώτη καὶ δευτέρα κατὰ τὴν αὐτὴν τάξιν ταῖς φοραῖς τῶν ἄστρων, φανερόν· τὸ δὲ πλῆθος ἤδη τῶν φορῶν ἐκ τῆς οἰκειοτάτης φιλοσοφίᾳ τῶν μαθηματικῶν ἐπιστημῶν δεῖ σκοπεῖν, ἐκ τῆς ἀστρολογίας· αὕτη γὰρ περὶ οὐσίας αἰσθητῆς μὲν ἀϊδίου δὲ ποιεῖται τὴν θεωρίαν, αἱ δ' ἄλλαι περὶ οὐδεμιᾶς οὐσίας, οἷον ἥ τε περὶ τοὺς ἀριθμοὺς καὶ τὴν γεωμετρίαν ("It is thus clear that these unmoved movers are substances and that one of them is first and another second in the order of the celestial motions. The number of the latter must be discussed in the light of the mathematical science most akin to philosophy, i.e. astronomy. For it studies sensible but eternal substances, whereas the other mathematical sciences, e.g. arithmetic and geometry, do not study any substances"). On this passage see Kouremenos (2010) 3.6.

primary beings, whose precise number has been left unclear by others, e.g. Plato and other members of the Academy, whom Aristotle singles out here for criticism (1073a14–23), but it is now clear that it might become known one day thanks to astronomy (1073b8–17). An echo of Aristotle's view on astronomy vis-à-vis philosophy can be read in Ptolemy's argument for the priority of astronomy to theology on account of its contribution to theology (*Alm.* 1, 7.5–10 Heiberg).[11]

2.2 Astronomy in Socrates' intellectual autobiography in the *Phaedo*

A link between astronomy and the Good seems to be hinted at in Socrates' philosophical autobiography in the *Phaedo*. He recounts his frustration with Anaxagoras' book, where he had expected in vain to find cosmological explanations based on what is good, since the author considered the mind to be the ultimate cause of everything. Socrates says that he was eager to learn why it is good for the earth to be at the middle of the cosmos if it is indeed situated there and that he expected to find in Anaxagoras' book similar explanations about the phenomena of the moon and the other celestial bodies such as their speeds relative to one another and solstices. Socrates expected to learn from Anaxagoras' treatise that a celestial body or phenomenon is as it is or occurs as it does because it is good for it to be as it is or to occur as it does, and he believed that an account of what is good in each case meshes with an account of the common good (97d5–98b6). We expect the good in each particular case to be the relations of each aspect of the heavens to the rest that bind all of them together into a unified whole of interconnections, the common good. Later on, returning to the problem of the position of the earth at the center of the cosmos and its immobility, Socrates denies that its position and immobility can be ultimately explained in mechanical terms,

---

11 τό τε γὰρ θεολογικὸν εἶδος αὕτη μάλιστ' ἂν προοδοποιήσειε μόνη γε δυναμένη καλῶς καταστοχάζεσθαι τῆς ἀκινήτου καὶ χωριστῆς ἐνεργείας ἀπὸ τῆς ἐγγύτητος τῶν περὶ τὰς αἰσθητὰς μὲν καὶ κινούσας τε καὶ κινουμένας, ἀιδίους δὲ καὶ ἀπαθεῖς οὐσίας συμβεβηκότων περί τε τὰς φορὰς καὶ τὰς τάξεις τῶν κινήσεων ("For astronomy is the branch of mathematics that can greatly help theology make progress since it is the only one that can make well-founded guesses about the unmoved and separated activity [that causes motion in the universe] on account of how closely related to the latter are the phenomena exhibited by the sensible substances that cause motion and are moved but are eternal and unchanging in their motions and in the arrangements of these motions"). Mansfeld (1998) 66 n. 226 notes that Ptolemy's ranking of astronomy relative to the other branches of theoretical philosophy looks like "an emendation of Aristotle's view that it is the mathematical discipline that comes closest to philosophy".

by hypothesizing a celestial vortex or simply that air holds the earth fast: the earth and everything else in the sensible cosmos are not forcefully held together by something like the mythical Atlas but are bound together coherently by what is good and fitting, by their mutual relations that really tie them together into a unified whole (99b6–c6).[12] Here Plato has Socrates talk about the Good of the *Republic* as manifested not in the soul and the city but in the heavens; moreover, the speeds of the celestial bodies relative to one another, the relative fastness and slowness of all eight celestial revolutions in the *Timaeus*, i.e. the relations among the periodicities in celestial motions, figure as a prominent aspect of this manifestation. The link with the *Republic* is evident in the imagery Plato has Socrates use. After his disappointment with Anaxagoras, he got tired of his search for beings and, fearing that he might suffer the fate of those who dare look directly at the sun during an eclipse, not at its image in e.g. water, and that he might blind his soul by looking with his eyes at the things themselves, he then decided to begin searching for the truth about beings indirectly, taking refuge in dialectic and thus starting out from the hypothesis of forms, that there is something which is the beautiful itself, the good itself etc. (99c6–100b9). In the *Phaedo* the Good is clearly manifested as much in the heavens as in the sphere of human affairs, as is shown by the account Socrates gives of why he sits in the prison after he reports his disappointment with Anaxagoras (98b7–99b6). But it is introduced with an implicit and unargued assertion of its counter-intuitive manifestation in the heavens. This might signal that the good in the celestial realm is in some sense prior to the good in human affairs and that, just as in Socrates' early frustrated search for the Good the heavens had a quite intimate connection with it, they are implicitly assumed to also have a privileged relation to the Good in the dialectical philosophy of forms, to which Socrates is presented as having decided to turn after his disappointment with Anaxagoras.

2.3 Astronomy in the myth of the *Phaedo*

Such a relation is suggested by the version of the *Republic*'s cave simile in the myth at the end of the *Phaedo*. There Plato has Socrates replace the cave with one of the many depressions in the surface of the earth. It is inside this pit that we

---

[12] In a similar manner Aristotle denies in *Cael*. B 1 that the rotating spherical shell of the first simple body whose fixed and luminous parts are the stars is constrained by a motive soul to undergo an eternal counter-natural motion, an erroneous notion which in his view the ancients turned into the myth of the heavens-supporting Atlas (284a11–284b5).

happen to live, around the water pooled in the chasm's depths under a dense cover of air and mist filling the rest of this wretched place, where everything is corroded by moisture, though we wrongly think that we live on the earth's true surface and that the foggy and unclear air surrounding us is the true heavens in which the celestial objects move. In fact, however, the earth's true surface is only the non-depressed part of its surface that lies untarnished in the bright true heavens where the celestial objects as they really are move.[13] Just as a sea creature

---

13 Plato has Socrates call αἰθήρ the rarefied analogue to our air for the blessed inhabitants of the true surface of the earth (111a7–b1). The true heavens where the celestial objects move is thus not the unclean air surrounding us as we wrongly believe (109b5–7 and d5–110a1) but a different substance called αἰθήρ which presumably also constitutes all celestial bodies. In poetry αἰθήρ is used indiscriminately in the sense "air", "sky" or "heavens", and in the fragments of his didactic epic Empedocles employs it for air (see Wright [1981] 23). Etymologically the noun is related to nouns such as αἰθρία and αἴθρη, which designate the clear and bright sky or weather, and to the adjective αἴθριος, -ον used to describe such sky or weather. Aristotle thinks that αἰθήρ is an ancient word for the first simple body, the substance he introduced initially as matter of a diurnally rotating shell in the mass of which the stars are fixed as its bright parts and which is the crust of the rest of the cosmos, the next cosmic stratum of the simple body fire reaching up to the lower boundary-surface of the shell of the first simple body, filling up the remaining part of the heavens and also constituting the planets, the sun and the moon; later Aristotle extended the cosmological role of the first simple body into that of a single filler of the heavens and matter of all celestial objects. On Aristotle's first simple body see Kouremenos (2010) ch. 2; for αἰθήρ as an ancient name of this body (and for Aristotle's belief that infinitely often in the past scientific knowledge, of the constitution of the heavens in this case, has been obtained and lost with the exception of small traces) see *Cael.* A 3, 270b16–25, and *Mete.* A 3, 339b19–30. The use of this word in the *Phaedo* as name of a substance which seems to be different from water and air, and in all probability from the other two Empedoclean elements as well, and makes up bodily symbols of the forms related to the heavens and the luminaries moving therein is particularly intriguing in view of Aristotle's cosmology, all the more so since this first simple body shares certain similarities with the Platonic forms and is often described by Aristotle in an appropriately exalted manner. In the *Timaeus* αἰθήρ is the name of the purest air which is distinguished from the muddier and darker sort (58d1–4) but, since in the *Timaeus* the celestial bodies consist mainly of fire (40a2–b8), the use of the word αἰθήρ in the *Timaeus* does not seem to be presupposed in the myth of the *Phaedo*. Aristotle objects to Anaxagoras' use of the noun as a name of the element fire, apparently based on the paretymology of αἰθήρ from the verb αἴθειν, "to kindle", in the transitive form, or "to blaze", in the intransitive (see the passages from *Cael.* and *Mete.* cited in this n.). αἰθήρ could be a name of fire in the *Phaedo* but the tenor of the myth seems to call for a fictional substance that is radically different from all crass matter found in the depths where we live and incomparably brighter than fire, for a substance that would have been suitable as sole constituent of the forms if they had been material things, which they are not. Aristotle derives the noun αἰθήρ from the phrase ἀεὶ θεῖν, "to be perpetually in motion" (see the two passages cited above), which in his cosmology is a feature only of the first simple body, not of any of the traditional Empedoclean simple bodies; this paretymology occurs in Plato's *Cratylus* (410b6–8).

would realize how much clearer our place is if it could only raise its head above the surface of the sea, of which it thinks as the heavens because it is through water that this creature sees the sun and the other celestial objects, similarly, if we only could fly beyond the air, we would realize what the true heavens and the true light and the true earth are, provided that our nature could bear to look at them (109a9–110b2). Flying beyond the unclean distorting air to reach the true surface of the earth answers to leaving the cave of the *Republic*. What one would see on and from the true surface of the earth, away from the distorting influence of the unclean air, corresponds to everything outside the cave looked at directly by the freed prisoner, i.e. to the forms as they are approached in philosophy. Plato has Socrates say that everything around us here in our hole of corruption exists on the true surface of earth too but beautiful and perfect, as befits symbols of forms qua intelligible paradigms resembled by sensibles. It is a sight suitable to spectators who are *eudaimones*, just as is expected of those who are capable of seeing the true light, the Good, and in it everything else. The blessed inhabitants of the true surface of the earth are, consequently, superior to us in wisdom but also in sight and hearing, since referring sensibles to forms can turn them into objects of knowledge: they see the sun, the moon and the other celestial objects as these happen to be, their *eudaimonia* in all other respects being consequent upon these facts (110a1–b2, d3–111c3).[14] The luminaries as seen through the distorting air and the tainted analogues of all things on the true surface of the earth existing in our misty pit seem to correspond to everything the freed prisoner looks at indirectly in the simile of the cave, to forms as studied in mathematics; as seen even more distortedly by the inhabitants of the sea through the water, they answer to the simulacra of the things outside the cave and their shadows, to the things seen by the prisoners in the cave (cf. 111a7–b1). Of the metaphors for forms as studied in philosophy, the variation on the *Republic*'s cave simile in the *Phaedo* accords pride of place to those for forms that are somehow related to the celestial objects: the sun, the moon and the other celestial objects themselves, the luminaries as they really are. It is with these metaphors that the account of the true surface of the earth opens and closes, and the concluding statement that

---

14 There seems to be no clear differentiation in the Homeric epics between Olympus and the upper sky (see Kouremenos, Parássoglou & Tsantsanoglou [2006] 189–190), and Plato can very well have in mind here that passage from the *Odyssey* which dwells on the inviolate stability and serenity perpetually enjoyed by Olympus, a place rid of all violent changes in its marvelously calm conditions, as befits the abode of immortal gods and goddesses, which is blissful in all respects (6.41–47). Probably due to this absence of a clear distinction between Olympus and the sky in Homer, in early Greek natural philosophy "Olympus" became synonymous with the heavens (see Kouremenos, Parássoglou & Tsantsanoglou [2006]189–190).

eudaimonia hinges on the facts about the celestial objects themselves corroborates the suspicion that Plato hints at an intimate relation of the heavens to philosophy and the Good earlier on in Socrates' philosophical autobiography. This is exactly what one would expect in a variation on the *Republic*'s cave simile if its imagery does suggest that, in the family of mathematics and all forms, astronomy and the forms this branch of mathematics actually studies have a special role to play in paving the way to the Good.

2.4 Astronomy and beauty in *Republic* 7

An important detail in the discussion of astronomy in *Republic* 7 as a propedeutic to philosophy leaves no doubt that this is indeed so. It is noteworthy that the relation of astronomy to the goal it must serve as a propedeutic to true philosophy, to the escape of the cave and the revolving of one's soul away from the false nocturnal day of becoming to the true day of being (521c1–d7), is stated in quite more exalted language than used for the relation of the other branches of mathematics to this goal (527d5–e3). It is, moreover, in the discussion of astronomy that Plato has Socrates touch upon some interesting and important points, which can be plausibly assumed to also signal the privileged position of this branch of mathematics in the family: the relations between the branches of mathematics, obliquely but clearly referred to here and emphasized twice after all branches of mathematics have been discussed as of paramount importance to the successful launching of the mind on its way to the Good and the Beautiful (531c5–d5 and 537b7–c8); the importance of problems to the growth of mathematics; the need for advances in mathematics and confidence that they will be forthcoming thanks to the beauty of mathematics despite the lamentable lack of public support for its study in contemporary Greek states (528a6–d1).[15] To say that astronomy is the most elaborately discussed field of mathematics is no exaggeration, the complexity of its treatment matching the compliment Plato has Socrates pay it: the most beautiful of all sensible things are the decorative patterns in the heavens (529c6–d6), the observed celestial motions that are the sensible subject matter of astronomy. All branches of mathematics have a sensible subject matter (cf. 522b5–e4, 526c7–d7, 530c6–531a3 and b8–c4), though they are really about non-sensible forms, the latter being participated in by sensibles; not even some of the sensible subject matter of harmonics, however, is said to be beautiful, let alone included in the most beautiful sensible things. Extolling the beauty of the sensible subject

---

15 On Plato's belief in the future progress of mathematics see 1.2.4.9.

matter of astronomy effectively singles it out from among the sensibles as the closest kin in the sensible realm to the Good, the cause of all beauty (517b7–c4), which in the *Phaedo* is said of beauty itself (100c10–e3), a form that seems to be identical with the Good (see 1.3.9). It is probably the latter that Plato has Socrates name allegorically the "demiurge", by whom only the celestial motions and all their aspects, the entire heavens, have been made as beautiful as sensibles can be (530a4–8). When Plato has Socrates say that the Good is the cause of all beauty, of all the sensible realm it is again in the sky that he has him clearly locate the most beautiful sensible effects of the Good, mentioning as such only sunlight and its author, the sun, the most prominent celestial object to which the Good is said to have given birth in a biological variation on the demiurgic allegory (cf. *R.* 6, 508b9–c2).

This mention of the demiurge in the *Republic* in connection with the making of the cosmos and the heavens as its most beautiful part inevitably brings to mind the *Timaeus*, and makes it likely that it was Plato himself who had interpreted the generation of the beautiful cosmos by a most good demiurge in this work as an allegory, probably of the eternal causal dependence of the cosmos on forms and hence the Good (cf. 1.4.2).[16] If this mention also clinches the hints in the *Republic* that astronomy has a privileged role to play in paving the way to the Good for philosophy, the virtual usurpation in the *Timaeus* of the role accorded in the

---

16 The status of the demiurge in the *Timaeus* has been much discussed. For a helpful survey of the various literal and non-literal interpretations of the demiurge see Carone (2005) 31 n. 19 (she too understands the demiurge as a symbol, of the soul of the whole cosmos; but in 36e5–37a2 this soul and the demiurge are distinguished in a way that rules out their conflation). For another recent interpretation of the demiurge as symbol see Johansen (2004) 79–91 who proposes that the demiurge is best understood as a personification of craftsmanship or, in Aristotelian terms, of efficient causation which accounts for the imposition of forms on space (cf. 1.3.4). Whereas the demiurge is said to be father and maker of the cosmos at the beginning of the cosmological part of the *Timaeus* (28c3–5), later on (50c7–e1) the role of the father is accorded to forms, that of the mother to space and that of the offspring to the product of the imposition of forms to receiving space. This suggests that the demiurge whose supreme goodness is emphasized is a symbol for the forms as a system, the Good that is itself the highest form. Johansen (2004) 81–82 thinks that the comparison of the forms with the father "applies to the world considered independently of the demiurge" since forms, space and generation are said next to have been there even before the cosmos came to be thanks to the demiurge (52d2–4), and that this is indicated by the temporal restriction ἐν τῷ παρόντι (50c7). The preposition, however, does not contrast its context as a discussion of a pre-cosmic state of reality independent of the demiurge with an earlier discussion of reality as a cosmos causally dependent on the demiurge: its context is a refinement of the earlier distinction at 27d5–29d3 between forms (intelligible, eternal and unchangeable paradigms) and their images (sensibles coming to be), and it contrasts this two-pronged distinction with its expansion into a three-pronged one by the addition of space (see 48e2–49a4).

Republic to philosophy and the Good by astronomy and the heavens seems to be just a clear statement of this role and the corresponding suppression, expected in a cosmological work, of the relation of philosophy to the Good that is emphasized in the *Republic*, not a real doctrinal shift.[17] It seems, that is, to be an unpacking of a position Plato espouses already in the *Republic*, assuming that the *Timaeus* is later than the *Republic*. The same seems to be the case in the *Laws*, reportedly Plato's last work, where the situation as regards the question of the relation of astronomy to philosophy might be taken to be closer to the *Timaeus* than to the earlier *Republic*.[18] We will turn first to the *Timaeus* and the *Laws* and then to the important question: why does Plato privilege astronomy over the other members of its family?

2.5 Astronomy in the *Timaeus*

According to *Republic* 6, the genuine lover of wisdom is one who strives towards beings, the forms, and whose burning desire will not be satisfied until he has laid hold of the nature of each thing as it is with the part of his soul kindred to it and, having become really one with the beings and produced understanding and truth, has finally obtained knowledge, lives the life of truth and receives nourishment (490a8–b8). Assimilation also features prominently in the description of the philosopher's goal in the justification of Socrates' belief that only philosophers can govern (*R.* 6, 500b8–d10). What philosophers desire to assimilate themselves to as far as possible is, as seen above, the eternally fixed and rational order of the forms: the Good that is the template for temperance, justice and all civic virtue. This human good is said in *Republic* 4 to consist in an ordering of the soul's parts, reason, appetites and emotions, and is likened to a harmony, the unifying ordering of distinct sounds by means of the ratios in which their pitches stand (443c9–444a2). In the *Timaeus*, the human good is broadly conceived as in the *Republic*: as a harmony in the human soul imitating another harmony, one above humans but accessible to their rational soul. But in the *Timaeus* this harmony is not of all three parts of the human soul but only of its rational part; moreover, the rational part of the human soul aspires to assimilate itself not to the

---

17 *Pace* Kucharski (1971) 319 and 326 but also Carone (2005) ch. 3 who proposes that astronomy is offered in the *Timaeus* as alternative to philosophy for the masses (see 2.7). For another unitarian reading of Plato's views on astronomy in the *Republic* and *Timaeus* see Johansen (2013).
18 Cf. Carone (2005) 75–76; see, however, 2.7.

unifying harmony of all forms but instead to celestial thoughts, harmonies and motions.

The relevant part of the *Timaeus* (90a2–d7) opens with the image of the human rational soul, which is housed in the head, as divine root anchoring a plant not to the ground but to the heavens, with which the rational soul is akin, for it was born in the heavens, as is explained in the cosmogonical part of the work (39e3–40a2 and 41a7–42e4), and is thus naturally drawn upwards, to its native place, accounting for human bipedalism (in 44d3–8 it is argued that the human head is approximately spherical because it contains the brain, which houses the rational part of the soul, and thus its shape must imitate that of the spherical heavens). A person can become exceptionally *eudaimōn* and achieve immortality to the fullest extent that it is humanly possible only if s/he has cultivated love of learning (φιλομαθία), which here is not to be distinguished from philosophy, "love of wisdom", as its association with *eudaimonia* makes clear: that is, if s/he has exercised and cared for and ordered well the soul's divine and rational part, with which as a *daimōn*, a guardian spirit, that person dwells together, *eudaimonia* being implicitly assumed to mean the well (εὖ) ordering of one's own *daimōn*, a word which here is assumed, tacitly again, to mean "knowing" part of one's soul (cf. *Cra.* 397e2–398c4). The proper care for the rational soul requires proper nourishment but, whereas in *Republic* 6 the rational soul is nourished by the forms with which it is akin, and ultimately by their unifying ordering into the Good, here the rational soul is depicted as a plant's root that draws nourishment from the heavens and it is to heavens that it is said to be kindred. Plato often speaks metaphorically of the forms as located "up", contrasting their "place" with "down", the realm of sensible and of human affairs, and of the rational soul's turning from the sensibles to the forms as "looking upwards" (see e.g. *R.* 6, 500b8–d10, and *R* 7, 528c4–529c2). But here the heavens are not a metaphor for the forms. They are the heavens observed by astronomers.

Whereas in the *Republic* the soil into which the rational soul as a root must extend to absorb nutrients is a metaphor for the forms with which the wisdom-lover's rational soul must become one in order for knowledge to be generated, its heavenly analogue in the *Timaeus* are the thoughts and revolutions of the universe, to which the wisdom-lover's rational soul must assimilate itself if truth is to be produced. It is these thoughts and revolutions that our rational soul is kindred with and nourished from. At issue are the thoughts of that soul which is purely rational (unlike the human soul which, apart from a part rational only in potentiality, has also irrational parts, appetites and emotions), and is introduced at the beginning of the cosmological part of the *Timaeus* (34b10–37c5): a cosmic soul interwoven with the body of the cosmos, it causes all celestial motions, soul being considered a self-moving cause of motion (as in *Phdr.* 245c5–246a2 and *Lg.* 10, 891e4–896b2). It has been constructed by the demiurge as eight concentric circular motions, the revolutions of the universe which are mentioned as the heavenly food of our rational soul together with the thoughts of the cosmic soul they constitute. Each of these motions accounts for a celestial motion: one which takes place on the plane of the celestial equator causes the diurnal rotation of the fixed stars and the whole cosmos; those taking place inside it at the appropriate angle bring about the zodiacal motions of the planets, the sun and the moon (37c6–39e2). We are perhaps to imagine these revolutions as motions of space itself, which receives certain forms and turns into elemental matter (51b7–52b5 and 53c4–56c7): they force matter to move almost globally (diurnal rotation of the whole cosmos with the sole exception of the immobile earth at the center of the cosmos) and, in a different way, locally too (zodiacal motion of the planets, sun and moon). It should be kept in mind, however, that in *Laws* 10 being in circular and uniform self-motion is said to be a mere appropriate metaphor for the unknown way by which rational soul causes all celestial motion (896d5–899a10), circularity of the path of self-motion and uniformity of its speed standing for the stability and order of reason itself as first cause of motion.[19] The circular motions

---

19 Assuming that in the *Timaeus* the cosmic soul and all souls are literally conceived as circular motions (cf. Arist. *de An.* A 3, 406b26–407a2), Sedley (1999) 317 n. 13 notes that a literal locomotive construal is neither confirmed nor excluded by *Lg.* 10. The text does seem to exclude it, however, though it is conceivable that it is presupposed in the *Timaeus*. See 897d3–e7, a passage which recalls e.g. *Phd.* 99c6–100b9: ΑΘ. Τίνα οὖν δὴ νοῦ κίνησις φύσιν ἔχει; τοῦτο ἤδη χαλεπόν, ὦ φίλοι, ἐρώτημα ἀποκρινόμενον εἰπεῖν ἐμφρόνως· διὸ δὴ καὶ ἐμὲ τῆς ἀποκρίσεως ὑμῖν δίκαιον τὰ νῦν προσλαμβάνειν. ΚΛ. Εὖ λέγεις. ΑΘ. Μὴ τοίνυν ἐξ ἐναντίας οἷον εἰς ἥλιον ἀποβλέποντες, νύκτα ἐν μεσημβρίᾳ ἐπαγόμενοι, ποιησώμεθα τὴν ἀπόκρισιν, ὡς νοῦν ποτε θνητοῖς ὄμμασιν ὀψόμενοί τε καὶ γνωσόμενοι ἱκανῶς· πρὸς δὲ εἰκόνα τοῦ ἐρωτωμένου βλέποντας ἀσφαλέστερον ὁρᾶν. ΚΛ. Πῶς λέγεις; ΑΘ. Ἧι προσέοικεν κινήσει νοῦς τῶν δέκα ἐκείνων κινήσεων, τὴν εἰκόνα λάβωμεν· ἣν συναναμνησθεὶς ὑμῖν ἐγὼ κοινῇ τὴν ἀπόκρισιν ποιήσομαι. ΚΛ. Κάλλιστα ἂν λέγοις ("ATH. Well, what is the nature of the motion of reason? It is difficult, my friends, to give a reasonable answer to this question, so now you should let me help you with the answer. CL. You are right. ATH. Let us not, therefore, answer by looking straight in the eye of the sun, bringing darkness to the noon, as if we could ever behold and understand reason satisfactorily with mortal eyes. It is safer to try to see it looking at an image of what our question is about. CL. What do you mean? ATH. Let us consider as image the one of the ten motions distinguished above to which reason is similar. I will remind you of it, and we will give the answer together. CL. Very nice"). On the ten motions see 893b6–894c9. Plato has the Athenian stranger dwell on circular (and uniform) motion as a mere image, a sign that we should take this seriously into account. Not only the circular motion of reason but also the very notion that reason consists in self-moving motion(s) seems to be an image, too, given the stranger's disavowal of knowledge about the nature of reason and the association in *Sph.* 249b12–c5 of staticity and reason. It seems to be a vivid

are supposed to have been made by the demiurge as a coherent whole, as a harmony into which they are unified by certain numerical ratios in which they are stand to one another, like those in which the pitches of sounds must stand so as to give rise to a harmony: Plato's harmonic image, now not only of the orderliness but also of the unity of reason, is appropriate in view of his depiction of rational soul as motions because, as he takes it, pitch depends on the speed of the sound-producing motion of air (676b2–6), though the motions that make up the rational soul in the heavens are not motions of air. To achieve the best life set by the gods before humankind for all time we ought to rearrange the disorderly motions that take place in our brains and are our own rational souls by understanding their orderly cosmic analogues, the harmonic revolutions making up the cosmic soul that enlivens the universe, hence the thoughts thought by these harmonic motions, which means to effect the assimilation of our rational souls to their celestial kin, thereby establishing in them the harmony that is proper to them (90c6–d7). Since the cosmic soul, which participates in thought and harmony, is invisible (36e5–37a2), however, this can be achieved only by our understanding of the celestial motions, the observable effects of the motions constituting the cosmic soul, and of their harmonies, a metaphor for the various relations among them.

Indeed, earlier on Plato has Timaeus say that the demiurge invented and gave us sight in order that we might observe the orderly revolutions of reason in the heavens and derive benefit from them as regards the disorderly revolutions of our own thought, which are akin to them: that is, by understanding the orderly revolutions of reason in the heavens and participating correctly in its thoughts according to nature, that we might replicate in our rational souls the totally fixed revolutions of god and put in order the wandering revolutions in ourselves (47a1–c4). Clearly, the orderly revolutions of reason in the heavens that can be observed by us and understood correctly thanks to our sight are not the invisible motions themselves that figuratively make up the cosmic soul but their effects, the visible motions of the celestial objects, through which we have only indirect access to

---

image of the unfathomable way by which a rational soul causes motion on the cosmic level: by being itself a motion, an image drawn from our everyday experience. The circularity (and uniformity) of this motion can be an appropriate symbol of the hallmark of rationality, static and symmetric order, thanks to the exceptional symmetry of the circle (and the orderliness of uniform motion). 898d9–899a10 suggests that Plato would exalt the rational soul as cause of motion by assuming that, no matter how it brings about motion, it does not do so mechanically or kinetically. For the literal interpretation of the circular motion of rational soul see also Carone (2005) 44–45 with nn. 79 and 81 for further references. See also next n.

the cosmic mind bringing them about.[20] Plato has Timaeus open the teleological account of sight by proclaiming that we see so that we can see the succession of day and night as well as of months and years and the phenomena of equinox and solstice, which have made it possible for us to develop the concepts of number and time and the inquiry into the nature of the universe (47a1–7): what is more important, all these have provided us with philosophy, the greatest good that gods have bestowed on humans (47a7–b2). If philosophy is the love of learning that one ought to cultivate if s/he is to become exceptionally *eudaimōn* according

---

[20] In *de An*. A 3, 406b26–407a2, Aristotle identifies the motions that constitute the rational cosmic soul with the celestial motions; cf. Sedley (1999) 317–318 who argues that the motions of the cosmic soul are invisible in themselves but have been rendered visible by the demiurge when he planted in each of them a celestial body to illuminate them. Sedley supports this claim by a reference to *Ti*. 38–9 but nothing is said there about the celestial objects' having been lit up by the demiurge in order for the circular revolutions of the cosmic soul to become visible. Moreover, the passage quoted and translated in previous n. rules out the visibility of both the cosmic soul and all souls (cf. *Lg*. 10, 898d9–e2), though it is conceivable that in *Lg*. 10 Plato does not operate with the same view on the nature of the cosmic soul as in the *Timaeus*, where this soul is viewed as a literal bundle of circular motions made visible by the celestial bodies with whose motions the cosmic soul is indeed identical. In the *Timaeus* the moon, the sun and the five planets are said to have been placed by the demiurge about the earth in seven of the eight concentric circular motions of the cosmic soul (38c3–e3). But, if the riding of the seven luminaries on the circular motions of the cosmic soul is not understood in light of *Lg*. 10 as a metaphor for the unknown way by which a rational soul causes all celestial motion (see previous n.), then in the *Timaeus* Plato has a rudimentary conception of celestial motions, whereby the planets move zodiacally along five concentric circles; the only reason why they are called planets, i.e. "wanderers", is that their participation in another circular motion, i.e. the diurnal rotation, combines with their zodiacal motion to follow each day a different turn of a spiral, as explained in *Ti*. 39a5–b2. Plato, in other words, ignores the most intriguing wanderings of the planets, the episodes of non-circular retrogradation during their zodiacal motions, which his conception of celestial motions cannot produce; this is also clearly shown by *Lg*. 7, 820e8–822d1, where the wanderings not only of the planets but also of the sun and the moon are their spiral motions. However, one is understandably unwilling to ascribe to Plato the notion that our participating correctly in the thoughts of the divine reason in the heavens is as simple a matter as realizing the unwavering circularity of all celestial motions, which can be observed: as he has the Athenian stranger say in *Lg*. 7, 821b5–822d1, this is something easy to learn and easy to teach, not something observable, easily or not, and elementary astronomy is to be taught to the young of the planned city up to the introduction of this view of celestial motions so that all citizens will learn to not blaspheme god, clearly by holding the erroneous belief that the soul producing the celestial motions is irrational since its effects are disorderly and wandering (cf. *Lg*. 10, 896d5–899c1). Not blaspheming god does not entail correct participation in the thoughts of god; and the means by which it is achieved, the conception of all celestial motions as circular, seems to be a mere teaching aid, a useful but crude model of celestial motion or an image like the related notion of the cosmic soul as circular motions. See also 2.10.

to the *Timaeus* account of the best life set by the gods before humankind, philosophy seems to be effectively equated with astronomy. What must be learned are the thoughts of the cosmic soul which causes the celestial motions and to the harmony of whose invisible constitutive revolutions the learner's rational soul aspires to assimilate its own unharmonious revolutions via learning. But the learner can achieve this goal only by understanding the observable celestial motions caused by the invisible motions making up the cosmic soul. The gods have thus literally bestowed philosophy on humans, for in the *Timaeus* the only gods are the celestial objects, which are enlivened by the cosmic soul (39e3–41d3).

It would be rash, however, to conclude that in the *Timaeus* astronomy is promoted from a propedeutic to philosophy in the *Republic* to the position of philosophy itself, with the celestial motions, and ultimately the thoughts of a cosmic soul which causes them, usurping the place of forms and the Good. Plato has the philosopher Timaeus conclude his account of metals by saying that questions of physics provide a welcome diversion from the important discourse about eternal beings (59c5–d2). This is the description of the subject matter of philosophy, the forms, familiar from the *Republic*, and undoubtedly in the *Timaeus* too it refers to what is studied in philosophy. The *Timaeus*, however, does not identify as eternal beings the cosmic soul and the celestial objects despite their exalted status. The cosmic soul is said to be the best among all things that have come to be, having been made by that of all intelligible and eternal beings which is the best (36e5–37a2), the demiurge (29d7–30a7); the celestial objects are said to be divine living beings but also to have been made by the demiurge, understandably so since he is presented as having made the cosmic soul enlivening them. Thus, if philosophy is the discourse about eternal beings, respite from which questions of physics can provide, its subject matter cannot really be what it seems to be from the teleological account of sight and the account of the human good, for in the *Timaeus* the celestial objects and the harmonic revolutions of the cosmic soul that enlivens the celestial objects causing their motions are not described as eternal beings.

The only things that are explicitly said to be eternal beings in the *Timaeus* are immutable and intelligible paradigms that are contrasted with those things that are sensible, come to be and pass away, and among whose images are all good and beautiful sensible things, of which the most good and beautiful is the cosmos: the noun used in the divided-line simile of the *Republic* for the direct, dialectical, approach to forms and the resulting cognitive condition (νόησις) is used once again in the *Timaeus* for the cognitive condition whose objects are the paradigmatic eternal beings, while the opposite term for the cognitive condition whose objects are sensibles (δόξα) reappears, as we expect, with the same meaning in the *Timaeus* (27d7–29d3). In this context, moreover, Plato has Timaeus make an unmistakable allusion (29c3) to the proportion-theoretic re-description of the divided line in *Republic* 7 (533e3–534a8). Given the description of forms as objects of true discourse and knowledge in Timaeus' introduction of the receptacle (48e2–52d1), we have thus strong reason to suspect that in the *Timaeus* nothing has changed since the *Republic* as regards the objects philosophy is about. If the *Republic* hints that astronomy as well as the forms it actually studies have a special role to play in paving the way to the Good, which in this dialogue is emphasized as the peak of the subject matter of philosophy, then it is not surprising at all to find the situation reversed in the *Timaeus*, a cosmological work: the main emphasis now falls on the special relation of the human good, hence of the Good, to astronomy, which thus appears to usurp the place of philosophy in the *Republic*, whereas the relation of the Good to philosophy is hinted at in the reference to the discourse about eternal beings and in their characterization as intelligible and immutable paradigms whose images are all good and beautiful sensible things. Forms fit self-evidently into the account of the best human life offered in the *Timaeus* if the thoughts of the cosmic soul which causes the celestial motions cannot but have as objects certain closely related forms, intelligible and immutable paradigms of the celestial motions, whose relatedness encapsulates the Good.

If so, when Plato has Timaeus say that various astronomical phenomena have made it possible for us to develop the concepts of number and time and the inquiry into the nature of the cosmos, all of which have provided us with philosophy, he means not that philosophy is actually astronomy, pursued as in the *Timaeus*, i.e. not only mathematically but also, and more importantly, cosmologically and ethically, but that it just sprang from marveling at the phenomena of the sky and wondering about the nature of the cosmos. The substitution of astronomy for philosophy is, however, presented as genuine Platonic doctrine at the end of the *Epinomis*, a short work probably written by Philip of Opus in the fourth century BC as an appendix to Plato's *Laws*.[21]

2.6 Astronomy in the *Epinomis*

The final part of the *Epinomis* begins with the Athenian stranger preparing to answer the question addressed earlier in the discussion (973a1–b6): what must one learn to be considered wise? He begins by equating platonically goodness with a wisdom acquired through systematic education and, before he tries to describe clearly to his codiscussant this wisdom as it has been revealed to him in his

---

[21] On Plato and the authorship of the *Epinomis* see the relevant section in Tarán (1975).

exhaustive search for it, he says that the nature of this wisdom is perplexing because the greatest part of virtue is not rightly practiced: for mortals there is no greater part of virtue than piety, but even the best people ignore this (988e6–989b1). Earlier on (984d3–8), the Athenian stranger has identified the celestial objects with visible gods, the greatest and most honorable ones, waving aside politely the traditional Greek gods such as Zeus and Hera (that the celestial objects are gods is already stated in 981b3–982a3).²² Thus the intimate connection between the wisdom sought after here and virtue, whose greatest part is piety, suggests that both are to be found in astronomy. The identification of the wisdom at issue with astronomy is made explicit shortly after this wisdom's implicit equation with piety. The Athenian stranger warns that "it is bizarre to hear this, but the name by which we at any rate call this wisdom, astronomy, would never be accepted by people, unfamiliar as they are with these matters and ignorant of the fact that the wisest person must be a true astronomer: one who is an astronomer not in the sense of Hesiod and all the rest like him, a student of morning and evening risings and settings of the fixed stars, but one who has studied the seven of the eight periodic motions, the zodiacal motions of the planets, the sun and the moon, each of them undergone along its own circle in such a manner that no ordinary people but only those of a marvelous nature can ever easily understand" (989e1–990b3).²³

---

22 Cf. Pl. *Lg.* 10, 899b3–9, and *Ti.* 39e3–40d5. According to the author of the *Epinomis*, knowledge of the planets had been first obtained by the peoples of the Near East, Egypt and Syria, due to the meteorological conditions there at summertime that allow easy observations of all celestial objects, and has then spread to Greece and everywhere else (986a8–987a6). In his view, however, the Greeks perfect all their borrowings from non-Greeks, and, although it is difficult to discover indisputably everything related to the planets and the other celestial objects, there are many good hopes that the Greeks, being reliant on their multifaceted education and the Delphic oracles, will be able to pay better and more just respect to all these divinities, the celestial objects, than the rumored service done to them by the pioneering foreigners (987d3–988a5). The author of the *Epinomis* seems to suggest that the conception of all celestial objects as divine is not Greek but Near Eastern. See also Morrow (1993) 445–448.

23 πειρώμεθα δὴ τῷ τε λόγῳ διεξελθεῖν ἅ τ' ἐστὶν καὶ οἷα καὶ ὡς δεῖ μανθάνειν, κατὰ δύναμιν τὴν τ' ἐμὴν τοῦ λέγοντος καὶ τὴν τῶν δυναμένων εἰσακοῦσαι, θεοσεβείας ᾧτινι τρόπῳ τις τίνα μαθήσεται. σχεδὸν μὲν οὖν ἐστιν ἄτοπον ἀκούσαντι, τὸ δ' ὄνομα αὐτοῦ λέγομεν ἡμεῖς γε, ὅ τις οὐκ ἄν ποτε δόξειεν δι' ἀπειρίαν τοῦ πράγματος–ἀστρονομίαν–ἀγνοεῖ τε ὅτι σοφώτατον ἀνάγκη τὸν ἀληθῶς ἀστρονόμον εἶναι, μὴ τὸν καθ' Ἡσίοδον ἀστρονομοῦντα καὶ πάντας τοὺς τοιούτους, οἷον δυσμάς τε καὶ ἀνατολὰς ἐπεσκεμμένον, ἀλλὰ τὸν τῶν ὀκτὼ περιόδων τὰς ἑπτὰ περιόδους, διεξιούσης τὸν αὐτῶν κύκλον ἑκάστης οὕτως ὡς οὐκ ἂν ῥαδίως ποτὲ πᾶσα φύσις ἱκανὴ γένοιτο θεωρῆσαι, μὴ θαυμαστῆς μετέχουσα φύσεως. ὃ νῦν εἰρήκαμεν ἐροῦμέν τε, ὥς φαμεν, ὅπῃ δεῖ τε καὶ ὅπως χρεὼν μανθάνειν. For the reference to Hesiod see Kouremenos (2015) 1.3.2–3.

Next follows a short discussion of four branches of mathematics whose study is propedeutically required for one's becoming wise and good, equivalently a competent astronomer: arithmetic, plane geometry, stereometry, and harmonics (990b5–991b4). These are only four of the five propedeutics to philosophy in the seventh book of Plato's *Republic*, the fifth, astronomy, missing exactly because it has usurped the place of philosophy.[24] Indeed, the author of the *Epinomis* views arithmetic as the study of the numbers themselves, not of those numbers which have bodies, in an unmistakable allusion to Plato's own description of arithmetic as a propedeutic to philosophy (525d5–8). Philip of Opus, moreover, employs the term *geometry* for plane geometry following Plato's usage in the discussion of stereometry as a propedeutic to philosophy (528a6–10 and d1–10). He also notes that this term *geometry* is ridiculous (γελοῖον), recalling the adverb used by Plato in his discussion of geometry as a propedeutic to philosophy for the ridiculousness of the geometers' talk about squaring, applying areas and adding, which gives the false impression that geometry is concerned with what is generated, not with beings (527a6: λέγουσι μέν που μάλα γελοίως). There can thus be no doubt that in the *Epinomis* astronomy has usurped the place of philosophy in the *Republic*, the propedeutics of astronomy in the *Epinomis* being described in terms recalling the description of the propedeutics to philosophy in the *Republic*, among which astronomy is included.[25]

---

24 On mathematics in the *Epinomis* see Mueller (1991) 99–104 and Kouremenos (2015) 2.2.4.
25 Cf. Dillon (2003) 187 (cf. also 196) and Nightingale (2004) 184. Philip's inversion of the relationship between astronomy and philosophy in Plato's *Republic* could allow Ptolemy to go a step further than the close relationship posited by Plato and Aristotle between astronomy and the highest science, Plato's dialectic and Aristotle's first philosophy (see above n. 10), and elevate the former to the position of the latter (on Ptolemy see above n. 11), all the more so if he accepted the attribution of the *Epinomis*, or at least of the views put forth in it, to Plato himself. Platonic dialectic studies being, and corresponds to what Aristotle calls the highest part of theoretical philosophy, the first philosophy, which is also theology, for it studies both being as such and a particular kind of beings, divine substances or the gods. In the *Epinomis*, however, the latter are studied by astronomy, and the priority of philosophy to astronomy put forth in the *Republic* is inversed: astronomy occupies the position of dialectic in the *Republic*, though an emasculated dialectic still appears next to it (see below). Fed into the Aristotelian tripartition of theoretical philosophy, this yields Ptolemy's elevation of astronomy to the highest place in it if the identification of astronomy and theology in the *Epinomis* is disregarded together with dialectic or the study of being in order for astronomy to be exalted to the highest degree possible. To decouple astronomy and theology, all Ptolemy had to do was adopt a radical Pyrrhonist attitude towards the objects of theology as unknowable. Dialectic is not integrated with astronomy in the *Epinomis* and can easily be left out of consideration, which applies to Aristotle's study of being since it can be assumed to sit uneasily next to theology as first philosophy's second strand.

Whereas in the *Republic* arithmetic, plane geometry, stereometry, astronomy and harmonics pave the way to philosophy, according to Philip of Opus arithmetic, plane geometry, stereometry and harmonics pave the way to astronomy. Philosophy is famously described in *Republic* 7 as the cornice of the building of mathematics (534e2–535a1), the supreme science in which all five branches of mathematics find their completion (τέλος). In the *Epinomis*, however, arithmetic, plane geometry, stereometry and harmonics find their completion (τέλος) in astronomy, the study of the celestial objects that are the most divine created things, whose nature is the most beautiful of all sensibles (991b6–c6).[26] It is in this context of extolling astronomy as the wisdom in which the other branches of mathematics find their completion that philosophy, which allows one to relate particulars to their forms, is mentioned as indispensible part of this wisdom, insofar as it is a useful tool to be employed in discussions for questioning and examining wrong views. Although philosophy is thought to provide the finest and first test we can use for questioning and examining what has been wrongly said, while anything else pretending to be such a test is nothing but the vainest of all efforts, its appearance in the *Epinomis* as an add-on to wisdom only highlights the demotion from the high position it occupies in the *Republic* in favor of astronomy.

2.7 Astronomy in the *Laws*

That wisdom and goodness are inseparably linked with piety and astronomy harks back to a passage in the twelfth book of Plato's *Laws*, where the Athenian proclaims to his codiscussants that true piety presupposes, first, realizing the superiority of soul over all generated things; second, knowledge of the fact that the phenomena of the divine celestial bodies do not occur haphazardly but are sub-

---

[26] τὸ δ' ἐπὶ τούτοις τέλος, εἰς θείαν γένεσιν ἅμα καὶ τὴν τῶν ὁρατῶν καλλίστην τε καὶ θειοτάτην φύσιν ἰτέον, ὅσην ἀνθρώποις θεὸς ἔδωκεν κατιδεῖν, ἣν οὔποτε ἄνευ τῶν νῦν διειρημένων μὴ κατιδὼν ἐπεύξηταί τις ῥᾳστώνῃ παραλαβεῖν. πρὸς τούτοις δὲ τὸ καθ' ἓν τῷ κατ' εἴδη προσακτέον ἐν ἑκάσταις ταῖς συνουσίαις, ἐρωτῶντά τε καὶ ἐλέγχοντα τὰ μὴ καλῶς ῥηθέντα· πάντως γὰρ καλλίστη καὶ πρώτη βάσανος ἀνθρώποις ὀρθῶς γίγνεται, ὅσαι δὲ οὐκ οὖσαι προσποιοῦνται, ματαιότατος πόνος ἁπάντων ("Now, for their completion we must go to the created things that are divine, by nature the most beautiful and divine of visible things, to the extent that god granted humans to behold their nature, which nobody will ever boast of having easily beheld without the propedeutics just laid down. Also, we must relate the particular things to their forms in our discussions, questioning and examining what has been wrongly said, for this is rightly the finest and first test we can use, while anything else pretending to be such a test, without being so, is the vainest of all efforts").

ject to reason, which presupposes the first and knowledge of astronomy (see 7, 820e8–822c9, and 10, 888e4–899d3); third, training in the other two branches of mathematics that are required for astronomy, in arithmetic and geometry (see 7, 817e5–820e7); fourth, understanding the whole 'music' of the close interrelationships among all branches of mathematics, their unity, which will be used for the similar arrangement of customs and laws; fifth, the ability to give an account of what has an account, training in philosophy (967d4–968a4).[27] Plato has the Athenian say that one who is unable to achieve the above in addition to possessing the civic virtues could never become a true ruler of a city but merely a servant for others who rule. The true rulers of a city here are the members of the so-called nocturnal council, the highest governing body in the planned Cretan colony whose laws are discussed in the *Laws*. Like the famous philosopher-rulers of the *Republic*, they will study higher mathematics (cf. *Lg.* 7, 817e5–818a3). Astronomy is clearly singled out from among the branches of mathematics, and philosophy seems to be regarded as secondary to astronomy, as in the *Epinomis*, but Plato's preceding discussion of the nocturnal council (960e9–967d3) leaves no doubt at all that in the late *Laws*, as in the earlier *Republic*, he regards not astronomy but philosophy as the master science.

There is no better way of studying and seeing anything, the Athenian says, than by being able to look up from the many and dissimilar to one unifying form: an expert craftsman and guardian must be not only able to look at the many but also eager to know a unity and, having obtained knowledge of it, must then be able to put the many together in the pattern of this unity, looking at them synoptically (965b7–c8). Concerning what is beautiful and also what is good in many

---

27 Οὐκ ἔστιν ποτὲ γενέσθαι βεβαίως θεοσεβῆ θνητῶν ἀνθρώπων οὐδένα, ὃς ἂν μὴ τὰ λεγόμενα ταῦτα νῦν δύο λάβῃ, ψυχή τε ὡς ἔστιν πρεσβύτατον ἁπάντων ὅσα γονῆς μετείληφεν, ἀθάνατόν τε, ἄρχει τε δὴ σωμάτων πάντων, ἐπὶ δὲ τούτοισι δή, τὸ νῦν εἰρημένον πολλάκις, τόν τε εἰρημένον ἐν τοῖς ἄστροις νοῦν τῶν ὄντων τά τε πρὸ τούτων ἀναγκαῖα μαθήματα λάβῃ, τά τε κατὰ τὴν μοῦσαν τούτοις τῆς κοινωνίας συνθεασάμενος, χρήσηται πρὸς τὰ τῶν ἠθῶν ἐπιτηδεύματα καὶ νόμιμα συναρμοττόντως, ὅσα τε λόγον ἔχει, τούτων δυνατὸς ᾖ δοῦναι τὸν λόγον· ὁ δὲ μὴ ταῦθ' οἷός τ' ὢν πρὸς ταῖς δημοσίαις ἀρεταῖς κεκτῆσθαι σχεδὸν ἄρχων μὲν οὐκ ἄν ποτε γένοιτο ἱκανὸς ὅλης πόλεως, ὑπηρέτης δ' ἂν ἄλλοις ἄρχουσιν ("No mortal man can ever truly respect the gods who has not grasped these two truths now stated. First, soul is the most important of all things that come to be, and is also immortal and rules over all bodies. In addition to that, as we have often said by now, he must also grasp the rationality in the celestial objects that governs existing things as well as the subjects that necessarily come before their study and, having grasped as a whole the music of their close ties, he must use them to arrange customs and laws in the same way, being also able to give an account of what has an account. One who cannot achieve the above in addition to possessing the civic virtues could never become a competent governor of the city as a whole but be merely a servant for others who rule").

ways, the true guardians of the laws of the city must know not only that each of these is a plurality but also in what sense and how they are each a unity, and they must also be able to give an account of this and judge and act accordingly (966a5–b9). Nothing seems to have changed in the *Laws* since the seventh book of the *Republic* with the description of the philosopher as a comprehensive viewer trained propedeutically in mathematics with the final goal to grasp the unity of mathematics so as to be prepared for the highest unities studied in philosophy, the Beautiful and the Good (531c6–d5 and 537b7–c7); or since the sixth book of the *Republic*, where only philosophers are declared to be capable of ruling in a city since they know in each case one form over the bewildering multiplicity and dissimilarity of its participants, among which the vast majority of people wander, and behold it as exemplar of rational arrangement in order to legislate about the beautiful, just and good in the city and preserve its already existing legislation (484b4–d9 and 500b8–d10). As a most important manifestation of the Beautiful, hence the Good, Plato has the Athenian stranger mention the gods, whose existence and power is established, to the extent that they can be humanly ascertained, by arguments for the superiority of soul and the order inherent in the celestial motions and everything else controlled by reason, which has arranged the universe into a cosmos (966c1–967a5): as the Athenian has demonstrated in *Laws* 10, the motions of the celestial bodies are caused by one or more rational and good souls enlivening the celestial objects that can thus only be gods executing orderly motions (888e4–899d3). However, the Athenian reminds his codiscussants that the majority of the citizens in the planned Cretan colony are to know about these matters only so far as the law prescribes (966c1–6): their education in elementary astronomy will be up to the demonstration of the orderliness of the celestial motions (*Lg.* 7, 820e8–822d1), presumably by arguments of the type showcased in the tenth book of the work, which aim to dissuade an average citizen from disbelief in the existence of gods. On the other hand, the members of the nocturnal council are supposed to engage in an intensive study not only of higher mathematics but also of all matters that are related to gods (966c6–d2).[28] They can only be supposed to do this in the best way for examining and viewing anything: by looking up from multiplicity and dissimilarity to the unifying form or forms ultimately imparting to celestial motions order and harmonious relations that are the most important manifestations of the Beautiful and, like those tying all mathematics together, allow one to transcend multiplicity and grasp an overarching unity. The goal of this undeniably philosophical approach to astronomy by the members of the nocturnal council is to see how everything in the

---

[28] On the nocturnal council see Morrow (1993) 500–515.

heavens is caused by thoughts willing the manifold realization of the Good (967a1–5), clearly those of the rational soul or souls enlivening the luminaries that can only have the relevant forms as their objects. It is only if approached in this way that astronomy and the rest of mathematics it presupposes will not be thought to promote impiety, so its strong link with piety in the *Laws* indicates that, far from usurping the position of philosophy as in the *Epinomis*, astronomy is exalted in Plato's last work thanks to philosophy, the queen of the sciences in the *Laws* as in the earlier *Republic*.[29]

It cannot be accidental that in *Laws* 4 the Athenian defines piety, conduct dear to and in conformity with god, in terms of a person's being like to what has measure, for things that do not have measure are dear neither to one another nor to those in measure (716c1–4). It is unlikely that here being in measure is measurability and not *com*mensurability: *sym*metry in the sense of relatedness, of magnitudes' having a common measure relating them to one another with ratios and proportions. This is indeed hinted at by the fourth requirement for true piety, grasp of the 'music' of the close interrelationships that unite all mathematics into the pattern for the successful arrangement of laws and customs. Piety is thus defined in terms of the trait that makes a philosopher an expert craftsman of temperance, justice and all civic virtue in *Republic* 6, of all likeness to the Good that is the unity into which all other forms are related: the assimilation of oneself to the pattern of divine things that, neither wronging nor being wronged by one another, are well-ordered by relations described as rational and at the same time likened to ratios (500b8–d10). Having measure and symmetry, in the original sense of the term, appears in the *Philebus* as definiens of what is good (64e5–65a5). By depicting the Athenian as defining piety in terms of assimilation to things in measure, Plato hints that, at least for those few citizens in the planned Cretan colony who will be fit for membership in the nocturnal council, piety and god(s) are not substitutes for but equivalent to philosophy and its cynosure, the Good, as befits the counterparts of the philosopher-kings in the much more famous city of the *Republic*. Indeed in *Laws* 4 Plato has the Athenian define god as the measure of all things paraphrasing the Protagorean dictum (716c4–6), while in *Republic* 7 it is the Good that is implicitly defined as measure, when Socrates stresses with a mathematical simile the importance of training in philosophy for the future philosopher-rulers who must know the Good if they are to know its manifestations (534b3–e1): those who will have the highest power cannot be irrational, as they will be if they do not know the Good, like irrational lines, i.e.

---

29 Cf. Morrow (1993) 573–590. *Pace* Carone (2005) ch. 3 the *Laws* do not support the view that in the *Timaeus* astronomy is offered as alternative to philosophy for the masses.

those that are incommensurable with a given line (cf. Euc. *El.* 10 Def. 3). Lack of knowledge of the Good is illustrated here by lack of a common measure, a mathematical metaphor for the Good, the standard for the arrangement of laws, customs and everything in the state, as unifying relatedness like that which a common measure imparts to the magnitudes it measures. As it is, Plato's call in *Laws* 12 for astronomy to serve piety is a simple reformulation of the call in *Republic* 7 for astronomy to serve the approach of philosophy, the master science in both the late *Laws* and the earlier *Republic*, to the Good and the Beautiful (530c3–6; cf. 531c5–8). This is also hinted by the fact that astronomy and the branches of mathematics it presupposes are assumed in the *Laws* to promote piety only if they are linked to the realization of the Good.

It is true, of course, that in the *Laws* the importance of philosophy and the Good is hinted at rather than emphasized, let alone heavily, as in the earlier *Republic*; nor is there even the slightest hint at the nature of forms. But, assuming that in the *Laws* forms are conceived as in the late *Timaeus*, this is not surprising.[30] Mathematics too does not receive in the *Laws* the heavy emphasis that it does in the *Republic* despite its importance in the *Laws* too, made abundantly clear from the fact that it must be studied by all citizens of the planned Cretan colony at an elementary level, its in-depth study being required only of the members of the nocturnal council. After the Athenian stranger explains in *Laws* 7 why arithmetic, geometry and astronomy are worth studying (818b7–e2), one of his two Dorian codiscussants, the Cretan Cleinias, agrees reluctantly (818e3–4). Prompted perhaps in part by the guarded attitude of the Cretan towards his proposals, the stranger remarks next that, since it is difficult to make the educational program he advocates into law, its precise details are best left for a later occasion (818e5–7). Cleinias then observes that the Athenian appears scared by the habitual neglect in Dorian areas of the subjects just suggested to be most appropriate for the basic schooling of the citizens, and the stranger promptly agrees (818e8–819a1). What Plato has the sophist Hippias say in *Hippias Major* about the Lacedaemonians does apply to all Dorians: they cannot bear to listen about the stars and celestial phenomena, nor do they enjoy listening about geometry, most of them being unable even to count (285b5–c5)! Cleinias is presented as being blithely unaware of the fact that the morning and evening stars are a single celestial body and of the exact number of the planets classed together with the sun

---

30 Owen (1965) argued that the *Timaeus* should be considered a middle dialogue, and thus be grouped together with e.g. the *Republic* and placed before the *Parmenides*, exactly because he assumed that after the *Parmenides* Plato was forced to abandon his belief in separately existing forms as paradigms in which sensibles participate and which they thus resemble.

and the moon as the wandering celestial bodies (821b5–c5). A heavy emphasis on philosophy, the forms and the Good would, therefore, be very inappropriate in the *Laws*, given the choice of the Cretan Cleinias and another Dorian, the Spartan Megillus, as codiscussants of the Athenian stranger, Plato's mouthpiece, and of a Cretan setting for their discussion of government and laws, topics that motivated these choices since Plato certainly admired the Spartan and Cretan constitutions, though not uncritically, and thought of them as kindred. The closer relation that astronomy has to philosophy and the Good in comparison to the rest of mathematics, however, is clearly emphasized in the *Laws*, as in the *Timaeus*, much more prominently than in the *Republic* and the *Phaedo*.

2.8 Astronomy and the Good

But why is astronomy, according to Plato, more intimately related to philosophy and the peak of its subject matter, the Good, than the other branches of mathematics? All branches of mathematics are chosen as the only appropriate propeudetics to philosophy because they in fact introduce forms, though indirectly, and also constitute a family, a harmoniously arranged unity, on account of their various interconnections, which can only reflect the interrelationships among the forms that tie them together into the highest form of them all and the cynosure of philosophy, the Good. Nor does there seem to be any difference in importance between the forms which astronomy is really about and those really studied in the other branches of mathematics since in *Republic* 7 Plato believes that astronomy ought to be pursued as geometry if it is to turn into a propedeutic of philosophy (530b6–c4): as it is, the forms astronomy is really about are forms of certain geometrical objects, but Plato does not seem to have posited a privileged relationship of some 'geometrical' forms to the Good and philosophy. The answer to our question does not seem to lie in the forms astronomy really studies, whatever these might be. It lies rather in the fact that astronomy reveals a sensible realization of the Good as result of thought willing to bring it about, provided that this discipline is pursued mathematically so as to reveal unifying forms over the apparent arbitrary variability in celestial motions, whose form-derived and thus form-reflecting observable order, provided that it is mathematically and philosophically understood and appreciated, marks them as the best possible embodiment of goodness and beauty itself.

A Platonic philosopher is not merely interested in understanding all the other forms and the Good but also and most importantly in successfully bringing this understanding to bear on the human sphere. As Plato puts it in *Republic* 7, the prisoner who has been freed from the cave and seen everything outside it and the sun of the Good must then go back inside and apply the knowledge gained on the surface of the earth to everything appearing inside the cave to the wretched prisoners (519b7–520e3): philosophers not only mold themselves to the order of all the other forms that is the Good but also apply their knowledge of the Good to the sphere of private and public live as demiurges of human goodness (*R.* 6, 500b8–d10). As he puts it in the *Philebus*, pure knowledge of justice itself and the other forms such as those of the circle and the sphere are worthless without impure knowledge of the circles and spheres in human activities such as building, and thus by implication without impure knowledge of justice in private and public life (61d10–62b9). Similarly, in the twelfth book of the *Laws* true piety, i.e. understanding the Good, which requires grasping the rational order of the celestial motions and the kindred harmony of the relationships among all fields of mathematics, is explicitly said to aim at the similar arrangement of customs and laws (967d4–968a4). The importance Plato lays on the practical application of abstract knowledge is evident in his prescription in *Republic* 7 for future philosopher-rulers of fifteen years' administrative experience after their decade-long studies in mathematics and a five-year-long course in philosophy before they will be able to see the Good and use it as a template to arrange the state, the citizens and themselves (540a4–c2). The ultimate goal of their long mathematical studies is to see the Good first reflected in the relations of each field of mathematics with the others, all of which are thus viewed comprehensively as a unity, the philosopher's mark being comprehensive viewing (537b7–c7). But, even after they have sharpened with the aid of philosophy their view of the Good, their philosophical education is not complete: it will be completed only if the Good has been viewed fully comprehensively, not only in itself as the order of all other forms into a unity, first mathematically and then philosophically approached, but in all its realizations in private and public life too, something which needs extensive practical experience to be attained. In the symbolic terms of the cave simile, seeing the sun and realizing its power over the whole cosmos is not an end in itself: the former prisoner must also realize that the sun is responsible even for what the prisoners see inside the cave, where he will return to apply his knowledge to all that appears to these unfortunates.

However, the applied relevance of the objects of abstract philosophical knowledge is already prefigured in the propedeutic study of mathematics: not so much in the useful applications of all its fields including astronomy (522b5–e4, 526c7–d7 and 527d1–7), for all these applications concern human needs and desires and the production of material goods and their maintenance or care (533a10–c7), but mainly in the humanly independent realization of forms as the harmonious order of the celestial motions. Astronomy is that branch of mathematics which teaches that some of the forms studied in mathematics are observably realized at the largest scale of the sensible realm as beauty and goodness in the best possible way in which such realization is achievable (530a4–8). It is closer to the Good than the rest of mathematics not because it reveals more or most of the Good in the way that all mathematics does but rather because, approached not merely mathematically but also philosophically, it shows an objective realization of the Good in the heavens, whence the rest of the sensible realm is governed. Therefore, it introduces the objective dominance of the Good in all of the sensible realm, the entire human sphere included: the supremacy of the Good, in absolute terms and in our life, and the realization of the Good as best and broadly as possible in human affairs are the peak of the subject matter of philosophy, to which the subject matter of astronomy, philosophically approached, turns out to be much closer than that of pure geometry or arithmetic and its application in harmonics, a field of mathematics inextricably linked to human needs and desires. It is thus not surprising that in the cave simile the former prisoner first raises his eyes to the night sky and beholds directly the moon and the other celestial objects in it and then views directly the sun and realizes its dominance over the whole cosmos, including the cave.

The above account presupposes that observation is indispensible to astronomy. This seems to clash with the admonition in *Republic* 7 that astronomy cannot be of truly propedeutic service to philosophy unless it is practiced in a way radically different from the way it was pursued at the dramatic time of the dialogue, which presumably was also how this discipline was mainly understood when the work was written: astronomy must leave the things in the heavens alone and instead focus on problems as geometry does (530b6–c6). The astronomy of his time which Socrates is presented as rejecting from the propedeutic curriculum of the future philosopher-rulers is mired in what is observed in the sky, which is the reason why it is unsuitable for the curriculum.[31] "You seem to me," Socrates says when his codiscussant suggests this astronomy as a propedeutic, "to have a nice view of the study of the things up there! You appear to think that one sees not with his eyes but with his mind even if he tries to learn something by bending his head backwards to look at decorations on a ceiling! You might be right and I naïve. But I cannot help thinking that only the study of what is and the eyes cannot see can make the soul look upwards and, if someone attempts to study something sensible looking upwards open-mouthed or squinting downwards, I say that he will never learn anything, for there is no knowledge about any of these things, and that his soul looks not upwards but downwards,

---

31 On this astronomy see Kouremenos (2015) 1.3–5.

even if he attempts to learn lying on his back on the earth or in the sea" (529a9–c2; cf. 527d1–528a5).[32] Here Plato seems bizarrely to want to eliminate observation from a philosophical astronomy which will study not the sky but intelligible forms, collectively referred to as "what is". But this cannot be so.

2.9 Astronomy and observation

The forms that are at issue in *R.* 7, 529a9–c2, can only be those which the astronomers will study as geometers through problems. In the context of *Republic* 7 these geometrical problems are best understood as construction problems:[33] these, as Plato has Socrates make clear to Glaucon while discussing geometry, give the ludicrous impression that geometry is all about making what comes to be and passes away, though in fact it aims at obtaining knowledge about stable, intelligible forms (527a1–b11). Ridiculous as it might be, the focus in geometry on construction problems is also said to be unavoidable, and the most plausible explanation for this is that, as said in *Republic* 6 in the simile of the divided line, geometers can investigate their real subject matter, non-sensible forms, only aided by its visible representations they use (510c2–511a3); although the example of such a representation is a very simple one that does not come from a construction problem (it is a square with its diagonal, drawn obviously in a proof of the incommensurability of the side and diagonal of the square), Plato's point undoubtedly applies to the simple or complicated, visible or mentally visualizable, products of construction problems. Since Plato has Socrates parallel, on the one hand, visible representations of forms that might be seen by a geometer but in which he will be interested only in order to learn about these forms and, on the other hand, visible representations of forms observed by an astronomer in the heavens only in order to obtain knowledge of these forms (529d7–530a3), the *Republic* contains no radical proposal to ban observation from astronomy. The heavens bestow on us ready-made visible geometrical structures from which we can and should obtain knowledge of the forms sensibly represented therein, via

---

32 Οὐκ ἀγεννῶς μοι δοκεῖς, ἦν δ' ἐγώ, τὴν περὶ τὰ ἄνω μάθησιν λαμβάνειν παρὰ σαυτῷ ἥ ἐστι· κινδυνεύεις γὰρ καὶ εἴ τις ἐν ὀροφῇ ποικίλματα θεώμενος ἀνακύπτων καταμανθάνοι τι, ἡγεῖσθαι ἂν αὐτὸν νοήσει ἀλλ' οὐκ ὄμμασι θεωρεῖν. ἴσως οὖν καλῶς ἡγῇ, ἐγὼ δ' εὐηθικῶς. ἐγὼ γὰρ αὖ οὐ δύναμαι ἄλλο τι νομίσαι ἄνω ποιοῦν ψυχὴν βλέπειν μάθημα ἢ ἐκεῖνο ὃ ἂν περὶ τὸ ὄν τε ᾖ καὶ τὸ ἀόρατον, ἐάντε τις ἄνω κεχηνὼς ἢ κάτω συμμεμυκὼς τῶν αἰσθητῶν τι ἐπιχειρῇ μανθάνειν, οὔτε μαθεῖν ἄν ποτέ φημι αὐτόν, ἐπιστήμην γὰρ οὐδὲν ἔχειν τῶν τοιούτων, οὔτε ἄνω ἀλλὰ κάτω αὐτοῦ βλέπειν τὴν ψυχήν, κἂν ἐξ ὑπτίας νέων ἐν γῇ ἢ ἐν θαλάττῃ μανθάνῃ.
33 Cf. Procl. *in Euc.* 77.7–78.13 (Friedlein) on construction problems vs. theorems.

constructing these structures ourselves: how, though, can this ever be achieved without accurate observational knowledge of the heavenly geometrical structures to be constructed, i.e. without accurate observational knowledge of the sky? As it is, the mathematized astronomy that will provide aid to philosophy in its inquiry into the Good and the Beautiful (530b6–c6; cf. 531c5–8) will start out by observing the sky, though it will not be restricted to observation, and since Plato has Socrates stress that the structures observed in the sky are the most beautiful sensibles (cf. 529c6–d1 and 530a4–8), it certainly will do so not least insofar as it will help its students appreciate the sensible realization of the Beautiful in the sky, i.e. of the Good which is the cause of all beauty (517b7–c4).

If a geometer, Plato has Socrates explain to Glaucon, stumbles upon a beautiful geometrical structure exquisitely made by Daedalus or another craftsman, he will admit that it is most beautifully and expertly made but will also think that it is ridiculous to engage in a careful observational study of it as if he could find in it the truth about equality, doubleness or any other relationship of commensurability that might obtain in it (529d7–530a3). To use the example illustrating in the simile of the divided line the use of sensible representations of forms in geometry, no matter how long and accurately you observe a square exquisitely drawn with its diagonal, you will never learn whether its side and the diagonal are commensurable or not: to learn the truth about the relationship of the side and the diagonal of the square, you will have to prove whether they are commensurable or not and, since your conclusion can by no means be reached empirically, this goes a long way towards convincing you that your conclusion actually concerns something purely intelligible, whose mere sensible image is a square no matter how exquisitely drawn. Turning to construction problems that are more relevant to astronomy, we can illustrate the same point by using the problem of doubling the cube from solid geometry.[34]

In *Republic* 7 Plato has Socrates introduce solid geometry all of a sudden as an undeveloped field of mathematics which can be of propedeutic service to

---

[34] The problem of doubling of the cube, or the cube-duplication problem, seems to have come up in the work of the early mathematician Hippocrates of Chios, sometime before the end of the fifth century BC. Hippocrates asserted that, if between two given lines A and B are constructed two mean proportional lines X and Y, i.e. such that the proportion A : X = X : Y = Y : B holds, since it follows that $A^3 : X^3 = AXY : XYB = A : B$, if line B is two times line A, it turns out that line X is the side of a cube which is double the cube with line A as side; and since A and B can have to each other any ratio, we can evidently increase a cube in any ratio we please. Cf. the relevant testimony by Procl. *in Euc.* 212.24–213.11 (Friedlein). On the reduction to the construction of two mean proportionals see Saito (1995) and Netz (2004) 274–275. For the story because of which the problem came to be known as Delian see Kouremenos (2015) 2.2.

philosophy if it will make progress and solve open problems such as doubling the cube (528a6–e3): the point of Socrates' move is to suggest politely to Glaucon that the astronomy of their time, which Glaucon has proposed as the next suitable propedeutic to philosophy after plane, as it turns out, geometry, is unsuitable, and that what is needed is an astronomy as yet undeveloped, like stereometry, focusing on construction problems, as will be explicitly stated soon.[35] Again, no matter how long and accurately you observe two exquisitely made cubes of which the volume of one is double that of the other, you will never learn the truth about the relationships of their volume: you will do so only if you learn how to construct the side of a cube whose volume is double that of given cube. Given his emphasis in this context on the use of what is seen as a springboard to what is unseen but does reveal the truth about what is seen, Plato most probably expected those among his contemporary audience who were abreast of developments in mathematics to recall at least one of three constructions of the side of a doubled cube proposed in the fourth century BC by Archytas of Tarentum, Eudoxus of Cnidus and Menaechmus (of unknown origin).[36] Both Archytas and Menaechmus relied in their constructions on curves, Menaechmus on conic sections, their first known appearance in mathematics, whose unexpected connection with the length required to be constructed is hardly imaginable.[37] The same was in all probability true of the Eudoxean construction too, which our source for the fourth-century-BC solutions to the problem of doubling the cube does not detail.[38]

Plato has Socrates describe the celestial counterparts to those beautiful geometrical structures exquisitely made by an expert craftsman as "the diversity in the sky" (τῇ περὶ τὸν οὐρανὸν ποικιλίᾳ), which is clearly observable (529d7–8); it too has been made by an expert craftsman, the demiurge of the heavens (530a4–8) which, as said above (2.4), seems to be a personification of the Good which rules over the sensible realm (cf. 516b8–c1) and is the cause of all beauty (517b7–c4), production being a metaphor for the ultimate causal dependency of the heavens and the other sensible contents of the cosmos on the Good. The word

---

35 On solid geometry and astronomy in *R.* 7 see Kouremenos (2015) 1.7.
36 Our source for the early solutions to the problem of doubling a cube (in the fifth and fourth centuries BC) is very late, Eutoc. *in Sph. Cyl.* 3.88.13–90.11 (Heiberg). The commentator quotes a letter addressed by Eratosthenes of Cyrene to his patron, Ptolemy III. In his letter the polymath describes the construction of an ingenious instrument of his own design for doubling any given cube. See Knorr (1993) 17–24 for a plausible defense of the letter's authenticity against the objections of Wilamowitz (1962).
37 On their solutions see e.g. Kouremenos (2015) 1.7.2–3.
38 For reconstructions see Riddell (1979) 13–19 and Knorr (1993) 52–61. All reconstructions are speculative.

translated here as "diversity" (ποικιλία) has connotations of intricacy and beauty, and a cognate noun (ποικίλματα) is used by Socrates for the decorations on a ceiling which one studies with his eyes by bending his head backwards to look at them without having to use his mind, just as contemporary astronomers approach the heavens (529a9–c2). The geometrical structures made in the heavens thus exhibit diversity, which means that they are dissimilar and vary with respect to themselves (cf. *R.* 10, 611a10–b3): as it is, if astronomy is to ascertain the truth about them by learning how to construct them and thus seeing, however dimly, the intelligible forms realized in them, it cannot be plausibly assumed to even begin to attempt to do so without as accurate as possible an observational study of them. How can successful solutions to construction problems be possibly obtained if what is to be constructed is not known at least tolerably well?[39] Although observational data of a considerably high degree of accuracy seems to be needed for the project of astronomy if this field is to be of value to philosophy, Plato does not believe that perfectly accurate empirical knowledge of the sky can be obtained for all time, and thus views its pursuit as utterly futile. This is another aspect of his injunction to leave the things in the heavens alone: not only astronomy should not be limited to mere observation, important though it is to its project, it should also not labor under the false assumption that an eternally unaltered observational picture of the heavens can be built.

This important point is introduced by Socrates after his hypothesis of a geometer stumbling upon a beautiful geometrical structure made by an accomplished craftsman and before his statement that astronomy should leave the things in the heavens alone and follow the lead of geometry focusing on construction problems instead. The attitude of an astronomer to celestial motions, Socrates explains, should be like that of the hypothetical geometer who knows that the truth about doubleness or any other relation of commensurability obtaining in the beautiful geometrical structure he sees in front of him cannot be found in it; it is clear that the geometrical diversity in the heavens, the astronomer's counterpart to the geometer's beautifully crafted geometrical structures, are exhibited by all or some celestial motions. The astronomer will certainly think that celestial motions are made as beautifully as possible by the demiurge of the sensible heavens and everything in it (530a4–8). But he will know better than to try by all possible means to find the truth about the relative lengths of daytime and nighttime

---

[39] Nothing suggests that the observational component of the future astronomy will need not be taught to the philosopher-rulers in the making (Gregory [2000] 48–60) or that the mathematical/philosophical astronomers who will study astronomical problems arising from the results of observation will not have to do observational work (Vlastos [1981] 16).

during the year, the relation of the solar day, into which daytime and nighttime combine, to the synodic month and the tropical year, and the relations of these two calendrically important periods to those of the planets: the reason is that the celestial objects are sensible bodies and their motions are sensible too, but what is bodily and sensible cannot be assumed to always be in the same state and behave unvaryingly, hence the periods of celestial motions, observable motions of bodies, are subject to variations and thus trying to find observationally their true lengths for all time is meaningless (530a8–b5). Again Plato does not want to banish observation from astronomy. He simply makes on purely metaphysical grounds the important point that celestial periodicities are not constant but subject to variations and thus talk of their true lengths observationally determined for all time is wrong. He clearly thinks that they can be determined with a high degree of accuracy, presumably for quite long timespans, and he puts great stock in knowing them and their various relations, as is shown from his comment in the *Timaeus* that most people not only do not know the periods of the zodiacal motions of the planets, they are unaware even of the fact that these motions are periodic (39c2–d2; cf. 2.1).[40]

Since it is only by means of careful observations that the celestial periods and their relationships can be determined, Plato does not have Socrates propose that astronomy must try to construct the varying geometrical structures exhibited in the sky by celestial motions in order to ascertain the truth about the periods of these motions and their relationships. The solution to a construction problem effects the construction of a geometrical object and in its context relations of commensurability or incommensurability obtaining in the constructed object can also be determined. The emphasis Plato lays in *Republic* 7 and the *Timaeus* on the celestial periods and their commensurabilities might tempt us to conjecture that his radical call for astronomy to turn its attention to construction problems inspired by the geometrical diversity in celestial motions implies a no less radical

---

[40] Gregory (2000) ch. 4 argues that in the *Laws* and the *Timaeus* Plato thinks that all celestial motions are regular, stable and amenable to precise mathematical prediction, unlike in *R*. 7. But since reason is said in *Ti*. 47e5–48a5 to fail in completely persuading the recalcitrant material necessity to submit to it (cf. 29d7–30a6), it is not easy to see how celestial motions, which are undergone by material objects, can be exempted from this general principle even if the incomplete persuasive power of reason over material necessity is assumed to mean the incomplete instantiation of teleology due to initial conditions and logical possibility, as Gregory (2000) 113–115 suggests addressing this passage. Nothing, moreover, in the *Laws* hints that Plato abandoned his view in *R*. 7 that celestial bodies cannot possibly move in an undeviatingly regular manner since they are material, unless the celestial motions are the motions of the soul(s) producing them; see, however, above n. 19 and 20.

hope: solutions to these problems might determine invariable numbers and commensurabilities that are aspects of the unchanging forms varyingly realized in the geometrical dissimilarity of celestial motions and are themselves manifested as the inconstant periods of these motions and their commensurabilities. The parallel, however, between a geometer and astronomer strongly suggests that this cannot be so. Plato has Socrates point out to Glaucon that a geometer does not think that the truth about a commensurability obtaining in a sensible geometrical structure can possibly be found *in* this structure, no matter how beautifully and artfully it is made; it can be learned only if he tries to construct this structure using it as means to learn about an intelligible form realized in it. With respect to the astronomer, Plato has Socrates say that he thinks it makes no sense to try to ascertain by every means the truth for all time about the periods of celestial motions and their commensurabilities, although the celestial motions are exquisitely beautiful, without adding the crucial qualification "*in* the celestial motions": had it been added, there would have been little doubt that in Plato's view the truth about the observables at issue could have been obtained only mathematically in the sense conjectured above, from forms that are varyingly realized in the geometrical diversity exhibited by celestial motions and are accessed by solving construction problems arising from this diversity.

Since the aim of a construction problem is to produce a given geometrical structure, the varying geometrical structures that are exhibited observedly in the sky by all or some celestial motions and by which those astronomical construction problems will be inspired can only be the shapes of the paths of celestial motions. The solutions to construction problems will involve activity on the astronomer's part as if his goal were to make something and not to obtain knowledge of forms (527a1–b7). Guided by the astronomer's mind in the cognitive state called "mathematical thought" (διάνοια), whereby forms are approached not in themselves but indirectly via their sensible representations (*R.* 6, 510c2–511a3), this activity can be literally visible, if it is presented in drawing, or mentally visualizable, if geometrical objects are manipulated and operated upon in the astronomer's mind for the construction to be effected. In Archytas' solution to the problem of doubling the cube, probably the earliest of those put forth in the fourth century BC, the construction is effected by the intersection of two curves, one generated as the intersection of a cylinder and a semicircle rotating about one of the endpoints of its diameter, the other generated as the intersection of the cylinder and a triangle rotating about one of its sides: the kinematic construction of these curves could only have been mentally visualizable at the time, not represented in drawing. Moreover, in view of the emphasis Plato lays in this context on the inconstancy and variegation of the celestial motions that prompt the mind to learn about the forms visibly and variably realized therein, a difference between these motions and all mentally visualizable change used to investigate the forms at issue should be stressed. Unlike the observable motions of bodies, mentally visualizable changes involving mathematical objects, themselves mental realizations of unchanging forms, do not exhibit any variation: to use once again Archytas' solution to the problem of doubling the cube, the semicircle and the triangle rotate with constant speeds and periods of rotation, whatever these might be (and provided, or course, that one is interested in their rotations after the curves they describe on the cylinder have met), while the shape of the path they describe as they intersect the cylinder is fixed by the shapes of the intersecting surfaces. Unlike the observable motions of bodies, in other words, the mentally visualizable changes, to which the mental realizations of unchanging forms of mathematical objects are subjected in the production of solutions to geometrical construction problems, do resemble forms, though motion and all change are in fact completely foreign to forms.

It must be such motions that the diverse decorative patterns visible in the sky, which can only be all or some celestial motions, are unfavorably compared with as much deficient in the crucial passage where Plato has Socrates explain to Glaucon how the advanced astronomy he envisions will help the soul look really upwards, unlike contemporary astronomy which is unfortunately restricted to sensibles. It will do so in this manner: "Since these diverse decorative patterns in the sky have been made in what is visible, they will be regarded as the most beautiful and exact of their kind but as much inferior to the true ones, motions that are performed relative to one another and carry along what undergoes them with invariant fastness and invariant slowness, in true number and all true figures, all of which can be grasped by mathematical thought, not sight" (529c6–d5).[41] One

---

41 ταῦτα μὲν τὰ ἐν τῷ οὐρανῷ ποικίλματα, ἐπείπερ ἐν ὁρατῷ πεποίκιλται, κάλλιστα μὲν ἡγεῖσθαι καὶ ἀκριβέστατα τῶν τοιούτων ἔχειν, τῶν δὲ ἀληθινῶν πολὺ ἐνδεῖν, ἃς τὸ ὂν τάχος καὶ ἡ οὖσα βραδυτὴς ἐν τῷ ἀληθινῷ ἀριθμῷ καὶ πᾶσι τοῖς ἀληθέσι σχήμασι φοράς τε πρὸς ἄλληλα φέρεται καὶ τὰ ἐνόντα φέρει, ἃ δὴ λόγῳ μὲν καὶ διανοίᾳ ληπτά, ὄψει δ' οὔ. τὸ ὂν τάχος καὶ ἡ οὖσα βραδυτὴς φορᾶς φέρεται καὶ τὰ ἐνόντα φέρει is strange, but cf. φέρεται γὰρ καὶ ἐν φορᾷ αὐτῶν ἡ κίνησις πέφυκεν in *Tht.* 156d2–3, from which it is a small step to τὸ ὂν τάχος καὶ ἡ οὖσα βραδυτὴς φορᾶς φέρεται καὶ τὰ ἐνόντα φέρει in view of τάχος δὲ καὶ βραδυτὴς ἔνι τῇ κινήσει αὐτῶν in *Tht.* 156c8. τὰ ἐνόντα, sc. φοραῖς, in our passage can be identified as the generating objects; cf. ἡ γραμμὴ ἡ τοῦ κύκλου ἐν φορᾷ ἐστίν in [Arist.] *Mech.* 851b34–35. They are not the heavenly bodies visible in the sky, as Burnyeat (2000) 59 has it: τὰ ἐνόντα must be invisible, like the motions that carry them. Mourelatos (1981) 2–5 and 27–30 seems to assume that τὰ ἐνόντα are other φοραί, all of these motions being the revolutions of concentric circles and rotations of concentric spheres. But there is no reason to see circles and spheres in the passage; nothing in it or its context hints at these figures.

expects that the diverse decorative patterns in the sky are unfavorably compared with forms, the true decorative patterns (τῶν ἀληθινῶν, sc. ποικιλμάτων) that do not exhibit variability, unlike their sensible manifestations, and thus are not in the heavens, unless in a metaphorical sense, or anywhere else. One also expects that these forms are forms of geometrical objects visibly realized in a varying manner in the heavens as ever-changing shapes of paths of all or some celestial motions. Truth (ἀλήθεια) is indeed what geometry draws the soul to, insofar as the objects of its study are unchanging forms, though they are accessed via construction problems, as if they were subject to coming into being (527a1–b10); moreover, inferiority or deficiency is an attribute of sensibles compared to forms manifested in them (cf. *Phd.* 74d4–75a4). In a surprising move, however, Plato has Socrates make clear that the true decorative patterns are some motions.[42] This leaves no doubt that the visible and diverse decorative patterns in the heavens compared disparagingly with them are celestial motions, but it suggests that Plato is committed to forms of motions and that it is these forms that ought to be investigated in astronomy via geometric construction problems. Moreover, the invariance of the fastness and slowness of these true motions relative to one another is described by the present participle of the verb *is* (τὸ ὂν τάχος καὶ ἡ οὖσα βραδυτής), which suggests that they, just like those motions they belong to, are beings, i.e. forms. This is also suggested by the description of the numbers and the figures with which these motions are performed as true (ἐν τῷ ἀληθινῷ ἀριθμῷ καὶ πᾶσι τοῖς ἀληθέσι σχήμασι): the true numbers seem to be the invariant numerical measures of the fastness and slowness of the motions that are said to be the true decorative patterns, the true figures being the invariant shapes of the trajectories of these motions. As it is, given the context of the passage under discussion, Plato seems to posit in it forms of motions with fixed, as it could only befit them, speeds, periods and shapes of paths that could only be themselves forms, form-numbers and forms of geometrical shapes communing with one another and thereby constituting forms of motions: according to Plato, therefore, to help the soul look really upwards, astronomy ought to look up away from the visible and varying celestial motions to the intelligible and necessarily unvarying forms of motions that are realized visibly and, again necessarily, varyingly as celestial motions.

The concept of forms of motions seems to be untenable, however. Forms commune with one another intrinsically, but the shapes of paths of moving sensibles can participate in an indefinitely large number of forms of geometrical objects and, similarly, the measures of their speeds and periods, if their motions are

---

42 They cannot be constellations *pace* Bulmer-Thomas (1984) 108–109; cf. Burnyeat (2000) 60 n. 88.

periodic, can participate in form-numbers of an indefinitely large range: it would be a bit of a stretch to posit an intrinsic relationship between the measures of the speeds and periods of motions and the shapes of their paths, hence the communion of the relevant forms in which they participate and which thus jointly are some higher forms, the forms of motions.[43] Furthermore, it would be rather strange if Plato required of astronomy the investigation of forms of motions by means of geometrical construction problems. In this case what ought to be produced would certainly be kinematic models assumed to be better approximations to the forms of motions at issue than their shifting realizations as celestial motions. In Greek geometry, however, to which Plato clearly wants astronomy to be really reduced, motion enters constructions not as what is to be produced but as a means to it, and what is to be effected with such means is a geometric object or structure whose form, to put it in Platonic terms, can be indirectly approached only thereby.

Thus, since Plato strongly suggests that the astronomical construction problems will be inspired not by the kinematic but by the geometrical variation that is exhibited in celestial motions, it is preferable to assume that this variation is observed in the shapes of the paths of celestial motions, and that it is exactly these shapes that ought to be constructed by astronomers in order to glean forms of geometrical objects imperfectly realized as ever-shifting paths of celestial motions. As said above, the constructions can be plausibly assumed to be effected kinematically, by mentally visualizing geometrical objects undergoing motions which, in their idealized fixity, are different from the visible motions of bodies and form-like. It is compared with these motions, which are described in terms suitable to forms, that the visible and diverse decorative patterns in the sky, all or only some celestial motions, are said to be much deficient in the passage discussed in this section.[44]

---

[43] On the form of motion in *Sph.* 254b7–255e7, one of the five forms included among the greatest, see Silverman (2002) 158.

[44] If τὰ ἐνόντα in *R.* 7, 529c6–d5, are geometrical figures that move so as to generate other geometrical objects, which geometrical objects could be generators and which generated? There is no hint in this passage or in its context that Plato wanted to answer this question. Post (1944) 299 mentions lines produced by the movement of points, lines and planes (he also suggests that Plato's future astronomy will include mechanics, which can be ruled out as completely unlikely). τὰ ἀληθῆ σχήματα are identified by Burnyeat (2000) 59 with spherical shapes of paths of motion but he does not explain what it is that moves. Robins (1995) 373–378 thinks that τὰ ἀληθῆ σχήματα are circular paths traced out by the rotating regular, or Platonic, polyhedra inscribed in spheres. But circles or semicircles, spheres or other solids are not hinted at in *R.* 7, 529c6–d5, or in its context. As for the regular polyhedra, the astronomical significance accorded in the

This comparison highlights the superiority of approaching forms realized in various contents of the physical world not via the relevant sensibles and the senses but by means of mathematics, an approach which does not break away completely from the senses in that it cannot avoid treating its true subject matter, forms, as a kind of rarefied sensibles that are subject to change, motion and coming to be. All this has already been made clear in the similes of the divided line and the cave. The comparison, however, seems to serve another goal too, one more closely related to its context. Compared to the motions that will be used in their investigation, the visible decorative patterns in the sky, i.e. celestial motions, are deficient because, unlike those other motions, they exhibit variations in their fastness and slowness, equivalently in the numbers measuring their fastness and slowness, and in the figures that are the shapes of their paths. The motions that will be used in the investigation of celestial motions are "true". As in the case of forms, what holds of them does not change: they are so fast and slow as they are, without variation, hence the use of the present participle of the verb *is* for the description of their invariant fastness and slowness as if these motions were beings, forms; thus the numbers measuring the fastness and slowness of these motions do not change but hold true of them always as true numbers, and the properties of the figures that are the shapes of the paths of these motions also hold true of these figures always, making them true, i.e. unchanging, figures. In view of the reference to the inconstancy of the periods of the celestial motions a few lines after the comparison of celestial motions with those that will be used in astronomy to investigate them, it can be self-evidently assumed that fastness and slowness in the comparison refer to periods. The particle *and* (καί) in the phrase "invariant fastness and invariant slowness in true number" (529d2–3: τὸ ὂν τάχος καὶ ἡ οὖσα βραδυτὴς ἐν τῷ ἀληθινῷ ἀριθμῷ) can be used to link two alternatives irrespective of which one is the case:[45] the point seems to be that in geometrical

---

Timaeus only to the dodecahedron can be plausibly understood in a non-kinematic manner (see ch. 1 n. 87). There is no reason to think that Plato presaged Kepler and his *Mysterium Cosmographicum*. Given (a) the assimilation of the future astronomy to geometry in R. 7, 530b6–c6, (b) the emphasis in R. 7, 527a1–b11, on the fact that the objects really studied in geometry are not subject to change as well as generation and decay, and (c) Aristotle's description in *Metaph*. B 2, 997b12–998a6, of Platonic astronomy as a science of what is immobile, it is unlikely that the future astronomy will define uniform, circular motions (Mueller [1992] 192–194); or that it is to be identified with the elementary spherical astronomy e.g. in Autolycus' *On the Moving Sphere* ("spherics"; Mueller [1981] 103–111); or with a science of pure kinematics that will focus on the revolution of concentric circles and spheres (Mourelatos [1981] 2–5 and 27–30); or, in general, that the "geometrical" objects it will be really concerned with are in motion.

45 See Denniston (1954²) 292.

construction problems, such as those that will be inspired by the shifting figures of the paths of celestial motions, whether the periods of visualized revolutions are long or short does not matter at all: they are just assumed to be constant. When Socrates makes the comparison, however, no mention of periods has already been made, and fastness and slowness can just as well be understood to refer to the speed of motions at issue, about which the same point is made. Whether the speed of visualized motions, be they revolutions of not, employed in geometrical constructions is slow or fast is irrelevant: these motions are just assumed to be uniform, "in true number", though their magnitudes (the specific "true" numbers) are also irrelevant.

Plato might very well have intended his audience to draw this conclusion in order to help them recognize those specific celestial motions which, since they exhibit geometrical variety in the shifting shape of their paths, will inspire, as will appear soon, astronomy to turn its attention to geometrical construction problems. Compared with the motions that will be employed in the kinematic constructions of the future astronomy, the celestial motions that will inspire these constructions are inferior because they are not uniform but instead slow down and speed up. Now, the inconstancy of all celestial motions Plato will stress below with regard to their periods can be plausibly assumed to apply to their speeds as well. But, since he has not yet made Socrates point this out, one can be expected to understand the comparison only in light of astronomy and thus identify the celestial motions at issue here with the non-uniform zodiacal motions of the moon, the sun and the five planets. The comparison, that is, excludes the diurnal motion of the so-called fixed stars along their circles on the celestial sphere or, equivalently, the diurnal rotation of this sphere, on which the stars can be thought to be fixed, about its axis: this motion is uniform, for it reflects the actual uniform rotation of the Earth about its axis in the opposite direction, and is also self-evidently excluded because the shapes of the paths it describes, parallel circles on a sphere, do not exhibit any variation (by Plato's lights there is, of course, no truly everlasting constancy in any aspect of all celestial motions). The zodiacal motions of the moon, the sun and the planets, on the other hand, are non-uniform since they are actually motions in ellipses, whether real, in the case of the moon (about the Earth) and the planets (about the sun), or apparent, in the case of the sun, whose zodiacal motion reflects the annual motion of the Earth about the sun.[46] Moreover, given the geometrical variety the celestial motions at issue are

---

[46] There is no mention of or clear allusion to the phenomenon in Plato's works. But in the case of the sun it is manifested as the inequality of the seasons which was known to Euctemon and Meton in the fifth century BC (Simp. *in Cael.* 497.15–24 [Heiberg]). A papyrus dated to 190 BC lists

assumed to present in their paths, they can be plausibly identified with the zodiacal motions of the planets, the only celestial motions known in antiquity to exhibit striking variation in the shape of their paths due to retrograde motion.

2.10 Planetary retrograde motion and Plato

The generally eastward zodiacal motion of a planet is often seen to be interrupted. The planet appears to be stationary in the sky (first station), then begins to move again, though in the opposite direction, but after a while stops for a second time (second station), and when its motion resumes, the direction is once again to the east. As a result of this reversal in the direction of its motion (retrogradation), the planet is seen to trace out a looping or zigzag path; the shape of a retrograde path is not the same from one retrogradation to the next, a marked deviation from circularity in the path of the planet's motion in the background of the zodiac. Planetary retrogradations are as spectacular as they are puzzling within a geocentric worldview. The phenomenon is explained easily from a heliocentric point of view, given the different sizes of the orbits in which the planets move around the sun and their unequal orbital speeds. A planet's threading its way along the background of the zodiac, with variably shaped retrograde bends and loops distributed at irregular intervals, can be statically described in metaphorical terms as a "decorative design" (ποίκιλμα), i.e. as an intricate embroidered design or a tracery on a vault, the celestial sphere, against the background of which the zodiacally moving planet is observed to trace out its elaborately shaped and always changing path. On the other hand, the motions of the moon and the sun against the background of the zodiacal constellations appear to follow a plain circular path.[47]

---

the lengths of the seasons as determined by Euctemon and Aristotle's contemporary Callippus of Cyzicus; see Neugebauer (1975) 686–687. Perhaps Euctemon and Meton did not discover the phenomenon of the inequality of the seasons and its cause, the non-uniform zodiacal motion of the sun, based on observations. The lengths of the seasons attributed to Euctemon in the papyrus seem to be an attempt to come up with a scheme for distributing 365 days as evenly as possible over the seasons; see Neugebauer (1975) 628. The non-uniformity in the zodiacal motion of the moon is quite easy to observe (because it causes the interval between successive phases to vary considerably; see Kaler [2002] 246) and it could have led early Greek astronomers to suspect the anomaly in the zodiacal motions of the sun and the planets. Aristotle is aware that all zodiacal motion is not uniform; see *Cael.* B 6, 288a13–17, and Kouremenos (2010) 3.2.1.

47 On retrogradations see e.g. Bowen (2013) 20–25 with helpful diagrams.

Scholars have doubted that fourth-century-BC Greek astronomers had knowledge of planetary retrogradations and have argued that passages in texts that can be thought to show awareness of the phenomenon before the second century BC need not do so.⁴⁸ As for Plato, his knowledge of the phenomenon may be implicit where he has Timaeus say (40c3–d3) that to discuss the dances of the zodiacally moving celestial objects and their approaches to one another, "the circlings of their circles backwards in relation to themselves" (τὰς τῶν κύκλων πρὸς ἑαυτοὺς ἐπανακυκλήσεις) and their advances (προχωρήσεις), their conjunctions and oppositions and their coming to be behind and in front of one another, which are portents of things to come for the ignorant, would be a vain effort without seeing these images (τὸ λέγειν ἄνευ δι' ὄψεως τούτων αὖ τῶν μιμημάτων μάταιος ἂν εἴη πόνος). The passage leaves no doubt about the importance Plato attaches to observational knowledge of the sky, of the zodiacal motions and the related phenomena in this case, all of which are for him images of forms.⁴⁹ Nor is there any reason to doubt that in the case of the planets "the circlings of their circular motions backwards in relation to themselves" can refer to the reversals in the direction of planetary zodiacal motion before an episode of retrograde motion and after it:⁵⁰ in the *Statesman* the same noun (ἀνακύκλησις)⁵¹ is used for circular motion (rotation) in the opposite direction and the verb "to circle backwards" (ἀνακυκλεῖσθαι) for undergoing circular motion in reverse direction (269d5–270a8).⁵² The objection that *Ti.* 40c3–d3 refers not only to the planets but also to the sun and the moon whose zodiacal motions do not exhibit the phenomenon of

---

48 See Bowen (2013) 230–248; cf. Goldstein (1997) 4.
49 Cf. the use of the term μιμήματα at *Ti.* 50b5–c6 in the sense of εἰκών (as is clear from 52c1–5).
50 Zodiacal motion is assumed here to be simply the rotation of a circle, which carries the zodiacally moving celestial object, about its center; see below.
51 The absence of ἐπί does not seem to be significant; cf. Bowen (2013) 238 n. 40.
52 Bowen (2013) 238 n. 40 acknowledges the use of ἀνακύκλησις and ἀνακυκλεῖσθαι in *Plt.* but does not seem to consider it important, although ἀνακύκλησις is a *hapax* in the Platonic corpus and the cognate verb occurs only once again in it, at *Ti.* 37a5, where it is used in a related sense (the cosmic soul is said to be circling backwards in relation to itself [αὐτή τε ἀνακυκλουμένη πρὸς αὐτήν] because it is made up of eight homocentric circles of which the seven inner ones are revolving oppositely to the outermost one). ἐπανακύκλησις is another *hapax* in the Platonic corpus. All three words do not occur in surviving pre-Platonic texts and do not reoccur until much later. ἐπανακυκλήσεις and προχωρήσεις are usually assumed to be retrograde motions and direct motions (in the main, eastward, direction of zodiacal motion); cf. Bowen (2013) 233 n. 33. It seems preferable to understand these words in a general sense, ἐπανακύκλησις as reversal in the direction of a circle's rotation, from eastward (direct motion) to westward (retrograde motion) and vice versa, and προχώρησις as advance after a reversal.

retrogradation does not carry much force:[53] the zodiacally moving celestial objects that come to be behind and in front of one another purportedly sending portents of future things to the superstitious ignorant are clearly only the sun and the moon, not the planets, even if Plato knew, as Aristotle did, that the planets occult one another, a piece of knowledge acquired from the Egyptians according to Aristotle (*Mete.* A 6, 343b28–30). The passage can very well mix together phenomena peculiar to the planets such as retrograde motion and to the sun and the moon such as their purportedly ominous eclipses since all these phenomena are related to the zodiacal motion, which is common to this septet of celestial objects.

Nor is there any reason to suspect that, when in *Republic* 10 at least Mars is said in the intriguing myth of Er to have been seen "circling backwards" (ἐπανακυκλούμενον) as it was moving oppositely to the diurnal rotation with the third largest angular speed of zodiacal motion, the planet is said to have been seen returning to the main, eastward, direction of its zodiacal motion after a time of retrograde motion. The mechanism whose eight close-fitting circular components correspond each to a celestial motion (see above n. 9) is first said to have been rotating as a whole in the direction of the diurnal rotation, whereas the seven inner components, whose rotations answer to the zodiacal motions of the five planets, the sun and the moon, also rotated slowly each in the opposite direction:[54] of these inner components, the eighth moved most quickly (the Moon), the seventh, the sixth and the fifth all moved with the second largest speed (the sun, Venus and Mercury), the fourth, which, as was observed, had been circling backwards, moved with the third largest (Mars, 617b2–3: τρίτον δὲ φορᾷ ἰέναι, ὡς σφίσι φαίνεσθαι, ἐπανακυκλούμενον τὸν τέταρτον), the third moved with the fourth largest (Jupiter) and the second moved with the fifth largest (Saturn; 617a4–b4).[55] What is described here as backwards-moving can be understood to be simply the eastward rotation of the component carrying Mars, a rotation opposite to the diurnal rotation; if so, it is not a phenomenon peculiar to this planet and the other two planets mentioned after Mars is said to have been seen to be

---

53 The objection is put forth by Bowen (2013) 238.
54 On their slowness compared to the diurnal rotation cf. Arist. *Cael.* B 10, 291a34–b3.
55 κυκλεῖσθαι δὲ δὴ στρεφόμενον τὸν ἄτρακτον ὅλον μὲν τὴν αὐτὴν φοράν, ἐν δὲ τῷ ὅλῳ περιφερομένῳ τοὺς μὲν ἐντὸς ἑπτὰ κύκλους τὴν ἐναντίαν τῷ ὅλῳ ἠρέμα περιφέρεσθαι, αὐτῶν δὲ τούτων τάχιστα μὲν ἰέναι τὸν ὄγδοον, δευτέρους δὲ καὶ ἅμα ἀλλήλοις τόν τε ἕβδομον καὶ ἕκτον καὶ πέμπτον· τρίτον δὲ φορᾷ ἰέναι, ὡς σφίσι φαίνεσθαι, ἐπανακυκλούμενον τὸν τέταρτον, τέταρτον δὲ τὸν τρίτον καὶ πέμπτον τὸν δεύτερον. The bearing rings of the celestial mechanism are counted from the outside, first being the outermost ring whose rotation corresponds to the diurnal rotation. There is no reason to translate ὡς σφίσι φαίνεσθαι "as appeared to them". Nothing in the text suggests a concern with appearances in contrast to what is the case.

backwards-moving, all the more so since the particle referring to the phenomenon and the accompanying relative clause can be construed in common with the ordinals ("the third" and "the second") referring to Jupiter and Saturn.

The repetition, however, of what has been stated before the listing of the magnitude of the speed of zodiacal motion in decreasing order, i.e. that the components of the celestial mechanism producing all cases of zodiacal motion rotated in a direction opposite to that of the diurnal rotation, is unnecessary in the middle of the very short list. The relative clause, moreover, gives the strong impression that it is intended to draw attention to something peculiar that had been observed about the zodiacal motion of Mars at least and is not part of an otiose repetition of a point just made about the direction of this motion. We get rid of the repetition if we understand the backwards-circling as not simply eastward rotation but instead as eastward rotation which at the time of observation had just resumed after an episode of retrograde motion in the opposite direction. At that time all seven inner components of the celestial mechanism that produce the zodiacal motion the moon, the sun and the planets had been observed rotating oppositely to the diurnal rotation: but, when next in the narrative the magnitude of the angular speed of zodiacal motion eastwards is listed in decreasing order, the narrator adds that at least in the case of Mars the eastward, hence principal, direction of zodiacal motion had been seen to have just resumed after a period of retrograde motion westwards, whose end had thus also been observed. Since each planet, the sun or the moon is assumed to move zodiacally eastwards as it rides what resembles a rotating bearing ring of a mechanism made up of eight such close-fitting rings, in the myth of Er planetary retrograde motion is a simple circular backwards-moving and its invariable path, a circular arc, cannot account for the geometrical variation in the shape of the path of actual planetary retrogradations.

The myth includes personified causes of all celestial motion and one of these agents can produce simple planetary retrogradations by making the eastwards-rotating bearing ring of a planet rotate backwards for a while.[56] The model of the heavens whose close-fitting bearing rings correspond each to a celestial motion is moved by the three Fates: Clotho spins periodically its outermost part, whose rotation answers to the diurnal rotation, with her right hand; Atropos spins periodically the seven inner components, whose rotations answer to the zodiacal motions of the five planets, the sun and the moon, with her left hand (whether she

---

[56] The following is an elaboration of Knorr (1990) 313–317.

moves necessarily all of them each time she acts is left unspecified);[57] Lachesis, though, is said to use both hands in turn, each clearly moving a section of the contraption turned by one of her sisters with either the same or the opposite hand (617c5–d1).[58] It is a reasonable assumption that Lachesis is presented as stepping in between successive spinnings of the outermost component by her sister Clotho and between successive spinnings of (all or some of) the seven inner components by Atropos; but, apart from the use of both of her hands in contrast to her two sisters and her standing in for both of them, the text does not give further details on her role as mover. Now, the choice of Clotho's and Atropos' hands need not be accidental since in the *Timaeus* the direction of the diurnal rotation is assumed to be to the right and that of the zodiacal motion to be to the left (36c4–d1).[59] Which component of the celestial mechanism is moved by which of Lachesis' hands, and thus the direction of the motion imparted to each when she must exercise her motive capacity, is left unspecified in the text. But, if Plato assumes in the myth of Er, as in that in the *Statesman*, that periodically the direction of the rotation of the cosmos, the diurnal rotation, reverses (*Plt.* 268d5–270d1), it could well be with her left hand that Lachesis spins the outermost component of the celestial mechanism when her turn comes but with her right hand that she spins of all seven inner components only the five that carry the planets, thereby producing retrograde motion of each planet.

Singling out Mars as the only planet seen undergoing retrograde motion can be plausibly explained in view of the fact that, compared to Jupiter's and Saturn's, its retrograde motion is considerably more prominent and easily observed, the retrograde motion of the other two planets being also difficult to observe because it occurs when these planets are close to the sun.[60] The assumption that

---

57 By spinning periodically the outermost part of the mechanism with her right hand Clotho is assumed to move the entire mechanism in the same direction so as for the participation of the planets, the sun and the moon in the diurnal rotation to be taken into account. Atropos' hand is needed to impart to the inner parts a second motion in addition to that of the mechanism as a whole; see 617a4–7.

58 καὶ τὴν μὲν Κλωθὼ τῇ δεξιᾷ χειρὶ ἐφαπτομένην συνεπιστρέφειν τοῦ ἀτράκτου τὴν ἔξω περιφοράν, διαλείπουσαν χρόνον, τὴν δὲ Ἄτροπον τῇ ἀριστερᾷ τὰς ἐντὸς αὖ ὡσαύτως· τὴν δὲ Λάχεσιν ἐν μέρει ἑκατέρας ἑκατέρᾳ τῇ χειρὶ ἐφάπτεσθαι. After ἑκατέρας the genitive τῆς περιφορᾶς is to be supplied, sc. τῆς ἔξω and τῆς ἐντός, all inner parts of the celestial mechanism (περιφοραί) being referred to collectively as one; cf. Arist. *Cael.* B 2, 285b28, where the phrase ἡ δευτέρα περιφορά is used for the zodiacal motion of all five planets.

59 Cf., though, *Lg.* 6, 760d2, and [*Epin.*] 987b2–6.

60 Theo of Smyrna 145.18–19 (Hiller) paraphrases Plato's τρίτον δὲ φορᾷ ἰέναι, ὡς σφίσι φαίνεσθαι, ἐπανακυκλούμενον τὸν τέταρτον as τρίτον δὲ φορᾷ ἰέναι, ὅν φασι φαίνεσθαι ἐπανακυκλούμενον μάλιστα τῶν ἄλλων, i.e. Mars whose retrogradations are most prominent. It

Lachesis spins with her right hand only five of the seven inner parts of the celestial mechanism, and not all of them at the same time as not all planets are in retrograde motion simultaneously, is not problematic given the scant detail provided on her task; if so, Atropos too cannot move with her left hand all seven inner components of the celestial mechanism at the same time but nothing in the text entails that she applies her left hand simultaneously to all of them.

That Lachesis uses not her right but her left hand in Clotho's stead and likewise not her left but her right hand in Atropos' stead is apposite in a context full of riddling descriptions of details of the cosmic mechanism. Bringing from the *Statesman* the shift in the direction of the diurnal motion to bear on the myth of Er in *Republic* 10 might seem questionable. However, in the *Statesman* this reversal is an imaginative mythical device clearly intended to illustrate a variation on the point made in *Republic* 7 in relation to the instability necessarily inherent in the celestial periods (cf. 2.9): what is bodily and sensible like the celestial objects and their motions cannot be assumed to always be in the same state and behave unvaryingly even if it has been arranged as beautifully as possible by the demiurge, which is the case with the heavens (530a4–b5). According to the *Statesman*, even the diurnal rotation, the celestial motion that seems to be the most uniform and unvarying, will periodically reverse its direction, a phenomenon recorded in the myth of Atreus and his brother Thyestes, when the god by whom the cosmos has been put together will stop for some reason following and controlling it and the necessity inherent in the bodily cosmos will assert itself. Moreover, the period after which this shift is assumed to occur (*Plt.* 269c4–d2) must be that whose length is said in *Republic* 8 to be the "perfect number" (546b4–5) and which is the last of the celestial periods listed in *Republic* 7 (see above n. 6); the context in *Republic* 8 also suggests that great catastrophes occur on a global scale after this period has elapsed, as is explicitly said in the myth of the *Statesman*. It is not unlikely, therefore, that the reversal in the direction of the diurnal rotation, another of the ideas that inform this myth, is tacitly presupposed in the last book of the *Republic*. In the *Statesman* the cause of the reversal is a necessity that is innate in the bodily cosmos and takes over when god does not follow its rotation

---

is possible that the words μάλιστα τῶν ἄλλων had been present in Theo's edition of the *Republic*, and an easy emendation of the text by including them (proposed by Burnet [1914] 304 n. 1) would not be unattractive: τρίτον δὲ φορᾷ ἰέναι, ὡς σφίσι φαίνεσθαι, ἐπανακυκλούμενον μάλιστα τῶν ἄλλων τὸν τέταρτον. If so, the text contains an explicit reference to retrograde motion, not as something seen by the observers (apart from the fact that they compared the rates of lunar, solar and planetary zodiacal motions oppositely to the diurnal rotation, nothing in the text suggests that they spent so much time observing as they would need to compare the retrogradations of all five planets) but as a note to the reader.

guiding it, whereas in the myth of Er it will be the intervention of a mythical agent. In the myth of Er, however, the three Fates are said to be daughters of personified necessity, on whose lap the cosmic mechanism turns spun by her daughters (617b4–5) and as whose steely spinning spindle is described the shaft of light running through the poles of rotation of the cosmic mechanism, its axis (see above n. 9): if the reversal in the diurnal rotation of the cosmos is indeed tacitly presupposed in the myth of Er, the depiction of its cause is simply a different take on its depiction in the myth of the *Statesman*.

The upshot of the above is that there is no reason to deny that Plato was aware of planetary retrograde motion even if we assume in view of the simple mechanical model of the heavens rotating on Necessity's lap in the imaginative myth of Er that he did consider the paths along which the planets move zodiacally to be circles, like the paths of solar and lunar zodiacal motion. The moon, the sun and the five planets are said in the *Timaeus* too to have been placed by the demiurge in seven concentric rotating circles (38c3–e3), all of them in the same plane which is oblique to another concentric circle encompassing them and corresponding to the equator of the oppositely rotating celestial sphere or, in cosmological terms, to the equator of the diurnally rotating cosmos (cf. 36b6–d7 and 39c1–2). Thus one might conclude that, according to Plato, the zodiacal motions not only of the moon and the sun but also of the planets are circular. But it should be kept in mind that the circles at issue in this passage are actually the invisible circular motions constituting the soul that enlivens the cosmos and causes the visible celestial motions: even if the moon, the sun and the planets are made to move zodiacally by invisible circular motions, this does not entail that the visible zodiacal motions of all these seven celestial objects follow circular paths, no matter why this might be so in two cases. At any rate, in the tenth book of the *Laws* it is said that, being in circular and uniform self-motion is a mere image for the mysterious way by which rational soul brings about all celestial motion (896d5–899a10). Circularity of path and uniformity of speed symbolizes the stability and orderliness of reason itself as cause of motion: if motion is brought about by reason, it necessarily exhibits the hallmarks of its cause to whatever extent it does so, but from this it does not follow that its path is always necessarily a circle, like the symbol of its cause, as if no other shape than the circle had symmetry or symmetries, which is most probably why Plato uses the circle as the path of uniform motion symbolizing rational causality.

Indeed, circular and uniform motion seems to be an image not only for the mysterious way by which reason causes all celestial motion but also for some of the effect itself. If the deviations from uniformity in all zodiacal motion and from circularity of path in planetary zodiacal motion alone are ignored, then in a first approximation, and ignoring all random variations due to their being motion of bodies, the zodiacal motions of the moon, the sun and the five planets can be plausibly assumed to be circular, uniform and coplanar, just like the invisible motions symbolizing their causes. As seen above, Plato has Timaeus employ the term *images* to describe the dances of the planets, the sun and the moon as they undergo their zodiacal motions along concentric circles and exhibit various phenomena. The zodiacal dances, circular or not, and all their phenomena are images insofar as forms are manifested in them; at the same time, as images can very well be also described the circles in which all these seven celestial objects are approximately assumed to dance zodiacally, just like the invisible circular motions causing these visible motions that are naturally assumed to be of the same kind as their cause are said in *Laws* 10 to be an image of the reason bringing about all celestial motion.

As paths of the zodiacal motions, these circles are an abstract toy-model of the paths of zodiacal motions that captures only their broad features, as is suggested by the fact that all seven circles are assumed to be coplanar. It is a variation on the toy-model of the heavens in the myth of Er as a mechanical device whose eight components representing all celestial motions have their rims on the same plane (*R.* 10, 616d7–e2), as if the planets, the sun and the moon moved zodiacally on the plane of the celestial equator. As seen above, it can mimic in a rough fashion even the most complicated phenomenon of planetary retrograde motion. But its place is in myths such as that of Er or *Timaeus*, which Plato would call by the same name, images that are helpful for purposes of illustration but can by no means show the richness of what they dimly depict, and in introductions to elementary astronomy. Part of the main lesson of the astronomy that will be taught at school to all future citizens of the Cretan colony planned in the *Laws* is that the moon, the sun or each planet moves zodiacally in a circle, always one and the same (7, 822c7–d1): according to *Laws* 1, to train well young children in a trade one gives them toy-models of its tools to play pleasurably with, images of its real tools (643b4–d4), which is an apt description of the childish notion that the path of all zodiacal motion is circular compared with a professional's knowledge of how complicated the shape of this path can be in the case of the planets.

Leaving aside the myth of Er, if we abandon the notion that in Plato's *Timaeus* the planets move zodiacally along circles, just as the sun and moon do, we do not have to deny him knowledge of retrogradations when he says that Venus and Mercury have been placed in circular motions causing zodiacal motion of the same period as the sun's but also possess a power contrary to the sun's, which can only be due to the motions enlivening them, and, as a result, overtake the sun and each is in turn overtaken by it (38d1–6). The phenomenon is the change of Venus and Mercury from an evening star to a morning star, which means that the planet has moved westwards for some time. It can be thought to involve in Plato's view not a change in the direction of zodiacal motion made possible by the power peculiar to these two planets to reverse it but only their falling behind the sun as all three celestial objects race in concentric circular tracks: peculiar to Venus and Mercury is a power not to reverse the direction of zodiacal motion but to fall behind the sun, as it moves zodiacally eastwards at a steady pace, and then catch up with and even overtake it, which does not entail knowledge of retrogradations.[61] However, if Plato does not think that the planets too move zodiacally in circles, this reading is not compelling.

If Plato hints in the *Timaeus* passage just discussed that the zodiacal motion of Venus and Mercury changes direction and thus that these planets exhibit retrograde motion, a probable reference to the fact that the other planets also do so can be read in the immediately following lines: τὰ δ' ἄλλα οἷ δὴ καὶ δι' ἃς αἰτίας ἰδρύσατο, εἴ τις ἐπεξίοι πάσας, ὁ λόγος πάρεργος ὢν πλέον ἂν ἔργον ὧν ἕνεκα λέγεται παράσχοι. Ταῦτα μὲν οὖν ἴσως τάχ' ἂν κατὰ σχολὴν ὕστερον τῆς ἀξίας τύχοι διηγήσεως (38d6–e3). The passage clearly concerns the other three planets and the adverb οἷ is usually translated "where": "As for the other planets, if one were to explain in detail where the demiurge enshrined them and to give all the reasons why he did so, the account, though not our main topic, would give us more difficulty than that for the sake of which was given. These issues might receive the attention they deserve later on at our leisure." Indeed, it has already been said that the moon has been placed in the first of the concentric circular motions, near their center, the sun in the second, Venus and Mercury in the next two; moreover, the text following immediately below (38e3–5) leaves no doubt that in the preceding lines the ordering of the moon, the sun and the planets is the main issue (it is not the sole topic, as the reference to Venus and Mercury clearly shows even if it does not betray awareness of planetary retrogradations). Plato has Timaeus decline to do for the three remaining planets what he has already done for the moon, the sun, Venus and Mercury, i.e. to order them according to the length of their zodiacal periods, although a few lines below he will have the lecturer hint at this ordering principle (39a2–3). The reason is that, as he will have Timaeus lament, the periods of the planets are not widely known (39c5–d2). Timaeus, of course, is presented as taking for granted that Venus and Mercury have the same zodiacal period as the sun, though Plato also has him skip over the

---

[61] See Bowen (2013) 236–237.

crucial detail that exactly for this reason they cannot be ordered relative to one another.

The adverb οἷ, however, with which the first indirect question is introduced, means not only "where" but also "whither". Although a verb like ἱδρύσατο, "enshrined", after this adverb in the sense "whither" seems inappropriate, for one would expect a verb of motion, the verb in this context does denote motion: it likens the planets, which are gods, to statues of gods set up in shrines, but what are likened to shrines are the circular motions and what are likened to statues are the planets that move zodiacally because of these shrine-like circular motions. Since the verb is used here in the sense "set up in the circular motions, as if in shrines, the planets, as if they were statues of gods, to thereby undergo zodiacal motion", the sense "where" of the adverb before the verb is appropriate, in view of the aorist, for the ending of the setting up, the specific circular motions in which the demiurge put the three remaining planets Mars, Jupiter and Saturn to endow them with zodiacal motion; but its other sense, "whither", also fits since the enshrining brings about perpetual zodiacal motion and all motion has direction. The indirect question introduced by this adverb comes right after the reference to Venus and Mercury overtaking the sun and being overtaken by it which can suggest awareness of the changes in the direction of their zodiacal motion and thus of the phenomenon of retrogradation. If there is no reason to assume that Plato is either unaware of this phenomenon or denies its reality, the indirect question suggests that he is aware that the other planets also exhibit changes in the direction of their zodiacal motions: "As for the other planets, if one were to explain in detail where the demiurge enshrined them [to move zodiacally] and whither and to give all the reasons why he did so etc."

If so, then in the passage under discussion Plato has Timaeus politely decline not only to order the planets Mars, Jupiter and Saturn according to the widely unequal lengths of their zodiacal periods but also to give an account of the changes in the direction of the zodiacal motion of all five planets. This phenomenon has probably been alluded to above in the discussion of Venus and Mercury, whose change from evening to morning star hints at their retrograding unmistakably if one is aware that in each case one and the same zodiacally moving body appears as both evening and morning star. But its explanation should provide an answer to the natural questions how and why, unlike in the cases of the moon and the sun, a circular motion with only one direction causes zodiacal motion of changing direction: in other words, it should be an account of the mysterious but as yet unknown way by which rational soul, symbolically likened to invisible circular and uniform motion, brings about all visible celestial motion, not all of which is circular and uniform, though certainly at issue here are deviations from the constancy of circularity and uniformity that are wholly products of reason, unlike, of course, those random variations celestial motions must exhibit since they are motions of bodies.

Plato seems to allude to the non-circular paths of planetary zodiacal motion when he points out that, of all celestial periods, most people are unfortunately aware only of the solar day, the tropical year and the synodic month: "Men, with very few exceptions, have not understood the periods of the other celestial objects, have no names for them, do not compare their numerical measures and thus in effect do not know that their wanderings, bewildering many and marvelously variegated, constitute time" (39c5–d2: τῶν δ' ἄλλων τὰς περιόδους οὐκ ἐννενοηκότες ἄνθρωποι, πλὴν ὀλίγοι τῶν πολλῶν, οὔτε ὀνομάζουσιν οὔτε πρὸς ἄλληλα συμμετροῦνται σκοποῦντες ἀριθμοῖς, ὥστε ὡς ἔπος εἰπεῖν οὐκ ἴσασιν χρόνον ὄντα τὰς τούτων πλάνας, πλήθει μὲν ἀμηχάνῳ χρωμένας, πεποικιλμένας δὲ θαυμαστῶς). As said above (2.1), the passage concerns the periods, in all probability zodiacal as well as synodic, of the five planets, whose "wanderings" are thus the paths of their zodiacal motions. Why would these motions be described as "marvelously variegated" (πεποικιλμένας θαυμαστῶς) if Plato did not want to hint at the phenomenon of planetary retrogradations? The verb used here (ποικίλλω) is cognate with the noun (ποικίλματα) used in *Republic* 7 for the intricately diverse geometrical patterns in the sky that future advanced astronomy will study geometrically so as to help the soul look really upwards and prepare it for philosophy: this description is best understood as a hint that the planets, unlike the moon and the sun, do not really move around the zodiac in neat concentric circles.

Plato can, of course, assume in the passage just translated that they do move zodiacally in such paths and refer not to these circular motions themselves as wanderings but to their combination with the diurnal rotation, in which all planets participate just as the sun and the moon also do: these two simultaneous motions combine into a spiral motion, which in our very few sources for the early history of Greek astronomy is first mentioned and correctly explained in the *Timaeus* (39a5–b2). What Plato calls "wanderings" of the moon, the sun and the planets in *Laws* 7, their following not a single path but many (822a4–8), is their moving in successive days along parallel circular paths which are actually the connected turns of continuous spirals, since neither the sun nor the moon exhibits the phenomenon of retrogradations; in this context it is emphasized that each of these luminaries always moves in one and the same circular path. It is, however, unlikely that Plato would refer to the parallel turns of these spiral paths, which are symmetrically arranged on the surface of the celestial sphere, as "marvelously variegated". Moreover, in the *Timaeus* passage under discussion this description seems to pick out a feature peculiar to the zodiacal motion of the planets, but the spiral shape into which their zodiacal motion is twisted because of their simultaneous participation in the diurnal rotation does not in itself mark off their zodiacal motion from that of the moon and the sun. Nor is there any cogent reason to assume that in this passage Plato is interested not in the zodiacal motion of the planets itself and the marvelously variegated "wanderings" it exhibits, which can be plausibly identified with the phenomenon of retrogradation, but rather in its combination with the diurnal rotation and the resultant spiral movement.

At any rate, however, in *Laws* 7 that the moon, the sun and the planets move zodiacally each always in one and the same circle and just appear to move in many paths because this motion combines with the diurnal rotation into a resultant spiral motion is said to be the main lesson of the astronomy that will be taught at an introductory level to all citizens of the planned Cretan colony (822c7–d1). The use of an approximate image, circular motion, for the zodiacal motion of the planets is indeed suitable for an introductory course on astronomy. It is unlikely, however, that the celestial geometrical variation featuring in such a course, the spiral paths of the moon, the sun and the planets, are those intricately diverse geometrical patterns in the sky that a mathematically advanced astronomy will study geometrically in order to help the soul look really upwards (cf. n. 20).

"Helix" (ἕλιξ) is the word Plato uses in the *Timaeus* for the spirals traced out by the planets, the sun and the moon as they move zodiacally and at the same time participate in the diurnal rotation, and it also occurs in an aporetic Aristotelian passage where the belief in the existence of the so-called intermediates as objects studied in mathematics (see 1.2.3) is aporetically defended after it has been criticized. If the existence of intermediates is not posited, which objects astronomy studies is a question that arises naturally since one could argue that "astronomy is concerned neither with sensible lines nor with these heavens [we observe]. For sensible lines are not like the lines in geometrical proofs (because nothing sensible is as straight or circular [as in geometry], given that a ruler touches a circle not at a point but instead as Protagoras used to say taking exception to the geometers), nor are the motions and helixes of the heavens like those in astronomical proofs, nor do the celestial objects have the same nature as points" (*Metaph.* B 2, 997b34–998a6).[62] The helixes of the heavens are evidently

---

62 ἀλλὰ μὴν οὐδὲ τῶν αἰσθητῶν ἂν εἴη μεγεθῶν οὐδὲ περὶ τὸν οὐρανὸν ἡ ἀστρολογία τόνδε. οὔτε γὰρ αἱ αἰσθηταὶ γραμμαὶ τοιαῦταί εἰσιν οἵας λέγει ὁ γεωμέτρης (οὐθὲν γὰρ εὐθὺ τῶν αἰσθητῶν οὕτως οὐδὲ στρογγύλον· ἅπτεται γὰρ τοῦ κανόνος οὐ κατὰ στιγμὴν ὁ κύκλος ἀλλ' ὥσπερ Πρωταγόρας ἔλεγεν ἐλέγχων τοὺς γεωμέτρας), οὔθ' αἱ κινήσεις καὶ ἕλικες τοῦ οὐρανοῦ

the paths of some celestial motions but it is unlikely that they are the spirals of the *Timaeus*. Aristotle implies a mismatch between the observed paths of some celestial motions and their handling in the astronomy of his day but, since contemporary astronomers can be plausibly assumed to have interested themselves only in the overall shape of the paths of the celestial motions, it is unlikely that anybody at the time would have been concerned with a mismatch between the spirals of the *Timaeus* and the actual paths of the motions whose shapes these spirals were supposed to be. On the other hand, the paths of planetary retrograde motions are good candidates for Aristotle's observed helixes of the heavens whose shapes were not satisfactorily resembled by their theoretical counterparts in contemporary astronomical proofs, early attempts at a mathematical handling of the puzzling phenomenon of planetary retrograde motion. *Helix* is not inappropriate as a description of the shape of the path of retrograde motion: in anatomical contexts Aristotle uses the term to describe the twists of the intestines (*PA* Γ 14, 675b22–27) as well as the epididymis and the vas deferens (*GA* A 3, 717a23–29).[63]

ὅμοιαι περὶ ὧν ἡ ἀστρολογία ποιεῖται τοὺς λόγους, οὔτε τὰ σημεῖα τοῖς ἄστροις τὴν αὐτὴν ἔχει φύσιν.

63 In *Cael.* B 10, 291a34–b3, Aristotle assumes that each planet moves zodiacally along its own circle, as do the sun and the moon, and he calls all celestial objects τὰ ἐγκύκλια σώματα or τὰ ἐγκυκλίως φερόμενα σώματα (*Cael.* B 3, 286b6–7; *Mete.* A 2, 339a12–13). However, the unmoved and immaterial mover introduced in *Ph.* Θ as proximate cause of the first motion in the cosmos, and thus as ultimate cause of all motion and change eternally going on in the cosmos, is said to cause proximately the sole or most uniform motion (10, 267b3–4: καὶ ὁμαλὴς αὕτη ἡ κίνησης ἢ μόνη ἢ μάλιστα). The first motion has been shown to be uniform insofar as it is a circular motion (9, 265b11–16) and for Aristotle not only speed but also the shape of the trajectory is a feature in respect of which a motion can be called uniform (a motion is uniform if any part of its path coincides precisely with any other; see *Ph.* E 4, 228b15–28). As it is, when the first motion is said to be the sole or most uniform, it is implicitly compared with some other motions which lack uniformity, either in both respects or in one only, and compared to which the first motion is thus the sole or the most uniform motion respectively: but, since the first motion is the diurnal rotation, if it is implicitly compared with the zodiacal motions of the five planets, the sun and the moon, a comparison made explicitly in *Metaph.* Λ 8, 1073a23–34, which can be plausibly assumed to also be made implicitly in *Ph.* Θ, then in *Ph.* Θ Aristotle hints not only that zodiacal motion lacks uniform speed, as he says in *Cael.* B 6, 288a13–17 (see Kouremenos [2010] 3.2.1), but also that not all zodiacal motion is uniform with respect to the shape of its path and thus circular. Only the zodiacal motions of the five planets can be alluded to here to lack uniformity with respect to the shape of its path because of the episodes of retrograde motion, unless Aristotle suspected deviations from exact circularity in the case of solar and lunar zodiacal motion. Uniformity with respect to the shape of the path might also be implicitly denied to zodiacal motion wholesale or to most of its instances (in the case of the planets) in *Cael.* B 6, 288a13–17. The

2.11 Planetary retrograde motion and forms

Although the geometrical variation in the spiral paths of the moon, the sun and the five planets is much less intricate than that in the zodiacal paths of the five planets, realizing the existence of these spirals clearly serves for Plato the same purpose as will the advanced astronomy that, as he hopes, will study mathematically the much more elaborate geometrical variation in the zodiacal paths of the planets due to retrogradations. The Greeks certainly knew very early on that the place on the horizon where the sun rises gradually shifts from a southeastern point, where the sun rises at winter solstice, to a northeastern one, where the sun rises at summer solstice. Over the same period, the place of the sun's setting on the horizon is similarly displaced from a point in the southwest, where the sun sets at winter solstice, to a point in the northwest, where the sun sets at summer solstice (the sun rises and sets exactly in the east and west only at equinoxes, midway between the northernmost and southernmost limits to the motion of its rising and setting place). The direction of motion then reverses. The Greek word for solstice, *tropē* (see e.g. Hes. *Op*. 479 and 564), literally means "turning", and denotes the reversals in the direction in which the sun's rising and setting places on the horizon are observed to move, one occurring at summer solstice and the other at winter solstice (the English term "solstice", from the Latin *solstitium*, refers to the apparent standing still of the sun at the extreme northern and southern

---

passage announces as topic of the chapter the uniformity of the diurnal rotation, with respect to speed as will turn out, and contrasts the diurnal rotation with the zodiacal motion whose non-uniformity, though, is described in such a way that it could also be lack of uniformity with respect to the shape of its path (see *Ph.* E 4, 228b15–28). It would not be surprising at all if for Aristotle here too uniformity with respect to the shape of the path and lack thereof go together with uniformity with respect to speed and lack thereof. The uniformity of the diurnal rotation with respect to speed is shown in *Cael.* B 6 after it has been established in *Cael.* B 4 that the diurnal rotation is the rotation of a spherical object and is thus a uniform motion with respect to the shape of its path (see 287b14–20; *Cael.* B 5 is a quite short chapter about the direction of the diurnal rotation): as it is, when Aristotle announces at the beginning of *Cael.* B 6 that the diurnal rotation is uniform with respect of speed as well in stark contrast to the zodiacal motion, he might very well implicitly deny that zodiacal motion, whether in all or most of its instances, is uniform also with respect to the shape of the path. Two other relevant passages already referred to above, where the diurnal rotation is said to be uniform in contrast to the zodiacal motion, can thus be also assumed to concern uniformity with respect to both speed and the shape of the path (*Cael.* B 10, 291a34–b3, and *Metaph.* Λ 8, 1073a23–34: in both passages the diurnal rotation is said to be simple, i.e. uniform, as turns out from *Metaph.* I 1, 1053a8–12). A rotating object can be said by Aristotle to move circularly despite the fact that it is not assumed to be spherical (see *Cael.* B 4, 287a2–5 and 29–30); all celestial objects revolve, so they can be called τὰ ἐγκύκλια σώματα or τὰ ἐγκυκλίως φερόμενα σώματα even if some of them do not really move in circles.

limits to the motion of its rising and setting points along the horizon, before it reverses direction). The circular path of the sun in the sky, unlike that of a star, is thus not the same every day of the year. At equinoxes, it coincides with the celestial equator which is bisected by the observer's horizon (this is why at equinoxes the hours of daylight and darkness are equal). At solstices, it coincides with two small circles of the celestial sphere parallel to, and equidistant from, the celestial equator, one to the north, with its largest part above the horizon, and the other to the south, with its largest part below the horizon. These circles are the tropics: of Cancer, where the sun is at summer solstice, when the time of daylight is the longest during the year, and of Capricorn, where the sun is at winter solstice, when the time of daylight is at its annual minimum. Between a solstice and an equinox, the successive diurnal paths of the sun coincide with parallel, small circles of the celestial sphere sandwiched between a tropic and the celestial equator. Over the course of a year, therefore, the sun's path appears to be a collection of disconnected parallel circles, in each of which the sun finds itself twice a year: these are the many paths in which it seems to wander according to *Laws* 7.

However, as soon as it has become understood that the sun does not just follow the diurnal rotation, as if it or rather its center were fixed in the celestial sphere, but at the same time undergoes a slower motion in the opposite direction across the field of stars in a circular path inclined to the celestial equator, the mystery of the sun's wandering in many different ways disappears. The sun does move in one and the same path, one which is as circular as the diurnal path of a fixed star, though the direction of its motion in it is opposite to that of the diurnal motion and a circuit is completed in a year. But the plane of this path is slanted to the plane of the celestial equator, the reference plane of the faster diurnal rotation in which the sun participates: as the angular distance of the sun from the celestial equator continually changes due to its annual motion in the slanted path, the path of its sharing in the diurnal motion is twisted into a spiral, palindromically traversed twice in a year, whose connected turns are the diurnal 'circles' of the sun. The wandering of the moon and the planets in a different path from day to day admits of the same explanation since all of these celestial objects also move oppositely to the diurnal rotation and across the same field of stars as the sun, though not all of them complete a circuit in the same time as the sun and in the case of the planets the path of this motion is only approximately circular. Puzzling multiplicity and disconnectedness are, therefore, replaced by unitary connectedness: a bewilderingly large multitude of disconnected paths become united into turns of a continuous spiral by a path of a much simpler, circular, shape, in which the celestial object moves as it undergoes simultaneously a second, also circular, motion. It goes without saying that intriguing unity in celestial multiplicity and variation is also revealed by the various relations between celestial periods in which, as seen above (2.1), Plato puts much stock.

These are clearly examples of the order said in *Laws* 12 to be inherent in both celestial motions and everything else controlled by reason, which has arranged the universe into a cosmos, and to also furnish an argument for the existence and power of the gods, one of the greatest manifestation of the Beautiful and the Good, alongside the arguments for the superiority of the soul (966c1–967a5): for, as has been shown in *Laws* 10, the orderly celestial motions must be caused by one or more rational and good souls enlivening the luminaries that can thus only be gods executing orderly motions (888e4–899d3), an orderliness proven by astronomy, training in which, and thus necessarily in arithmetic and geometry too, is a prerequisite for true piety. It is an example of the paradigmatic order in the celestial motions whose observation is, according to the *Timaeus*, the reason why god has bestowed on us the gift of sight: for it is through sight that we have access to the invisible and completely orderly revolutions of reason in the heavens, the thoughts of the soul causing the celestial motions, by first observing and then understanding mathematically which we can imitate their cause and order the wandering revolutions of our own souls, thereby becoming rational ourselves (47a1–c4). Given the demonstration of order in the wanderings of the moon, the sun and planets from day to day, it would only be natural for Plato to require the same for the wanderings of the planets in their zodiacal motions alone, independently of their participation in the diurnal rotation, wanderings whose paths exhibit much more elaborate geometric variation than those of the daily wanderings and which make the overall paths of planetary zodiacal motions only roughly circular.

In the reference case of the daily solar wanderings, multiplicity and disunity are packaged into a single object by the form of a geometrical object, the circle, as content of the thought of the soul which causes the luminary to move zodiacally in an imperfect manifestation of this form as circular path. In the case of planetary wanderings due to retrogradations, there must be one or more closely related forms of geometrical objects that are contents of the thought of this soul and along whose imperfect manifestations as ever-shifting paths inducing retrogradations this soul causes the planets to undergo their puzzling zodiacal motions. Taking our cue from the form of the regular polyhedron that doubles as the form of element comprising the forms of all four elements in nature (see 1.3.4), even if Plato did envisage a multitude of forms of planetary retrograde path, as we can plausibly call them, he could have viewed all of them as a single form: the form of path of celestial motion that comprises the form of the circle too and provides a coherent account of the geometry of all celestial motion and, as envisaged in the *Phaedo*, all related celestial phenomena in terms of intelligible unity and ultimately of the Good, the much wider intelligible unity to which this form contributes. It is this form of path of celestial motion, and through it the Good, that Plato urges astronomers in *Republic* 7 to begin to investigate mathematically by learning how to construct the shapes of the retrograde paths of the planets, thereby imitating as much as humanly possible the sole paradigmatically rational soul in the cosmos that causes the planets to move along them and all celestial motion.[64]

2.12 Conclusion

As said above (2.9), we do not know how Eudoxus managed to solve the problem of doubling the cube. We know, however, that a solution can be effected with his astronomical theory of homocentric spheres.[65] The nested spheres, after which this famous theory takes its name, rotate simultaneously and uniformly. What matters here is that, as a point of the innermost of four homocentric spheres orbits the center of the system, it can trace out a curve vaguely similar to the one which a planet is observed tracing out as it moves zodiacally: the combined rotations of all three inner spheres cause the point to describe above and below the equator of the outermost sphere, which stands for the ecliptic, a closed curve that

---

64 In *Metaph*. B 2, 997b12–20, Aristotle says that for Plato the true subject matter of astronomy is a static spherical cosmos which exists apart from its sensible diurnally rotating counterpart and is complete with a static sun, moon and all other celestial objects. ἔτι δὲ εἴ τις παρὰ τὰ εἴδη καὶ τὰ αἰσθητὰ τὰ μεταξὺ θήσεται, πολλὰς ἀπορίας ἕξει· δῆλον γὰρ ὡς ὁμοίως γραμμαί τε παρά τ' αὐτὰς καὶ τὰς αἰσθητὰς ἔσονται καὶ ἕκαστον τῶν ἄλλων γενῶν· ὥστ' ἐπείπερ ἡ ἀστρολογία μία τούτων ἐστί, ἔσται τις καὶ οὐρανὸς παρὰ τὸν αἰσθητὸν οὐρανὸν καὶ ἥλιός τε καὶ σελήνη καὶ τἆλλα ὁμοίως τὰ κατὰ τὸν οὐρανόν. καίτοι πῶς δεῖ πιστεῦσαι τούτοις; οὐδὲ γὰρ ἀκίνητον εὔλογον εἶναι, κινούμενον δὲ καὶ παντελῶς ἀδύνατον ("Again, if one posits intermediates apart from forms and sensibles, he will face many difficulties. For it is evident that there will be lines apart from the lines themselves and sensible lines, and similarly with the objects studied in each of the other sciences. Thus, since astronomy is one of them, there will be a cosmos existing apart from the sensible cosmos and a sun, a moon and all other celestial objects. But how can one believe these things? It is implausible that the cosmos is static and that it moves is completely impossible [if it is assumed to be an intermediate as object of astronomy]"). The context is again the criticism of the belief in the existence of the so-called intermediates as objects studied in mathematics. Nothing suggests that Plato posited the existence of an abstract counterpart to the spherical cosmos and all celestial objects within it, however, irrespective of whether the subject matter of astronomy is viewed as forms or intermediates, unless, of course, one interprets literally the imaginative myth in the *Phaedo* (see 2.3).

65 See Riddell (1979) 13–19.

regularly turns back on itself and whereupon the point's motion is principally in the direction of the rotation of the outermost sphere but occasionally reverses and then resumes its principal direction.⁶⁶ This configuration of nested rotating spheres allows the construction on a plane of both the required length that doubles the cube and the projection of the point's path during an event of retrogradation. The fact that the doubling of the cube can be effected with the astronomical theory of homocentric spheres makes it likely, in view of the connection between this stereometrical problem and astronomy in *Republic* 7, that this is how Eudoxus doubled the cube, that his stereometric and astronomical work had been done by the time Plato wrote his comments in *Republic* 7 on the undeveloped state of solid geometry at the dramatic date of the dialogue and that it is hinted at by Plato's remarks. Those among his contemporary audience who were abreast of the advances in mathematics after the dramatic time of the dialogue, and also realized that Plato considered propedeutic to philosophy an astronomy of mathematical sophistication comparable at least to that of contemporary

---

66 The classic reconstruction of Eudoxus' theory is due to Schiaparelli (1875); an interesting alternative reconstruction has been proposed by Yavetz (1998) and (2001). For an outline of both reconstructions see Kouremenos (2010) 1.4. They are undeniably speculative. The theory is outlined by Aristotle in *Metaph.* Λ 8, one of the two available sources on which reconstructions of the theory are based; the other is Simplicius' extensive commentary on *Cael.* B 12, for detailed discussion of which see now Bowen (2013). Bowen rejects the reliability of both Aristotle and the commentator as sources for early Greek planetary theory, thereby rejecting modern reconstructions of a Eudoxean theory of the planets from their testimony; see also Bowen (2002). In his view, Eudoxus spoke only of planetary motions and the phenomena of the planets at the horizon but not of planetary retrograde motion, which, as Bowen assumes, was unknown at the time in Greece; Aristotle simply tried to imagine how many rotations of nested spheres would be required to produce the planetary phenomena at issue and the production of planetary retrograde motion is an unfortunate incident of this attempt (Bowen [2002] 163–166). Knowledge of the phenomena of the planets at the horizon, for which there is no fifth- or fourth-century-BC Greek evidence, could have been imported from Mesopotamia in Bowen's view, but he sees no reason to assume the same for planetary retrograde motion, arguing that the transmission of astronomical knowledge from Mesopotamia to Greece was a very fragmentary process prior to the second century BC. I find this argument unconvincing. Representing retrograde motion need not have been the sole or the primary motivation for the planetary part of Eudoxus' theory of homocentric spheres. This seems to be one of the available possibilities, alongside the representation of the distance from the sun of two planets, Mercury and Venus, and of the invisibility periods of all five planets; see Mendell (1998) 228–229. Mendell's study of the theory of homocentric spheres for the planets as traditionally reconstructed shows that the theory could represent to some degree a number of planetary phenomena, none of which, though, can be selected as the theory's empirical foundation in the light of the mathematics alone. This might be an artifact of the insufficient evidence at our disposal; alternatively, it might show the fertility of the theory, provided that the sources on which our reconstructions of it rest are mainly correct.

stereometry with its ingenious solutions to the problem of doubling the cube, would have guessed without any difficulty what he has Socrates intend to say about the future advanced astronomy that will really help philosophy propedeutically.[67]

Given Plato's belief in the future progress of mathematics (see 1.2.4.9), the absence of any allusion to spheres from the description of this astronomy can very well be an implicit warning to his contemporary audience against the hasty identification of the future astronomy with the Eudoxean theory.[68] The latter is to be brought in mind only to illustrate the character of the astronomy he has Socrates envision in mathematical terms, unavoidably, of their time: it will investigate complex geometrical configurations generating kinematically representations of some forms of mathematical objects that are approximated by the observed paths of planetary retrograde motion and all celestial motion. By Plato's lights, however, this study of what we could rightly call the mathematical laws of motion on the largest scales of the cosmos would in all probability be eventually carried out by a mathematics that would be unrecognizable to its primitive ancestor of his time.[69]

---

[67] See more extensively Kouremenos (2015) ch. 1.
[68] On the anecdote associating Plato with the origins of the theory see Kouremenos (2015) ch. 3.
[69] As Plato could conceive them, the laws of motion were not dynamical, i.e. they did not specify the development of a physical system in time given its state at a certain time, but only determined the geometrical shapes of paths of motion; cf. Penrose (2004) 686.

Bibliography

Allen, R.E. 1965. "Participation and Predication in Plato's Middle Dialogues", in Allen (ed.) 43–60 (originally published in *The Philosophical Review* 69, 1960, 147–164).
Allen, R.E. (ed.) 1965. *Studies in Plato's Metaphysics*. London.
Allen, R.E. 1970. "The Generation of Numbers in Plato's *Parmenides*", *Classical Philology* 65, 30–34.
Annas, J. 1975. "On the Intermediates", *Archiv für Geschichte der Philosophie* 57, 146–165.
Annas, J. 1976. *Aristotle's* Metaphysics, *Books M and N*. Oxford.
Anton, P. (ed.) 1981. *Science and the Sciences in Plato*. Buffalo, NY.
Arsen, H.S. 2012. "A Case for the Utility of the Mathematical Intermediates", *Philosophia Mathematica* (III) 20, 200–223.
Barker, A. 1978. "Σύμφωνοι ἀριθμοί: A Note on *Republic* 531C1–4", *Classical Quarterly* 73, 337–342.
Barker, A. 2007. *The Science of Harmonics in Classical Greece*. Cambridge.
Becker, O. 1931. "Die diairetische Erzeugung der platonischen Idealzahlen", *Quellen und Studien zur Geschichte der Mathematik, Astronomie und Physik*, Abt. B: Studien, Band 1, Heft 4, 464–501.
Blyth, D. 2000. "Platonic Number in the Parmenides and Metaphysics XIII", *International Journal of Philosophical Studies* 8, 23–45.
Borwein P., S. Choi, B. Rooney & A. Weirathmueller (eds.). 2008. *The Riemann Hypothesis. A Resource for the Afficionado and Virtuoso Alike*. CMS Books in Mathematics/Ouvrages de mathématiques de la SMC 27. N. York.
Bostock, D. 2009. *Philosophy of Mathematics. An Introduction*. Malden, MA & Oxford.
Bowen, A.C. 2002. "Simplicius and the Early History of Greek Planetary Theory", *Perspectives on Science* 10, 155–167.
Bowen, A.C. 2013. *Simplicius on the Planets and Their Motion. In Defense of a Heresy*. Philosophia Antiqua 133. Leiden & Boston.
Brentlinger, J.A. 1963. "The Divided Line and Plato's 'Theory of Intermediates'", *Phronesis* 8, 144–166.
Bulmer-Thomas, I. 1984. "Plato's Astronomy", *Classical Quarterly* 34, 107–112.
Burnet, J. 1914. *Greek Philosophy*. Part I: *Thales to Plato*. London.
Burnyeat, M.F. 2000. "Plato on Why Mathematics is Good for the Soul", in T. Smiley (ed.), *Mathematics and Necessity. Essays in the History of Philosophy*, Oxford, 1–81.
Carone, G.R. 2005. *Plato's Cosmology and Its Ethical Dimensions*. Oxford.
Cherniss, H. 1944. *Aristotle's Criticism of Plato and the Academy*, vol. 1. Baltimore.
Cherniss, H. 1947. "Some war-time publications concerning Plato", *American Journal of Philology* 68, 113–146 and 225–265.
Cherniss, H.F. 1965. "The Relation of the *Timaeus* to Plato's Later Dialogues", in Allen (ed.) 339–378 (originally published in *American Journal of Philology* 78, 1957, 225–266).
Cleary, J.J. 2013a. "Science, Universals and Reality", in Dillon et al. (eds.) 333–378 (originally published in *Ancient Philosophy* 7, 1987, 95–130).
Cleary, J.J. 2013b. "Aristotle's Criticism of Plato's Theory of Form Numbers", in Dillon *et al.* (eds.) 415–439 (originally published in G. Damschen, R. Enskat & A.G. Vigo (eds.), *Platon und Aristoteles–sub ratione veritatis. Festschrift für Wolfgang Wieland zum 70. Geburtstag*, Göttingen 2003, 3–30).

Denniston, J.D. 1954². *The Greek Particles*. Oxford.
Deza, E. & M.M. Deza. 2012. *Figurate Numbers*. Singapore.
Dillon, J. 2003. *The Heirs of Plato. A Study of the Old Academy (347–274 BC)*. Oxford.
Dillon, J. 2014. "Pythagoreanism in the Academic tradition: the Early Academy to Numenius", in C. Huffman (ed.), *A History of Pythagoreanism*, Cambridge, 250–274.
Dillon, J., B. O'Byrne & F. O'Rourke (eds.). 2013. *Studies on Plato, Aristotle and Proclus. Collected Writings on Ancient Philosophy of John J. Cleary*. Ancient Mediterranean and Medieval Texts and Contexts 15. Leiden & Boston.
du Sautoy, M. 2004. *The Music of the Primes. Why an Unsolved Problem in Mathematics Matters*. London.
Evans, J. 1998. *The History and Practice of Ancient Astronomy*. N. York.
Findlay, J.N. 1974. *Plato. The Written and Unwritten Doctrines*. London.
Fine, G. 1995. *On Ideas. Aristotle's Criticism of Plato's Theory of Forms*. Oxford.
Fine, G. 1999. "Knowledge and Belief in *Republic* 5–7", in G. Fine (ed.), *Plato 1. Metaphysics and Epistemology*, Oxford, 215–246 (originally published in S. Everson (ed.), *Epistemology*, Companions to Ancient Thought 1, Cambridge, 85–115).
Fowler, D.H. 1990. *The Mathematics of Plato's Academy*, Oxford (first published: Oxford 1987).
Franklin, L. 2012. "Inventing Intermediates: Mathematical Discourse and Its Objects in *Republic* VII", *Journal of the History of Philosophy* 50, 483–506.
Gaiser, K. 1963. *Platons Ungeschriebene Lehre*. Stuttgart.
Geach, P. 1965. "The Third Man Again", in Allen (ed.) 265–277 (originally published in *The Philosophical Review* 65, 1956, 72–82).
Gerson, L.P. 2013. *From Plato to Platonism*. Ithaca, NY & London.
Goldstein, B.R. 1997. "Saving the Phenomena: The Background to Ptolemy's Planetary Theory", *Journal for the History of Astronomy* 28, 1–12.
Gowers, T. 2008. "The Language and Grammar of Mathematics", in T. Gowers, J. Barrow-Green & I. Leader (eds.), *The Princeton Companion to Mathematics*, Princeton, 8–16.
Gregory, A. 2000. *Plato's Philosophy of Science*. London.
Hacking. I. 2014. *Why is There Philosophy of Mathematics At All?* Cambridge.
Hardy, G.H. 1921. "Srinivasa Ramanujan", *Proceedings of the London Mathematical Society* 19, xl–lviii.
Harte, V. 2002. *Plato on Parts and Wholes. The Metaphysics of Structure*. Oxford.
Harte, V. 2008. "Plato's Metaphysics", in G. Fine (ed.), *The Oxford Handbook of Plato*, Oxford, 191–216.
Heath, T.L. 1956. *The Thirteen Books of Euclid's Elements*, 3 vols. N. York (reprint of the second edition: Cambridge 1926).
Heath, T.L. 1981. *A History of Greek Mathematics*, 2 vols. N. York (first published: Oxford 1921).
Ilting, K.-H. 1965. Review of Gaiser (1963), *Gnomon* 37, 131–144.
Johansen, T.K. 2004. *Plato's Natural Philosophy. A Study of the* Timaeus-Critias. Cambridge.
Johansen, T. 2013. "Timaeus in the Cave", in G. Boys-Stone, D. El Murr & C. Gill (eds.), *The Platonic Art of Philosophy*, Cambridge, 90–109.
Kahane, J.-P. 2015. "Bernoulli Convolutions and Self-similar Measures after Erdős", *Notices of the American Mathematical Society* 62, 136–139.
Kahn, C.H. 2013. *Plato and the Post-Socratic Dialogue. The Return to the Philosophy of Nature*. Cambridge.
Kaler, J.B. 2002. *The Ever-Changing Sky*. Cambridge.

Katz, V.J., M. Folkerts, B. Hughes, R. Wagner & J. Lennart Berggren (eds.). 2016. *Sourcebook in the Mathematics of Medieval Europe and North Africa*. Princeton.

Klein, J. 1968. *Greek Mathematical Thought and the Origin of Algebra*, transl. by E. Brann. Cambridge, MA (first published in *Quellen und Studien zur Geschichte der Mathematik, Astronomie und Physik*, Abt. B: Studien, Band 3, Heft 1 [1934] 18–105, 2 [1936] 122–235).

Knorr, W.R. 1990. "Plato and Eudoxus on the Planetary Motions", *Journal for the History of Astronomy* 15, 113–123.

Knorr, W.R. 1993. *The Ancient Tradition of Geometric Problems*. N. York (originally published: Boston 1986).

Kouremenos. Th. 2003. "Aristotle on Geometric Perfection in the Physical World", *Mnemosyne* 56 (fourth series), 463–479.

Kouremenos, Th. 2010. *Heavenly Stuff. The constitution of the celestial objects and the theory of homocentric spheres in Aristotle's cosmology*. Palingenesia 96. Stuttgart.

Kouremenos. Th. 2015. *The Unity of Mathematics in Plato's* Republic. Palingenesia 102. Stuttgart.

Kouremenos, Th., G. M. Parássoglou & K. Tsantsanoglou. 2006. *The Derveni Papyrus*. Studi e testi per il corpus dei papiri filosofici greci e latini 13. Florence.

Kucharski, P. 1971. "Eschatologie et connaissance dans le *Timée*", in P. Kucharski, *Aspects de la spéculation platonicienne*, Publications de la Sorbonne, Série: Études 1, Paris & Louvain, 307–337 (originally published in *Archives de philosophie* 29, 1966, 5–36).

Langlands, R. 2010. "Is there beauty in mathematical theories?", available at: http://publications.ias.edu/sites/default/files/ND.pdf.

Lear, J. 1982. "Aristotle's Philosophy of Mathematics", *The Philosophical Review* 91, 161–192.

Lowe, E.J. 2002. *A Survey of Metaphysics*. Oxford.

Mansfeld, J. 1998. *Prolegomena Mathematica. From Apollonius of Perga to the Late Neoplatonists*. Philosophia Antiqua LXXX. Leiden, Boston & Köln.

Mendell, H. 1998. "Reflections on Eudoxus, Callippus and their Curves", *Centaurus* 40, 175–275.

Mendell, H. 2008. "Plato by the Numbers", in D. Follesdal & J. Woods (eds.), *Logos and Language. Essays in Honor of Julius Moravcsik*, London, 125–160.

Meyer, C. & J.-F. Wicker. 2000. "Musique et mathématiques au XIVe siècle: le *De numeris harmonicis* de Leo Hebraeus", *Archives internationales d'histoire de sciences* 50, 32–67.

Miller, D.R. 2003. *The Third Kind in Plato's Timaeus*. Hypomnemata 145. Göttingen.

Mohr, R.D. 1985. *The Platonic Cosmology*. Philosophia Antiqua XLII. Leiden.

Moravcsik, J. 2000. "Plato on Number and Mathematics", in P. Suppes, J. Moravcsik & H. Mendell (eds.), *Ancient & Medieval Traditions in the Exact Sciences. Essays in Memory of Wilbur Knorr*, Stanford, 177–196.

Morrow, G.R. 1993. *Plato's Cretan City. A Historical Interpretation of the Laws*. Princeton (originally published: Princeton 1960).

Mourelatos, A.P.D. 1981. "Astronomy and Kinematics in Plato's Project of Rationalist Explanation", *Studies in History and Philosophy of Science* 12, 1–32.

Mourelatos, A.P.D. 2006. "The Concept of the Universal and Some Later Pre-Platonic Cosmologists", in M.L. Gill & P. Pellegrin (eds.), *A Companion to Ancient Philosophy*, Oxford UK & Malden MA, 56–76.

Mueller, I. 1970. "Aristotle on Geometrical Objects", *Archiv für Geschichte der Philosophie* 52, 156–171.

Mueller, I. 1981. "Ascending to problems: Astronomy and harmonics in *Republic* VII", in Anton (ed.) 103–122.

Mueller, I. 1991. "Mathematics and Education: Some Notes on the Platonic Program", *Apeiron* 24, 85–104.
Mueller, I. 1992. "Mathematical method and philosophical truth" in: R. Kraut (ed.), *The Cambridge Companion to Plato*, Cambridge, 170–199.
Mueller, I. 2006. *Philosophy of Mathematics and Deductive Structure in Euclid's* Elements. N. York (first published: Cambridge, MA 1981).
Netz, R. 2004. "Eudemus of Rhodes, Hippocrates of Chios and the Earliest Form of a Greek Mathematical Text", *Centaurus* 46, 243–286.
Neugebauer, O. 1975. *A History of Ancient Mathematical Astronomy*. Berlin & N. York.
Nightingale, A.W. 2004. *Spectacles of Truth in Classical Greek Philosophy. Theoria in its Cultural Context*. Cambridge.
Nikulin, D. 2013. *The Other Plato. The Tübingen Interpretation of Plato's Inner-Academic Teachings*. Albany, NY.
Owen, G.E.L. 1957. "A Proof in the *Peri Ideōn*", *Journal of Hellenic Studies* 77, 103–111.
Owen, G.E.L. 1965. "The Place of the *Timaeus* in Plato's Dialogues", in Allen (ed.) 313–338 (originally published in *Classical Quarterly* 3, 1953, 79–95).
Panza, M. & A. Sereni. 2013. *Plato's Problem. An Introduction to Mathematical Platonism*. Houndmills, Basingstoke (UK), & N. York.
Penrose, R. 2004. *The Road to Reality. A Complete Guide to the Laws of the Universe*. London.
Popper, K. 2002. *Conjectures and Refutations. The Growth of Scientific Knowledge*. London & N. York (first published: London 1963).
Post, L.A. 1944. Review of J.B. Skemp, The Theory of Motion in Plato's Later Dialogues (Cambridge 1942), *American Journal of Philology* 65, 298–301.
Pritchard, P. 1995. *Plato's Philosophy of Mathematics*. International Plato Studies 5. Sankt Augustin.
Ramanujan, S. 1915. "Highly Composite Numbers", *Proceedings of the London Mathematical Society* 14, 347–409.
Riddell, R.C. 1979. "Eudoxan Mathematics and the Eudoxan Spheres", *Archive for History of Exact Sciences* 20, 1–19.
Robin, L. 1908. *La théorie platonicienne des idées et des nombres d'après Aristote*. Paris.
Robins, I. 1995. "Mathematics and the Conversion of the Mind", *Ancient Philosophy* 15, 359–391.
Ross, D. 1951. *Plato's Theory of Ideas*. Oxford.
Saito, K. 1995. "Doubling the Cube: A New Interpretation of its Significance for Early Greek Geometry", *Historia Mathematica* 22, 119–137.
Schiaparelli, G.V. 1875. *Le sfere omocentriche di Eudosso, di Callippo e di Aristotele*. Pubblicazioni del R. Osservatorio di Brera 9. Milan.
Schindler, D.C. 2008. *Plato's Critique of Impure Reason. On Goodness and Truth in the Republic*. Washington, D.C.
Schofield, M. 1972. "The Dissection of Unity in Plato's *Parmenides*", *Classical Philology* 67, 102–109.
Scolnicov, S. 2003. *Plato's* Parmenides. *Translated with Introduction and Commentary*. Berkeley, Los Angeles & London.
Sedley, D. 1999. "The Ideal of Godlikeness", in G. Fine (ed.), *Plato 2. Ethics, Politics, Religion and the Soul*, Oxford, 309–328.
Sedley, D. 2007. "Philosophy, the Forms and the Art of Ruling", in G. R. F. Ferrari (ed.), *The Cambridge Companion to Plato's Republic*, Cambridge, 256–283.

Seel, G. 2007. "Is Plato's Conception of the Form of the Good Contradictory?", in D. Cairns, F.-G. Herrmann & T. Penner (eds.), *Pursuing the Good. Ethics and Metaphysics in Plato's* Republic, Edinburgh Leventis Studies 4, 169–196.
Silverman, A. 1991. "Timaean Particulars", *Classical Quarterly* 42, 87–113.
Silverman, A. 2002. *The Dialectic of Essence. A Study of Plato's Metaphysics*. Princeton.
Silverman, A. 2014. "Plato's Metaphysics", in J. Warren & F. Sheffield (eds.), The *Routledge Companion to Ancient Philosophy*, N. York, 213–226.
Smith, J.A. 1917. "General Relative Clauses in Greek", *Classical Review* 31, 69–71.
Stenzel, J. 1933^2. *Zahl und Gestalt bei Plato und Aristoteles*. Leipzig.
Sorabji, R. 1983. *Time, Creation & the Continuum*. London.
Tarán, L. 1975. *Academica. Plato, Philip of Opus, and the pseudo-Platonic Epinomis*. Philadelphia, PA.
Tarán, L. 1981. *Speusippus of Athens*. Philosophia Antiqua XXXIX. Leiden.
Tarán, L. 1991. "Ideas, Numbers and Magnitudes: Remarks on Plato, Speusippus and Aristotle", *Revue de philosophie ancienne* 9, 199–231 (reprinted in *Collected Papers [1962–1999]*, Leiden 2001, 247–278).
Taylor, A.E. 1955^6. *Plato. The Man and His Works*. London (first published: London 1926).
Toeplitz, O. 1929. "Das Verhältnis von Mathematik und Ideenlehre bei Plato", *Quellen und Studien zur Geschichte der Mathematik, Astronomie und Physik*, Abt. B: Studien, Band 1, Heft 1, 3–33.
Turnbull, R.G. 1998. *The* Parmenides *and Plato's Late Philosophy*. Toronto, Buffalo & London.
van der Wielen, W. 1941. *De ideegetallen van Plato*. Amsterdam.
Vlastos, G. 1965. "The Third Man Argument in the *Parmenides*", in Allen (ed.) 231–263 (originally published in *The Philosophical Review* 63, 1954, 319–349).
Vlastos, G. 1981. "The Role of Observation in Plato's Conception of Astronomy", in Anton (ed.) 1–31.
Wedberg, A. 1955. *Plato's Philosophy of Mathematics*. Stockholm (reprint: Westport, CT 1977).
Wilamowitz-Moellendorff, U. von. 1962. "Ein Wehgeschenk des Eratosthenes", in *Kleine Schriften* vol. 2, Berlin, 48–70 (originally published in *Nachrichten der K. Gesselschaft der Wissenschaften zu Göttingen*, Phil.-hist. Klasse, 1894, 15–35).
Wright, M.R. 1981. *Empedocles. The Extant Fragments*. New Haven, CT & London.
Yang, Moon-Heum. 1999. "The 'square itself' and 'diagonal itself' in *Republic* 510d", *Ancient Philosophy* 19, 31–35.
Yavetz, I. 1998. "On the Homocentric Spheres of Eudoxus", *Archive for History of Exact Sciences* 52, 221–278.
Yavetz, I. 2001. "A New Role for the Hippopede of Eudoxus", *Archive for History of Exact Sciences* 56, 69–93.

Index of passages

Alexander of Aphrodisias
in Metaph. (Hayduck)
56.33–57.11: 71 n. 110
57.9–10: 71 n. 111
79.5–11: 17 n. 16
79.11–15: 17 n. 16
80.8–15: 20 n. 26
83.6–16: 17 n. 16

Aristotle
APo.
  Α 7 75a38–b20: 47
        27: 68
APr.
  Α 39 46a17–27: 45
de An.
  Α 2 405a8–13: 49
      3 406b26–407a2: 93 n. 19, 95 n. 20
      4 409a3–5: 18 n. 23
Cael.
  Α 3 270b16–25: 87 n. 13
      10 279b32–280a10: 73
  Β 1 284a11–284b5: 86 n. 12
      2 285b28: 123 n. 58
      3 286b6–7: 131 n. 63
      4 287a2–5: 132 n. 63
        287b14–20: 133 n. 63
      6 288a13–17: 119 n. 46, 131 n. 63
      10 291a34–b3: 121 n. 54, 131 n. 63
  Γ 1 299a3–6: 41
        299b23–300a19: 69
      4 303a8–10: 68
EE
  Α 8 1218a1–8: 31, 32
        1218a15–28: 30, 32, 68 n. 102

EN
  Α 4 1096a10–18: 22, 25, 30, 31, 32
GA
  Α 3 717a23–29: 131
Metaph.
  Α 2 982a19–28: 68
      6 987a29–b9: 48
        987b13–14: 9 n. 1
        987b14–18: 24
        987b18–21: 70
        987b33–988a1: 71
      9 990b8–15: 22, 23
        991b6–7: 22
        991b9: 68
        992a10–18: 70
        992a19–24: 18 n. 23, 42
        992a32–b1: 68
  Β 2 997b12–20: 135 n. 64
        997b12–998a6: 117 n. 44
        997b35–998a4: 17 n. 16
  Ι 1 1053a8–12: 132 n. 63
  Λ 3 1070a18–19: 22 n. 30
      8 1073a14–23: 85
        1073a23–b1: 84
        1073a23–34: 131 n. 63
        1073b1–8: 84
        1073b8–17: 45, 85
  Μ 1 1076a19–22: 69
      2 1077a20–24: 33
      3 1078a9–12: 68
        1078a31–b6: 30 n. 49, 68 n. 102
      4 1078b7–12: 68 n. 105
        1078b9–36: 48
        1078b19–21: 49
      6 1080a12–35: 34
        1080b16–20: 34
      7 1081a5–12: 34

		1081b21–22: 71
		1082b24–28: 34
	8	1083b8–17: 34
		1084a3–4: 72
		1084a3–7: 71 n. 112
		1084b22–23: 32
	9	1085a31–34: 76
		1086a31–34: 10 n. 4
N	1	1087b4–9: 75
		1087b33–1088a14: 35, 38
	3	1090b20–26: 69, 70, 75 n. 121
		1090b24–25: 75

Mete.
A	2	339a12–13: 131 n. 63
	3	339b19–30: 87 n. 13
	6	343b28–30: 121

PA
A	5	644b22–31: 45
Γ	14	675b22–27: 131

Ph.
B	2	193b22–194a12: 34
Γ	2	209b11–16: 74
		209b33–210a2: 74
	6	203a1–16: 70
		206b27–33: 70
Δ	2	209b14–15: 68 n. 104
E	4	228b15–28: 131 n. 63
Θ	9	265b11–16: 131 n. 63
	10	267b3–4: 131 n. 63

Po.
	4	1449a9–15: 46

SE
	34	183b15–184b8: 46

Fragments
  53 Rose: 45

[Arist.]
LI
1 968a9–14: 19 n. 24

Mech.
851b34–35: 114 n. 41

Aristoxenus
Harm. (da Rios)
39.8–40.4: 64 n. 99

Claudius Ptolemy
Alm. (Heiberg)
1 7.5–10: 85

Democritus
DK 68 A 36: 49
        A 57: 48
        A 67: 48
        A 101: 49
        A 102: 48
        B 124: 48
        B 141: 48

Empedocles
DK 31 B 17.30–35: 54

Euclid
Elementa
1 Def. 1: 18 n. 23
    Def. 2–7: 18 n. 23
    Def. 3: 42
7 Def. 1: 34, 39
    Def. 1–2: 18 n. 23, 29, 40 n. 68
    Def. 2: 28, 34, 39
    Def. 3: 51
    Def. 3–4: 29
    Def. 4: 51
    Def. 5: 29, 51
    Def. 6–10: 29
    Def. 11–14: 29
    Def. 15–19: 29
    Def. 20–21: 29

	Def. 22: 29	4	716c1–4: 103
4	Prop. 16: 56 n. 87		716c4–6: 103
10	Def. 3: 19 n. 24, 104		718b5–723d4: 5
11	Def. 14: 18 n. 23		722d4–6: 5
	Def. 18: 18 n. 23		723a4–b8: 5
	Def. 21: 18 n. 23	5	737e1–738b1: 1
13	Prop. 18: 58 n. 89		737e7–738a2: 1

Eutocius
in Sph. Cyl. (Heiberg)
3.88.13–90.11: 110 n. 36

Hesiod
Op.
479: 132
564: 132

Homer
Od.
6.41–47: 88 n. 14

Philolaus
DK 44 B 1–6: 49

Plato
Cra.
397e2–398c4: 92
Euthd.
290b7–c6: 6
Euthphr.
5d1–5: 48
6d9–e1: 48
Grg.
503d6–504a5: 25
Hp.Ma.
285b5–c5: 104
Lg.
1   628a4–b5: 5
     643b4–d4: 126

4	716c1–4: 103
	716c4–6: 103
	718b5–723d4: 5
	722d4–6: 5
	723a4–b8: 5
5	737e1–738b1: 1
	737e7–738a2: 1
	739b8–e7: 65 n. 100
6	771a5–c7: 1
7	793a9–d5: 65 n. 100
	817e5–818a3: 2, 101
	817e5–820e7: 101
	818b7–e2: 104
	818e3–4: 104
	818e5–7: 104
	818e8–819a1: 104
	820e8–822c9: 101
	820e8–822d1: 95 n. 20, 102
	821b5–c5: 105
	821b5–822d1: 95 n. 20
	822a4–8: 129
	822c7–d1: 126, 130
10	888e4–899d3: 101, 102, 134
	891e4–896b2: 93
	893b6–894c9: 93 n. 19
	896d5–898d5: 63
	896d5–899a10: 93, 125
	896d5–899c1: 95 n. 20
	897d3–e7: 93 n. 19
	898c1–10: 61 n. 93
	898d9–e2: 95 n. 20
	898d9–899a10: 94 n. 19
	899b3–9: 98 n. 22
12	960e9–967d3: 101
	965b7–c8: 2, 24, 101
	966a5–b9: 102
	966c1–6: 102
	966c6–d2: 102
	966c1–967a5: 102, 134

967a1–5: 103
967d4–968a4: 2, 101, 106
Prm.
129d6–e1: 50 n. 80
129d6–130e4: 21
130e5–133a10: 9 n. 1
140b7–c4: 51
142a1–8: 29
142b1–143a3: 27
142b1–144a9: 28, 73
143a4–144a9: 28
144a4–7: 69
144b1–e9: 28
144e8–145b5: 29, 69
145b3–5: 29
Phd.
74a9–c3: 10 n. 6, 51, 52, 53
74a9–76e7: 53
74c1–5: 53 n. 84
74d4–75a4: 115
78d1–9: 54
78d1–79a11: 10
97b8–98b6: 65
97d5–98b6: 85
98b7–99b6: 86
99b6–c6: 66, 86
99c6–100b9: 86, 93 n. 19
100c10–e3: 9, 68, 90
101b4–c9: 50
101b9–c9: 12, 35, 36 n. 57
101c9–102a2: 44
103c10–e8: 57, 60
104a7–b4: 12 n. 10
104d1–8: 12
106d5–7: 61
109a9–110b2: 88
109b5–7: 87 n. 13
109d5–110a1: 87 n. 13
110a1–b2: 88

110d3–111c3: 88
111a7–b1: 87 n. 13, 88
Phdr.
245c5–246a2: 93
247c3–d1: 9
247c6–8: 19, 52 n. 83
265d2–e3: 22 n. 30, 27
Phlb.
15a1–b8: 9, 32
16c5–17b10: 11
16c5–18c6: 36 n. 57
17b11–e6: 13
18a7–c6: 11
18c7–d2: 13
23c9–d1: 73
24b10–25b4: 74
51b1–52b9: 26
55c4–57e5: 1, 56
55d1–56a8: 16
56d4–e6: 36
61d10–62b9: 106
61d10–62d3: 1, 15, 56
62c1–2: 16
63b7–c4: 65 n. 100
63e7–64a3: 26
64e5–65a5: 68 n. 102, 103
Plt.
262c8–263a1: 22, 27 n. 39
268d5–270d1: 124
269c4–d2: 124
269d5–270a8: 120
310e5–311c8: 65 n. 100
R.
4   430d3–432b2: 64, 80
     432a2–7: 84 n. 9
     441d11–442d7: 64, 80
     443b9–444a9: 9, 23
     443c9–444a2: 64, 80, 84 n. 9, 91
5   462a2–b3: 65, 80

Index of passages

6
- 473c11–e4: 8, 78
- 475b4–476d6: 9
- 476a5–9: 67
- 476b4–7: 9
- 478e7–479b7: 51, 52, 53
- 478e7–480a13: 10, 16 n. 16, 37
- 484b4–d9: 79, 102
- 490a8–b8: 91
- 500b8–d10: 4, 24, 26, 80, 91, 92, 102, 103, 106
- 504e6–505b3: 26
- 505a2–509d5: 78
- 506d5–e1: 26
- 507b4–7: 67
- 508b9–c2: 90
- 508d10–509a8: 67
- 509b1–4: 78
- 509b5–c2: 66, 67, 80
- 509d1–4: 78
- 509d6–511e5: 3, 16, 24 n. 37, 52 n. 83
- 510c2–d3: 5
- 510c3–511b1: 39
- 511b2–c2: 10
- 511c2–e5: 38

7
- 516b8–c1: 110
- 517b7–9: 67
- 517b7–c4: 67, 90, 109, 110
- 518a1–b6: 25
- 519b7–520e3: 106
- 519c8–520d5: 16
- 519e1–520a5: 4, 65, 80
- 521c1–d7: 89
- 521d4–525c7: 17 n. 16
- 521d4–526c6: 3
- 521c5–8: 45
- 522b5–e4: 89, 106
- 522c1–9: 28
- 522c1–e4: 4
- 522c5–7: 37 n. 61
- 522c5–525b8: 37
- 523c10–524c14: 51, 52, 59
- 524d8–525a9: 10 n. 6, 16 n. 16
- 525a5–8: 50
- 525b9–c7: 38
- 525c8–d1: 37 n. 61
- 525c8–526b3: 18 n. 23, 38
- 525d5–8: 99
- 526a1–b4: 39
- 526d6–e5: 67
- 526c7–d7: 89, 106
- 527a1–b1: 3, 17 n. 18
- 527a1–b7: 113
- 527a1–b11: 3, 16 n. 16, 17 n. 21, 40, 108, 117 n. 44
- 527c10–d3: 82 n. 4
- 527d1–7: 106
- 527d1–528a5: 108
- 527d5–e3: 89
- 528a6–10: 99
- 528a6–c7: 3, 42, 45
- 528a6–d1: 89
- 528a6–e3: 110
- 528d1–10: 99
- 528c4–529c2: 92
- 529a9–c2: 108, 111
- 529c6–d1: 109
- 529c6–d5: 43, 61 n. 93, 89, 114, 116 n. 44
- 529d7–8: 111
- 529d7–530a3: 108, 109
- 530a4–8: 90, 107, 109, 110, 111
- 530a4–b5: 81, 82 n. 6, 124
- 530a8–b5: 112
- 530b6–c4: 3, 42, 105
- 530c3–4: 4
- 530c6–531a3: 89
- 531b2–c5: 3, 42
- 531c2–3: 43
- 531c5: 4

531c5–8: 104, 109
531c5–d5: 65, 67, 77, 83, 89
531c9–d5: 4, 42, 66
531d6–7: 4
531d6–e5: 5, 40, 44
532d2–533a9: 66
532d7–533c6: 3
533a10–c6: 3, 18
533c9: 40, 44
533e3–534a8: 97
534b3–e1: 103
534e2–535a1: 3, 100
537b7–c3: 11
537b7–c8: 4, 6, 20, 42, 56 n. 88, 65, 66, 77, 83, 89, 102
537c6–7: 11
540a4–c2: 78, 106
546b4–5: 82 n. 6, 124
596a5–b3: 20
611a10–b3: 111
616b2–6: 83
616b4–5: 84 n. 9
616b6–c4: 84
616c4–7: 84 n. 9
616b7–c2: 84 n. 9
616d1–e3: 84 n. 9
616d7–e2: 126
617a4–b4: 121
617b1–2: 81 n. 3
617b2–3: 121
617b4–5: 125
617b6–8: 84 n. 9
617c5–d1: 123

Sph.
238a10–b1: 69
238b2–3: 35
246a7–c3: 9
252e9–253d4: 12, 26

253d5–e7: 12
254b7–255e7: 68 n. 103, 116 n. 43

Smp.
209e5–211b5: 2, 9, 10 n. 6, 67

Tht.
185d1: 35 n. 56

Ti.
27d5–29d3: 90 n. 16
28c3–5: 90 n. 16
29c4–d3: 55 n. 87
29d7–30a7: 96
30c2–31b3: 62
31c2–4: 79 n. 2
31c2–32a7: 65 n. 99
33c1–4: 61
34b10–36d7: 61
34b10–37c5: 92
36c4–d1: 123
36b6–d7: 125
36d8–37c5: 61
36e5–37a2: 90 n. 16, 94, 96
37c6–39e2: 93
37c6–40e2: 61
37d1–38b5: 9
38d1–3: 81 n. 3
38d1–6: 127
38d6–e3: 127
38c3–e3: 95 n. 20, 125
39a5–b2: 95 n. 20, 129
39b2–c1: 81
39c1–2: 125
39c2–d2: 81, 112
39c5–d2: 127, 129
39d2–7: 82 n. 6
39e3–40a2: 61, 92
39e3–40d5: 98 n. 22
39e3–41d3: 96
40a2–b8: 87 n. 13
40c3–d3: 120

41a7–d7: 61
41a7–42e4: 61, 92
42e5–44d2: 61
44d3–8: 61, 92
47a1–7: 95
47a1–b2: 4
47a1–c4: 61 n. 94, 94, 134
47a7–b2: 95
47e5–48a5: 112 n. 40
48e2–49a4: 90 n. 16
48e2–52d1: 97
48e2–53c3: 52 n. 83, 54 n. 85
50a5–c6: 53 n. 83
50c7–e1: 62, 90 n. 16
51b7–52b5: 53, 93
51b8: 55
51d3–e6: 76
51e6–52b5: 9, 10 n. 6
52a8–b5: 52 n. 83
52d2–4: 90 n. 16
53c4–d7: 74
53c4–56c7: 54, 93
53d7–e8: 55 n. 87
55c4–6: 56 n. 87
55d7–56c7: 59
57c7–d3: 56
57d3–5: 57
58c5–d4: 57
58d1–4: 87 n. 13
58d4–61c2: 57, 58
59c5–d2: 96
59d4–e5: 57
61d5–62b6: 60
62b6–c2: 60
62c3–63e7: 59
68e1–69a5: 16
69a6–70d6: 62
70d7–73a8: 62
73b1–d1: 61

73b1–e1: 62
73b1–76e6: 58
76e7–c5: 62
76e7–77c5: 61
90a2–d7: 92
90b6–d7: 61
90c6–d7: 94
90e1–91d5: 62
91a1–b7: 62

[Plato]
Epin.
973a1–b6: 97
981b3–982a3: 98
984d3–8: 98
986a8–987a6: 98 n. 22
987b2–6: 123 n. 59
987d3–988a5: 98 n. 22
988e6–989b1: 98
989e1–990b3: 98
990b5–991b4: 99
991b6–c6: 100
Ep.
7   342a7–d3: 19 n. 24
      342a7–344d2: 25 n. 37
      343a5–b3: 17 n. 16

Proclus
in Euc. (Friedlein)
54.1–8: 19 n. 24
77.7–78.13: 108 n. 33
212.24–213.11: 109 n. 34
269.8–21: 56 n. 87

Protagoras
DK 80 B 7: 17 n. 16

Simplicius
in Cael. (Heiberg)
496.4–9: 81 n. 3
497.15–24: 118 n. 46
in Ph. (Diels)
453.25–454.16: 71 n. 108

Speusippus
fr. 74: 69
fr. 82a: 73
fr. 84: 75
fr. 87: 75
fr. 94: 73
fr. 122: 74

Theon of Smyrna
Expositio (Hiller)
145.18–19: 123 n. 60

Xenocrates
fr. 2: 75
fr. 99: 73
fr. 100: 75
fr. 107: 69
fr. 153: 73
fr. 188: 73
fr. 260: 75

www.ingramcontent.com/pod-product-compliance
Lightning Source LLC
Chambersburg PA
CBHW031225170426
43191CB00031B/520